Renaissance Dramatists

FEMINIST READINGS / SERIES EDITOR: SUE ROE

Renaissance Dramatists

KATHLEEN McLUSKIE

Lecturer in English
University of Kent

HUMANITIES PRESS INTERNATIONAL, INC.
Atlantic Highlands, NJ

First published in 1989 by
Humanities Press International, Inc.,
Atlantic Highlands, NJ 07716

Library of Congress Cataloging-in-Publication Data

McLuskie, Kathleen.
Renaissance dramatists.

(Feminist readings)
Bibliography: p
1. English drama—Early modern and Elizabethan,
1500–1600—History and criticism. 2. Feminism and
literature—Great Britain—History—16th century.
3. Women and literature—Great Britain—History—16th
century. 4. Women and literature. I. Title. II. Series
PR658. F45M35 1989 822'.3'09 88–32899
ISBN 0–391–03520–7
ISBN 0–391–03521–5 (pbk.)

Printed in Great Britain.

Feminist Readings

Series Editor: Sue Roe

The *Feminist Readings* series has been designed to investigate the link between literary writing and feminist reading by surveying the key works of English Literature by male authors from new feminist perspectives.

Working from a position which accepts that the notion of gender difference embraces interrelationship and reciprocity as well as opposition, each contributor to the series takes on the challenge of reassessing the problems inherent in confronting a 'phallocentric' literary canon, by investigating the processes involved in the translation of gender difference into the themes and structures of the literary text.

Each volume surveys briefly the development of feminist literary criticism and the broader questions of feminism which have been brought to bear on this practice, from the initial identification of 'phallocentrism', through the tendency of early feminist critics to read literature as a sociological document, through to feminist criticism's current capacity to realign the discoveries of a wide range of disciplines in order to reassess theories of gender difference. The tendency of the feminist critic to privilege texts written by women and the notion that it might be possible to identify an autonomous tradition of 'women's writing' can offer a range of challenges to current feminist criticism, and the key texts by male authors surveyed by the series are considered in this light.

Can there be a politics of feminist criticism? How might a theory of sexual difference be seen to be directly applicable to critical practice? The series as a whole represents a comprehensive survey of the development by various theories of gender difference, and, by assessing their applicability to the writing of the most influential male writers of the literary tradition, offers a broadly revisionary interpretation of feminist critical practice.

Louise DeSalvo	*Nathaniel Hawthorne*
Bonnie Kime Scott	*James Joyce*
Julia Briggs	*Shakespeare*
Jacqueline Di Salvo	*Milton*
Sandra Gilbert	*T. S. Eliot*
Patricia Ingham	*Thomas Hardy*
Kathleen McLuskie	*Renaissance Dramatists*
Jill Mann	*Geoffrey Chaucer*
Marion Shaw	*Alfred Lord Tennyson*
Margarita Stocker	*Marvell*
Janet Barron	*D. H. Lawrence*
Ruth Nadelhaft	*Joseph Conrad*

Contents

Acknowledgements

I would like to thank all those who made this book possible. The English Board at the University of Kent granted me study leave and the British Academy and the Shakespeare Association of America awarded travel grants to attend conferences in Berlin and Boston. Those conferences provided valuable contacts and contexts for this work and I am grateful to Carol Neely, Lisa Jardine and Nancy Hodge for inviting me to join in the discussions. The fierce questioning of Cora Kaplan and the students in the Sussex English department graduate seminar made me think harder about history and feminism, continuing the process begun in the lively debate between Kate Belsey and Jim Sharpe at the HETE conference in 1987.

These subjects and many others have been talked through with Andrew Butcher, Jill Davis, Rod Edmond, Jean Howard, Lyn Innes, Pat Macpherson, Jan Montefiore, Marion O'Connor and, especially, David Turley. For their continual moral, intellectual and practical support, much thanks. Anna, Hilary and Celia Turley kept the whole enterprise in limits and in perspective.

CHAPTER ONE
'Such a lady at such a time'

In 1983 the Royal Shakespeare Company opened its Stratford season with a main house production of Middleton and Dekker's *The Roaring Girl,* directed by Barry Kyle and starring Helen Mirren. By itself this was not an especially remarkable occurrence: though Middleton and Dekker's play had not been performed since the seventeenth century, the Royal Shakespeare Company and others had been producing a steady diet of other plays by Shakespeare's contemporaries.[1] Some critics, however, did feel that something new was afoot. In attempting to discern why the company had produced 'this tedious and ill written Jacobean citizen melodrama' Gareth Lloyd Evans, writing in the *Stratford upon Avon Herald,* mockingly surmised that 'they thought of it as a substitute panto'. He then suggested that the company was trying to repeat its international success with Nicholas Nickleby. Finally the truth hit him:

> a third possible reason suddenly rears its head, militant and loud – Women's Lib! With a painful emphasis, one speech of Moll's is turned into a clarion call which amounts in crude terms to the statement – 'I won't be laid by you, you bloody male chauvinist pig, because you don't respect women'. (*Stratford upon Avon Herald,* 21 January 1983)

The extent to which Barry Kyle's production could be described as feminist was mooted by a number of critics. Kyle had been responsible for a number of productions (most notably Beaumont and Fletcher's *The Maid's Tragedy* and Dekker, Ford and Rowley's *The Witch of Edmonton*) which raised the issues of women in the courtly and rural worlds of Jacobean England, and

1

was currently directing Shakespeare's *The Taming of the Shrew*. He himself, however, disclaimed any hint of a feminist conspiracy:

> I didn't sit down to do a *grande oeuvre* of quasi feminist Jacobean dramas, but one of the things that appeals to me is that after Queen Elizabeth died, dramatists began to write about the world outside the window. *The Roaring Girl* and *The Witch of Edmonton* have working class heroines and women who really lived in the London of their day.
> In all these plays the leading figure is a woman, victimised for a number of reasons, often just because she is a woman. (*Ms London*, 25 April 1983)

The play itself struck a chord with notes sounded by contemporary feminism. Its eponymous heroine, Moll Cutpurse, was a larger-than-life historical character who was notorious for wearing men's clothes as she smoked and swaggered through the male world of taverns and London low life. In the play she is given a number of speeches which seem to plead for more equitable relations between men and women and for women's rights to free behaviour without the imputation of sexual availability. In the course of the action, she violently resists the pass made at her by a lecherous gallant, denouncing him as

> one of those
> That thinks each woman thy fond flexible whore
> If she can but cast a liberal eye upon thee
> (III.i.70–72)[2]

However, as many critics pointed out, her own singular behaviour is used in the plot to help the hero marry his true love and to prevent rather than assure the citizens' wives' attempts to find sexual satisfaction outside marriage. Her appeals are less for feminist autonomy in the sense of power for women than for more moral behaviour on the part of men – an opposition feminism had tangled with on many occasions since.[3] The play, in other words, made no claims for feminism as a political movement for social change; it made no appeal for women in general but presented Moll as a maverick figure whose position outside society gave her the scope to solve plots and speak for a new morality but posed no threat to existing social institutions.

The essentially individualist character of Moll was fully recognised by Barry Kyle:

The one thing about Moll is that she's a real one-off. She has a strong sexual effect on all the men around her either of immediate response or of hatred, because she's a slut, because she chooses to live and fight like a man. She's not a conceptual feminist, but she begins to put into words how badly women are treated when they are sexually attractive. But she's also tremendously innocent in a way, very idealistic and romantic about marriage. (*Ms London,* 25 April 1983)

His views were echoed by the actress Helen Mirren who also distanced herself from feminism as an organised political movement.

She's simply doing what she wants to do. She's not doing it for the sake of any theory about how life ought to be. (*Avantgarde International,* 3 July 1983)

It was hardly surprising, as a result, that the design of the production reproduced theatrically exciting but familiar ways of representing women on the stage. The femininity of all the women apart from Moll was played up. The citizens' wives were all frills and ruffs and nodding feathers while Mary Fitzallard, the lady love, though dressed as a boy for part of the action, wore her doublet firmly buttoned up with a little ruff and a charming beaver hat as signifiers of femininity. At the end of the play Sebastian, her betrothed, daringly suggests that kissing her in men's clothes 'In this strange form, is worth a pair of two' (IV.i.55).

The notion that male clothes increase rather than subvert women's sexiness spilled over into the presentation of Moll herself. Helen Mirren played the part with a dynamic, loose-limbed physical energy. Her adapted Jacobean costume, with its full breeches, allowed her to move easily over the many levels of the set, and a characteristic pose was an open, full-faced stance with legs wide apart and arms raised – a pose reproduced in the publicity photographs. She wore a loose ruffled shirt with no ruff; when she wore a doublet it was unbraced, and when it was removed, her sleeves were rolled up to her armpits revealing leather sweat bands on her wrists. It was an image which owed as much to the current fashion for 'jogging chic' as to the contemporary representations of Moll Cutpurse herself in seventeenth century pictures: though it may have fitted into the rational dress strand within feminism it also cast shadows from a much more long-lived tradition of the 'breeches part' on the English stage.

Part of the attraction of these 'breeches part' roles from the eighteenth century onwards was that they allowed attractive actresses to show their legs to the appreciation of men in the audience as well as the characters on stage. Occasionally, in the work of such skilled performers as the music hall male impersonator Vesta Tilley, a woman in male dress could subvert sexual stereotypes and even mock masculine styles.[4] In Kyle's production, sexual ambivalence on stage was haunted by images taken from pantomime. Gareth Lloyd Evans fairly accurately described Helen Mirren's style as the 'thigh-thrusting strut of a principal boy' while another Stratford critic preferred the image of a pantomime dame to allay the sexy effect:

> a sort of Peter Pan leaping about the stage didn't help. There must be plenty of scrubbers more suitable. A rough, tough looking and strongly built woman was called for. Why not use a male as in the original version? It didn't call for an attractive woman. (*Stratford upon Avon Midweek News,* 25 January 1983)

Helen Mirren was not only a dynamic and beautiful actress with long experience in classic roles, sexiness was part of her stage and publicity image. The resulting confusion between the world of classic actresses and the world of the commercial exploitation of women parallelled debates over the relationship between feminism and sexuality which was echoed in the language of some of the reviews of her performances. Of her performance as Cleopatra, running concurrently with *The Roaring Girl* in the Stratford Studio, the Other Place, it was noted:

> There's nothing grand about her, even her bosom (long time a measure of interpretations of the role) is more provocative than enveloping. She moves like a cat – but a frisky pussy, not a full furred, yellow eyed lynx. (*Drama,* Spring 1983)

The confusion of sexual discourses and the blatant voyeurism of such remarks revealed the problems around the representation of women and the debates on heterosexuality which were currently preoccupying the women's movement at large.[5] However, for critics who were, to say the least, uninterested in the contradictions of feminist theory, the opposition was much more clear cut. For some, the play's 'rumbustious' quality softened the impact of the feminist message and made 'the Roaring Girl a more entertaining figure than most of the more modern feminist heroines' (*Bedfordshire on Sunday,* 3 July 1983). For others there was a clear, and hypocritical, opposition between feminism and sexual attraction:

> Moll spends a good deal of time flinging her provocative body around – a circumstance which rather takes the edge off her militancy.
> (*Stratford upon Avon Herald,* 21 January 1983)

This production and the critical response it occasioned raised a number of important questions about the possible relations between Elizabethan drama,[6] modern drama and feminism. Given that the play, like many others, dealt with sexual relations and that marriage is both a social and a narrative solution to its plots, there was clearly an overlap with the concerns of contemporary feminism. However, given that feminism is a movement committed to a *change* in the relations of power between men and women and to an analysis of the fundamentally oppressive character of patriarchy, it might seem that the movement has little to hope for from a drama in which marriage is a happy ending and the subordination if not the oppression of most women is a necessary element for the continuation of peace and love and quiet life, an awful rule and right supremacy. Feminism, it seems, could only deplore the continued representation of women in such forms and such contexts and as such their disruptive opposition was in turn deplored by critics who were committed to the continued existence of this theatre and its plays.

This was certainly the view taken by Gareth Lloyd Evans. Reviewing Barry Kyle's production of *The Shrew* he announced:

> It will not have escaped the notice of some Shakespearean theatre-goers that some of his plays have, in the past few years, not so much been directed as victimised by bands of literary wild eyed mobsters. On nothing but bizarre, fashionable, or totally wrong evidence they hack at the heart and guts of the plays while relieving their less coherent din with cries that Shakespeare shall be revitalised and (wait for it) made to speak to the 20th century. (*Drama,* Spring 1983)

For him the inappropriateness of this kind of meddling was less
to do with the pressing concerns of the modern age than the
presumption of challenging the truth of the Shakespearean text.[7]
Middleton, Dekker and Shakespeare, he averred, 'had never
heard of Women's Lib'. Nevertheless in producing *The Shrew* at
the same time as *The Roaring Girl*, Barry Kyle was challenging
those truths in his own terms. The play was explicitly produced
as the other side of a debate in which *The Roaring Girl* took part.
The programme for *The Shrew* carried an advertisement for the
Middleton play and also quoted Moll's final speech in which she
held off from marriage until the other ills of society had been
recorded:

> When you shall hear
> Gallants void from sergeant's fear,
> Honesty and truth unslandered,
> Woman manned but never pandered,
> Cheaters booted but not coached,
> Vessels older ere they're broached.
> If my mind be then not varied,
> Next day following I'll be married.
> (V. ii. 217–24)

Nonetheless, Kyle's production of *The Shrew* offered an image of
patriarchy restored through Petruchio and Kate forging a friendly
alliance necessary for a successful companionate marriage:

> they respect one another in both anger and love (an absolute necessity
> for a comedy of true love) and they stand in sharp contrast to their
> friends and relations whose only measure of values is goods and
> chattels. . . . *The Shrew* survives . . . till next time. (*Drama*, Spring
> 1983)

However, the relation to debates both within modern feminism
and theatre criticism were also kept alive. The programme also
quoted an interview with Caryl Churchill whose *Top Girls* had
attracted a good deal of attention in the previous year. In *Top
Girls* Churchill had explored the case of a successful woman
whose achievements had been at the expense of her own daughter
and sister and in the quoted interview she declared:

> Achievement is about winning, but what about those women who

don't win? Women should be allowed to have adventures, but if it involves oppressing other women, feminism doesn't work.

The question of the particular relations between modern feminism and Elizabethan drama was also introduced by a quotation from Michael Billington's review of a previous RSC production of *The Shrew*. That production, directed by Michael Bogdanov, had played up the violence of Petruchio's taming and presented Kate's final acquiescence as a tragic defeat which made Billington raise

> a larger question at stake than the merits or otherwise of this particular production. It is whether there is any reason to revive a play that seems totally offensive to our age and society. My own feeling is that it should be put back firmly and squarely on the shelf.

Billington's comment showed that in spite of the insistence on the 'truth' of Shakespeare, the questions of the modern world, among them feminism, were not only a relevant but an inevitable consideration in the reproduction of these plays. Their representation on the modern stage is necessarily a part of the present. The styles in which they are performed, the images of women which they perpetuate and the relations of power which they enact are part of a political dynamic which has to include the issues raised by feminists.

The practical resolution of this dynamic between the historical text and the modern moment of its recreation has been most creatively addressed in the writing and the productions of the influential director Jonathan Miller. In *Subsequent Performances,* an account of his work in the theatre, he argues for the creative role of a director in recreating an 'afterlife' for works from different historical periods.

> I was very excited by this idea that the productions of the classics need no longer be slavish reconstructions but are recreations. The past, which is in many ways unvisitable, no longer reduces the director to the role of a failing archeologist but offers the actor and director alike the possibility of remaking a work of art that is essentially emergent. (Miller 1986; p. 75)

Nevertheless Miller makes a clear distinction between the

'emergent' dynamic of the work he is directing and the 'form of historical provincialism . . . a belief that the past is on probation and has to prove itself by its capacity to accommodate current interests' (ibid. p. 170). He sees this process as particularly evident in plays like *The Taming of the Shrew* 'which suddenly become a test case for feminism' (ibid. p. 119).

Miller's resistance to feminism, like Gareth Lloyd Evans's irritation with 'Women's Lib', was no crude misogyny. It was, rather, an impatience with what he saw as a clichéd and old-fashioned sentimentality about women in the plays. Miller's alternatives are almost-Shavian 'new women', argumentative, like his Portia, or rejecting any automatic acquiescence in marriage, like his celebrated Isabella, who rejected the Duke's implied offer of marriage at the end of the play. What Miller claims is different is that he arrives at this characterisation not in the service of any preconceived modish dogma but out of an openness to the possibilities of hearing the lines in a different voice. He describes, for example, his thoughts on the trial scene of *The Merchant of Venice:*

> As a director I often respond negatively to a precedent and, in this case, I recoiled from the sentimental radiance that actresses bring to Portia's famous mercy speech. I could imagine the speech being delivered in a much more argumentative and impatient way. . . . In my mind's eye I saw Portia leaning impatiently across the table to say, 'The quality of mercy is not *strained*' as if having laboriously to explain what should have been self evident to someone too stupid to understand. (ibid. p. 107)

A similarly new way of hearing a line occurred in the rehearsals for his television production of *The Shrew:*

> Their first encounter, when Kate tries to attack Petruchio, is usually presented as a tremendous rough and tumble on stage. During the course of rehearsing the scene when Kate slaps Petruchio, something very interesting emerged. Instead of Petruchio suddenly throwing himself violently on her, John Cleese leant considerately towards her and simply went 'Hm, mm!' as if this was an interesting move on her part which had to be considered. He then said very quietly, 'I swear I'll cuff you if you strike again.' This is a disconcerting move for which the character of Kate is unprepared, and it forces her to visualize her behaviour in a way that she would not have time to do if

Petruchio had responded immediately with some comparable loud and violent move. The very fact that Kate might be ruffled by such a gesture is interesting. She looks at him then, perhaps for the first time, and sees that he is not quite like the other suitors as he is neither frightened, nor is he simply provoked into a display of rumbustious bad temper. By unpredictable behaviour in that moment he gives her back a self-image that she can evaluate. Kate begins to realize that someone who is prepared to devote so much time to her must be prompted by affection rather than by a selfish determination to have his own authority observed. But even with this slightly more subtle performance of Petruchio, his absolute commitment to the idea that there must be rule in a household can be seen throughout the play underlying the humour and sympathy.

We no longer share this view of domesticity, which is framed by theological dogma, but as a director, approaching these plays from the past, I must recognize and accommodate the production to those theological assumptions. The alternative is to frog-march Shakespeare into the twentieth century and make the plays address our problems, and literally identify with our values. The language then seems wrong and artificial. If, however, you allow such differences in attitudes to be visible in the production, the play comes alive and Kate's final speech is rather moving as it is an agreement to abide by the rules within a framework in which it is possible to enjoy a close affection. In contrast to Kate's rather graceful submission, the disagreeable behaviour of her sister Bianca becomes repugnant and you can then see that the real shrew is Bianca and not Katharina at all. (ibid. p. 122)

Miller, with his characteristic intellectual eclecticism, found the historical support for his reading in Michael Walzer's account of Puritan culture, *The Revolution of the Saints*. However, in claiming this historical authority, he fudged the issue of the afterlife of the play. In rejecting feminism as 'a kind of historical provincialism' and claiming that he was dealing with the *Elizabethan* need for order as outlined by Walzer, he neglected the extent to which 'the need for order' is a live political issue in Britain today and one which feminism actively addresses. The idea of Petruchio providing 'a course of tuition as a result of which Kate learns the necessity of obedience' (ibid. p. 121) presents an image of order restored in public and private life which is exciting and original theatre because it goes against the familiar and expected grain. However, it does so in the service of a reactionary ideology which is the more served by the production's theatrical success. For Miller's procedure in that production was to reopen one of the traditions of *Shrew* interpretation – the rollicking violence of Petruchio's domination of Kate – while leaving closed another – the happy ending in marriage. He finds historical authority for the latter interpretation and uses it to close off the text's contradiction that the happy marriage is bought at the expense of Katherine's humiliation. A closer examination of the history would, of course, have revealed that the need for order was a matter for as keen debate by Elizabethans as it is today and the play, though its dramatic structure closes the argument, is an intervention in that debate.

Miller uses history more imaginatively than those critics for whom it is a way of closing off debate about a text's meaning. Nevertheless he uses it primarily as a source which he can mine to sustain his creative imagination rather than as an element in analysis. A similar co-option of history was evident in two of the inaugural productions at the Swan Theatre, a new theatre devoted to productions by the RSC of plays by Shakespeare's contemporaries. In the programme/text for *The Fair Maid of the West*, an adaptation of Heywood's two-part play, the director Trevor Nunn defends his choice of Heywood's plays by invoking the historical moment of their first theatrical production and the continuity of the ideas which they present:

> So why is Heywood worth our consideration today? Not only because of his whirling narratives and demanding dramaturgy, and not only because he was an entirely accessible, popular entertainer whose achievements provide a fascinating context for his greater but more obscure contemporaries; but because in his adventure stories he conveys a disarming innocence, an uncomplicated childlike directness which is revealing of the nation's character at the beginning of the English colonial parabola. Indeed it is sometimes difficult to believe his notions of Englishness are of the sixteenth and not the nineteenth century, so familiar is the national self-portraiture. Bess is a heroine, like Indiana Jones is a hero, unambiguous and admirable. The standards of moral firmness and self-denial Heywood requires of his characters are intended to be inspirational and formative and the effect is more of wish fulfilment than propaganda. (Heywood 1986; p.5)

Nunn's remarks reveal the ease with which the seventeenth century is invoked as both the favoured ancestor and the familiar brother of the twentieth.[8] They also show that history is used to suppress the question of gender which is in fact central to the play. Bess Bridges, unlike Indiana Jones, is a heroine; her actions are made necessary by the fact that she is left alone when her lover, Spencer, kills a man in a duel defending her reputation against an impertinent customer. Throughout the play the same reputation is assailed by men who assume that a woman alone is sexually available. She overcomes them all by a combination of physical courage and entrepreneurial acumen but these signs of independence are controlled by the constant reminder of her love for and faithfulness to Spencer with whom she is united in the end.

History was present in the production, not as a foreground for this preoccupation with a woman's reputation but as an energetically realised local colour. Before the performance the audience were welcomed to the theatre with glasses of beer as the inn which was the setting incorporated both the audience and the characters. The play opened with a witty induction in which an unfortunate company of players, trying to perform an old-fashioned production of Shakespeare's *Henry V,* were booed off the stage by the inn's customers who took over to perform Heywood's adapted play.

The performance stressed the historical distance of *The Fair Maid* but simultaneously suggested that the audience were part of its historical moment, not least in sharing the experience of its physical energy. The staging used the whole theatre with great inventiveness; it transformed the stage from inn to ship in full sail to the Court of Mullysheg King of Feg and conducted a sea fight and a chase through the Moorish town around and over the heads of the delighted audience. Throughout this participation in costume drama, the relations between men and women, the action of the plot, remained comfortably familiar. Bess was an attractive heroine who mourned her lover and fought off her suitors like any heroine of romance and, to render her even more familiar, sang the (interpolated) songs in a sweet country-and-western style, for all the world like Loretta Lyn.

The relationship between the modern and the historical in creating a theatrical effect was also explored in the same season's production of *The Two Noble Kinsmen.* This dramatic version of Chaucer's *The Knight's Tale* by Shakespeare and Fletcher was first performed at the Blackfriars Theatre in 1613 and shows both dramatists responding to the new style of romance which the King's Men developed at that theatre. Barry Kyle, and his designer Bob Crowley, responded to the ritual elements in the staging and the play's preoccupation with male honour. They dressed the main plot in brilliant costumes of black, white and red in a style which was part Japanese samurai but which also visually echoed modern Japanese high fashion. The sub-plot of the gaoler's daughter who falls in love with one of the aristocratic heroes was dressed in more familiar Elizabethan-style clothes.

Throughout the production sexual relations and sexuality were clearly to the fore, taking up a dominant theme of the play. The opening lines of the prologue make the connection clear:

> New plays and maidenheads are near akin,
> Much followed both, for both much money gi'en,
> If they stand sound and well.[9]

Both the narrative of the play and the slow, ritualised mode of its setting, including frequent scenic set pieces, made it impossible to treat sexuality with the familiar psychological realism. In the main action, Emilia, committed to a life of chastity, is loved at first sight by two knights, Palemon and Arcite, when they are prisoners at her brother Theseus' court. They fight a duel for her and are both condemned to death. She pleads for their lives but refuses to choose between them, so they are set to compete in a formal tournament. Arcite wins, but before he can enjoy Emilia he is thrown from his horse and killed, so that she ends up marrying Palemon.

The play denies the realist pattern of motivation which derives from character and issues in action. The knights fall in love with an almost comic suddenness and are consumed by every passion that they feel. The play's conflict between a high-flown notion of male friendship and the equally all-demanding power of love is expressed not through psychological anguish but by a poetic rendering of paradox which can only be resolved by the equally paradoxical irony of the denouement. For example, when the knights prepare for their first duel, the anticipated violence is contained by the formality of their preparation. Each combatant chooses his armour, each arms his adversary, then 'They bow several ways, then advance and stand' (SD III. vi. 93). Kyle developed these hints from text and stage direction to a visually striking display of elaborate formal courtesy which gave a theatrical meaning to Palemon's arcane assertion that the 'blood we desire to shed is mutual;/In me, thine, and in thee, mine; (III. vi. 95–6).

Both the play and the production, however, located these rarified emotional concepts and the forms in which they are contained as symbolic and characteristic of the liminal moment in which the characters find themselves. All of them are on the point of marriage; but marriage, although expected by each of them, is no simple, natural development of maturity. It is presented as alien to their most powerful feelings. Arcite, for example, lamenting his capture by Theseus, regrets that

> Here age must find us
> And, which is heaviest, Palamon, unmarried:
> (II. ii. 28–9)

But the ensuing speech on his expectations of marriage presents it in static and conventional poetic terms. The action begins on the eve of Theseus' and Hippolyta's wedding, but that match was no conventional romance[10] and our sense of this is further complicated by an excursus on the love between Theseus and his courtier Pirithous (I. iii. 33–47).

Emilia's chastity, too, is not presented as the expected pre-nuptial virginity but is rooted in the passionate memory of her friend, Flavina (I. iii. 50–87). Emilia's chastity is not only a refusal of marriage but also a resistance to the blame for male passion which attaches to women. When the knights declare their love for her she rejects Hippolyta's suggestion that

> That face of yours
> Will bear the curses else of after ages
> III. vi. 186–7)

saying

> In my face, dear sister,
> I find no anger to 'em, nor no ruin;
> The misadventure of their own eyes kill 'em.
> II. vi. 188–90)

However, she recognises the role of women as controllers of the damage caused by male passion. Just as she and Hippolyta pleaded in the opening scene for Theseus to avenge the three wronged queens, she pleads for the young knights, and in her soliloquy reluctantly accepts her role as both mediator and prize in the men's conflict:

> Yet I may bind those wounds up, that must open
> And bleed to death for my sake else: I'll choose
> And end their strife. Two such young handsome men
> Shall never fall for me; their weeping mothers,
> Following the dead cold ashes of their sons,
> Shall never curse my cruelty.
>
> (IV. ii. 1–6)

These questions about sexual relations and marriage are also stressed by the contrasting plot of the gaoler's daughter who falls in love with Palemon. The design and setting of this action more clearly suggested an Elizabethan social world, as the gaoler's daughter prepares to marry a man of her own class, approved by her father, and is flipped out of that safe society into madness by her love for the beautiful and exotic sight of Palemon – 'Lord, the difference of men'. The gaoler's daughter shows a rooted social sense of the limited possibilities of her world in the soliloquy where she first declares her love:

> To marry him is hopeless,
> To be his whore is witless.
>
> (II. iv. 4–5)

Her movement from naïve passion to complete derangement, however, is enacted in soliloquy; it is unconnected to social pressure, for the play presents the social world of the gaoler's daughter only in the holiday guise of may games and feats of strength. These are partly linked into the plot when the banished Arcite gains Theseus' favour through his prowess at a wrestling match. However, the scene of country festivity in which the village schoolmaster presents a morris to honour Theseus and Hippolyta is one of the set pieces which punctuate the action of the play.

Kyle used the opportunities provided by these scenes of rural merry-making to produce an extraordinary counter-image of sexuality to those of the formal main plot. In the action, the mad gaoler's daughter wanders into the preparations for the morris and replaces one of the dancers who had not appeared for the rehearsal. The morris includes a 'bavian' (baboon) whom the schoolmaster instructs to 'carry your tail without offense and scandal to the ladies' (III. v. 33–4) but otherwise consists of a fairly familiar cast of Lord and Lady of the May with accompanying servants, clown and fool. Kyle and Crowley ignored these references and presented instead a combination of mumming and charivari in which a bridled gaoler's daughter rode astride a huge wooden phallus which was carried, swaying, in a dance by garlanded young folk. At the climax of the dance a young man caught hold of the phallus tip and pulled from it a stream of white silk which he drew round the stage, completely enveloping Theseus, Hippolyta and their train. It was a stunning moment, a fantastic celebration of phallic power and a grotesque reminder of the physical sexuality which lay beneath both the high rhetoric of the aristocrats and the passionate derangement which afflicted the gaoler's daughter. In part it endorsed the doctor's view that the gaoler's daughter's malady could be cured by sexual consummation – a suggestion which caused consternation to her father – but it also indicated the dissonance between physical sexuality and the social and poetic forms which held its disruptive power in check.

This production did not locate its motifs of sexuality in a precise realisation of Jacobean social life. However, the contrast between the samurai aristocrat and the world of early modern social anthropology[11] did not affect the facile universalising which was evident in the production of *The Fair Maid of the West*. Rather, the style of the production made history evident by its absence. Its effects alienated the audience from simple engagement with the outcome of the story, making the action strange and potentially raising the question of what kind of society could have produced this strange account of its social forms and what conjunction of artistic and ideological pressures could have gone into its formation.

The historicity of the Elizabethan drama is not simply the difference of social ideas which may or may not speak to the twentieth century: it is also a difference of artistic form. Debates about historical ideas leave out of account the process by which ideological notions are mediated through the form of the theatrical text and the extent to which playwrights are actively engaged in modifying and adapting that form – as often in the interests of novelty as in the service of more direct ideological pressure. In her challenging 'Notes on an Elizabethan play' Virginia Woolf contrasts the realist tradition of the novel, dealing with Smith from Liverpool, with

> the land of the unicorn and the jeweller among dukes and grandees, Gonzaloes and Bellimperias, who spend their lives in murder and intrigue, dress up as men if they are women, as women if they are men, see ghosts, run mad, and die in the greatest profusion on the slightest provocation, uttering as they fall imprecations of superb vigour or elegies of the wildest despair. (Woolf 1971; p. 55)

Barry Kyle's production, by creating new versions of those images, reminded his audience of that tradition. However, by contrasting different models of historical forms he removed the production from the familiar 'Elizabethan World' in which costumes and customs are different but human beings much the same. The strangeness of the images Kyle created produced theatrical delight but also left the more intractable questions as a continued challenge to the audience.

III

This procedure was first developed theoretically and put into theatrical practice by Bertolt Brecht. Brecht worked towards a new form of theatre in which the audience would laugh when the characters wept, weep when they laughed.[12] They would thus, Brecht hoped, maintain an intellectual distance from the outcome of the narrative, discerning the social forms and the pressure of power which brought that weeping and laughter about. Brecht found the work of Shakespeare and his contemporaries full of examples of the epic theatre to which his own work aspired.[13] In 1946, while in exile in the United States, Brecht experimented with a production of Webster's *The Duchess of Malfi* in collaboration with W. H. Auden. Brecht's adaptation of the play was an attempt to render it more coherent while at the same time to insist on the material circumstances which lay behind the concern for family honour which motivated the Aragonian brothers' torture and murder of the Duchess in revenge for her unauthorised marriage.

Ferdinand's aristocratic status is insisted upon as he is introduced with 'Castruchio, courtiers, men at arms, standard bearers, all the appurtenance of a princely train'. His public character as a renaissance prince is also stressed in references to how 'the people line the streets awaiting progress to the haven'. A scene is added in which Antonio and Delio watch Ferdinand's triumphal procession through the streets after he has won the war, which Brecht introduced in order to explain the two-year gap in the action between the Duchess's marriage and the beginning of the brothers' revenge. Ferdinand's military honour is shown as an important part of his character, but it is also an aspect of aristocratic power, and Brecht stressed the conflict between the military and ecclesiastical arms of aristocratic power in an opposition between Ferdinand and the Cardinal. Bosola, in an added speech, tells us that the Cardinal 'steals enough land for five sons', and when the Cardinal excommunicates the Duchess, Ferdinand accuses him of a cynical move to take over her lands.

This economic motivation of the action is no crude personal explanation for it is related to the question of family honour in a complex way. We are shown a family caught in a historical dialectic between old notions of aristocratic image and a new individualism associated, in Brecht's view, with the bourgeois period of history. The Duchess had responded to the latter in marrying Antonio, but when he wishes to oppose Ferdinand with the new ideal of reason, she rejects his offer. As Antonio explains it:

> some strange enchantment, sprung
> From ties of blood has bewitched thee.
> (Adaptation Act 2, Scene 3)

For Brecht the plot was not merely the story of events but the meaning of a whole action: it could be understood only in terms of the conflicts of a particular moment in history rather than in terms of the moral or psychological dilemma of the individuals. The psychological was still present: Ferdinand's incestuous motivation was stressed with an excerpt from Ford's *'Tis Pity*

She's a Whore and the Duchess's wooing of Antonio is left intact in the adapted version. Nevertheless Brecht fiercely resisted the 'eternally human' element.

In the event, Brecht's hopes for the adaptation were not fulfilled. The English director George 'Dadie' Rylands, who had directed the influential post-war production with Peggy Ashcroft and John Gielgud,[14] was called in to direct the American production, and he insisted on restoring the original text, an understandable response in view of the poetic hash that Auden had made of the play. Brecht was characteristically contemptuous of the result:

> The production was supervised by an English director and involved old-style declamation in accordance with that so called Shakespearean tradition whose style derives from the nineteenth century and has, of course, nothing to do with the Elizabethan theatre. The shortcomings of this tradition could be clearly observed. The story narrated by the play was not performed; wherever it came through nonetheless, everything possible was done to damp down its startling twists. The characters were flattened out by the pernicious practice of stressing the 'eternally human' element while the shabby attempt to make each event a typical case purged of any operation of chance, so that the audience might blindly follow the workings of 'fate', stripped those events of all reality. The actors clung to their purple passages, their arias, for dear life, but without being able to ground them in the action.[15]

Brecht's production was not explicitly 'feminist', for he was less preoccupied with the fate of the women in the play than with the overall historical concerns. Nevertheless his account of the production's aims and the reasons for their failure show how a new reading of the play depends first on the reader and her other preoccupations and then on the style and context in which a performance takes place. His reading is potentially feminist in that it interrogates not only the torture and death of the Duchess but also her doomed passion for Antonio. He resists a simple emotional involvement with her heroism and her love and places her actions and those of her brothers in the larger historical frame.

An adaptation which addressed itself explicitly to the configurations of lust and power in Elizabethan drama was Howard

Barker's version of *Women Beware Women* directed by William Gaskill at London's Royal Court Theatre in 1986. Middleton's play had been the focus for a discussion of sexuality and the classic drama when it was revived by the Royal Shakespeare Company in 1962. Its revival coincided with the last, successful, phase of the effort to remove censorship from the English stage and the production was heralded as evidence of the modernity of the classic drama. Partly because of impatience with the petty prurience of the Lord Chamberlain's censorship of the stage, 'modernity' in 1962 was seen as synonymous with the new frankness about sex. T. C. Worsley in the *Financial Times* (5 July 1962) compared the play with Tennessee Williams and the Italian cinema, and *The Times* reviewer commented:

> what squeamishness of taste or inadequacy of enterprise has kept it off the boards so long is probably a matter of social history. It may be that a revival of vitality in English drama has made this the moment to put things right. (*The Times*, 5 July 1962)

Kenneth Tynan, one of the most vociferous critics of censorship and a champion of the New Drama, compared Middleton favourably with Shakespeare. Shakespeare, he said, 'lied about sex' and he praised, in contrast, the truth about sexuality presented in Middleton's plays:

> where sexual vagaries are concerned there is more authentic reportage in *The Changeling* and *Women Beware Women* than in the whole of the First Folio. (*Observer*, 8 July 1963)

In the twenty years between this production and Howard Barker's adaptation these 'truths' about sex had been challenged by new forms of representation of sexuality and by the feminist movement's attempts to make clearer connections between sexuality and politics. Barker's adaptation reflected this change of mood and clearly showed the influence of the revival of interest in the work of such sexual theorists as Wilhelm Reich, for whom sexual liberation was a subversive political force.[16] His adaptation of Middleton's play took the first three and a half acts, in which Bianca, who has eloped with the low-born Leantio, is raped by and then marries the Duke, as the starting-point for a drama in which lust is the knowledge necessary for political liberation.

The source for these ideas was certainly present in Middleton's
play. After Bianca has been raped she is first appalled and then
determined to accept the consequences of her betrayal:

> I saw that now
> Fearful for any womans' eye to look on
> Infectious mists and mildews hang at's eyes
> The weather of a doomsday dwells upon him.
> Yet since mine honour's leprous why should I
> Preserve that fair that caused the leprousy?
> Come poison all at once.
>
> (II. ii. 421–7)

The connection between sex and politics is manifest in the Duke's
use of his power for sexual ends but it is given a further dimension
in the other plots. Leantio, Bianca's husband, is also brought to
court, where he is humiliated by being forced to witness the
Duke's possession of his wife and is bought off with a court
sinecure. He, in turn, however, is lusted after by Livia, the
woman who had engineered Bianca's rape, and consents to a
liaison of convenience. This affair between the court procuress
and the low-born intruder is the catalyst for the final catastrophe
as it triggers the vengeance of her brother Hippolito, her exposure
of his incest with his niece, Isabella, and a finale of plot and
counterplot which kills them all off.

In the closing speech, the Cardinal, the Duke's brother,
moralises:

> Sin, what thou art, these ruins show too piteously!
> Two kings on one throne cannot sit together
> But one must needs down, for his title's wrong:
> So where lust reigns, that prince cannot reign long
>
> (V. ii. 220–23)

In the 1962 production these lines were declaimed by Ernest
Milton in the old Shakespearean style, so that, according to
Mervyn James (*Tribune,* 13 July 1962), John Gielgud, in the
audience, murmured 'beautifully spoken, Ernest'. In the more
cynical political world of the 1980s, they were once again taken as
the theme of the play, but the relations between lust and power
were separated from the notion of sin. Part II of Barker's play
posits a quite different end to the play in which Livia, awakened

to a true understanding of the politics of her situation by her sexual experiences with Leantio, conspires with Sordido (in the original a minor, comic figure, servant to the ward who is married to Isabella) to rape Bianca on the eve of her wedding, thus destroying the image of sexual prowess on which the Duke's status depends. Barker thus reversed the Jacobean moral opposition between lust and power, claiming, on the contrary, that aristocratic power both generated and depended upon an image of sexual omnipotence.

Barker's central thesis is echoed in a good deal of recent academic work[17] and would gain some support from feminist analyses of the role of sexuality in sustaining structures of power. However, its stage representation and the particular moment of its production set up a number of more complex resonances. The play was produced at a time when the British royal family included a number of eligible young men. The stock of romantic matrimony had risen considerably with the media hype surrounding the wedding of Prince Charles to Lady Diana, and Prince Andrew, soon himself to be married, had had his sexual exploits widely discussed in the tabloid press. A side-swipe at the royal family was not central to the play's political focus but it generated a facile, extra-diegetic, *frisson* nonetheless.

More problematic was the representation of sexuality on the stage. Barker abandoned the imagistic ambiguities of Jacobean poetic language and replaced them by revelling in the obscene physicality of coitus. In the startling opening lines of the second half of the play, Leantio, dishevelled and half-naked, announced:

> We fuck the day to death. And suffocate the night with tossing. Time stands still, she says so. Rolls back, even. As for the bed, it's our whole territory, the foot board and the headboard are the horizons of our estate, rank with the food of flesh.
>
> (Barker and Middleton 1986; p. 19)

Livia, in turn, celebrates the knowledge that this sex has given her. However, the knowledge is not arrived at by her own perception but by the overwhelming power of Leantio's phallic energy. Her language describes sexual experience in terms of male fantasies of the all-dominating phallus which hurts and tears, reaching the womb and the heart. The knowledge which this coitus brings fuels her determination for political change. However, the change is to be brought about by humiliating Bianca and destroying her as a false image of purity. The perpetrator of this act, Sordido, is presented as one whose lowly origins give him true knowledge, furthermore, as a homosexual, his rape of Bianca is a pure act, uncompromised by desire. Women, it seems, have to be raped into knowledge, men gain revolutionary knowledge and power by abstaining.

This frank misogyny is mitigated by a dramatic and theatrical procedure in which women act primarily as symbols. In a leaden line, the Cardinal informs Bianca:

> You are not a woman at all – but a symbol of the state
> (Scene 7)

and Sordido declares

> Stealing her toy virginity, all the poor of Florence grab their rights
> (Scene 6)

However, it is difficult to stage such an abstract thesis given the realist mode of the acting. The figure of Livia, undressed and moaning in the ecstasy of sexual bliss, is inseparable from images of pornographic fantasy and the on-stage rape of Bianca was performed with a distressing violence which blotted out the political symbolism.

At the end of the play the Duke, in a final effort to end the chaos, announces:

> *New duke* [he points to LEANTIO] *New duchess* [he points to LIVIA. LIVIA and LEANTIO go to hurry out]. Don't love . . .
> Don't love . . .!
> (Scene 7)

The play presents no reasoned political solution and, given the contempt for the masses, sexual inadequacy and craven credulity, it proposes no populist revolution. Sexuality alone cannot provide the basis for full political analysis but the sexual-political point about the agency of women in corruption and chaos has been firmly made once more.

IV

The sexual politics of Barker's play demonstrate the difficulties of using the stark oppositions of Elizabethan drama to present a political critique informed by feminist theory. The traditions of representation of women on stage, the extent to which those traditions are inevitably caught up in misogynist iconography, constantly come between the figure on stage and the meanings which plays impose upon her. These meanings are, of course, negotiable but that negotiation has constantly to be tested in performances which steer round the familiar and dominating images of principal boy, pantomime dame, pathetic victim and tragedy queen.

I have focused on these productions of Jacobean plays and the critical response to them not because they offer paradigms of feminist or anti-feminist readings but because they each demonstrate the process by which such readings are made possible. Each of the plays offers a moment in which the common-sense reading of the play, the smooth flow of the narrative, is disrupted, throwing it into relief and making questions about the action possible. Moll's androgynous presence and her proto-feminist speeches, John Cleese's determined calm, the phallic eruption of the may-game all call into question the commonplace understanding of sexual relations and the happy endings of marriage which are their expected conclusion. They create the space in which feminist readings are made possible: whether they are then developed or resisted depends upon the inclination of the viewer, aided or restrained by the context of the performance and the styles and traditions in which it is performed.

Feminist readings can, of course, be generated simply by feminist readers who will decide for themselves what they think of the torture of Tamyra or the patience of Griselda or the heroism of the Duchess of Malfi, using their feminism to resist[18] the text's meanings directly in the manner parodied by unsympathetic critics: 'Shakespeare bloody sexist. Petruchio bloody chauvinist pig. Kate rules OK' (*Drama*, Spring 1983).

A more reasoned and sympathetic account of this procedure is offered in Jonathan Culler's description of 'Reading like a woman',[19] which asserts

The first act of a feminist critic is 'to become a resisting rather than an assenting reader and, by this refusal, to assent to begin the process of exorcizing the male mind that has been implanted in us'. . . . In this second moment of feminist criticism there is an appeal to the potential experience of a woman reader (which would escape the limitations of male readings). . . .

The task of criticism in this third moment is to investigate whether the procedures, assumptions and goals of current criticism are in complicity with the preservation of male authority, and to explore alternatives. (Culler 1982; pp. 53, 58, 61)

Culler's somewhat overlapping categories all include the useful and important notion of resistance. However, they contain that notion firmly within the competing discourses of criticism and pay no attention to the problematic relationship between the reader and the text. The texts are seen as autonomous mechanisms asserting their authoritative readings across time, limiting their potential for feminist reading to the present moment in which the 'woman reader', by which Culler means 'woman critic', has sprung into being fully armed with her 'experience'. However tempting and effective such direct action might seem, it leaves the text intact and allows no analysis of the process which allows the text's continued reproduction. For feminism, as well as making specific interventions in modern political life, has also been concerned to analyse the structures of social and symbolic relations which make the oppression of women possible and necessary. A sense of history – of the present as well as the past – is vital for that analysis. The representations of women in Elizabethan drama took place and take place in specific historical contexts in which the development of the theatre, the use of literary and theatrical conventions and the ways of thinking and speaking about women are all important factors in the ways the stories are told upon the stage. The history which informs modern productions of these plays by the subsidised national companies and their reproduction in school and university syllabuses has been addressed elsewhere.[20] The history of their original methods and means of production is the subject of this book.

Notes

1. See Sally Beauman, *The Royal Shakespeare Company*, 1982. For a critical view of RSC policy see Alan Sinfield, 'Royal Shakespeare Theatre and the Making of Ideology' in Dollimore and Sinfield, *Political Shakespeare*, pp. 158–81.
2. Middleton and Dekker, *The Roaring Girl*, ed Andor Gomme.
3. See Sheila Jeffreys, *The Sexuality Debates*. This opposition also emerged in the seventeenth-century debate on women. See below, p. 49.
4. For a full discussion of transvestism on the nineteenth-century stage see Elaine Aston, 'Outside the Doll's House: A Study in Images of Women in English and French Theatre 1848–1914'. Ph.D. thesis, University of Warwick 1987.
5. See, for example, the 'sexuality' issue of *Feminist Review* II, 1982 and Elizabeth Wilson (1983).
6. Throughout this book I use the term 'Elizabethan' to refer to the drama written between 1580 and 1640 to avoid the clumsiness of 'Elizabethan/Jacobean/Caroline'.
7. For an extended discussion of alternative readings of Elizabethan drama, see Richard Levin, *New Readings vs Old Plays*. Faced with the plethora of 'alternative readings', Levin retreats into the comfort of the common-sense account offered by the narrative of the texts. The material which he discusses could equally bear witness to the open-ended quality of the texts and their potential for engagement with a variety of responses depending on an interaction of text and reader.
8. For a full account of the ideological appropriation of the seventeenth century by the twentieth see Don E. Wayne, 'Drama and Society in the Age of Jonson: An Alternative View' (1982) and Simon Barker, 'Images of the Sixteenth and Seventeenth Centuries as a History of the Present' (1986). The recent intellectual trend of 'New Historicism' in the United States is discussed in Jean E. Howard (1986).
9. Fletcher and Shakespeare, *The Two Noble Kinsmen,* ed G.R. Proudfoot (Edward Arnold, London, 1970).
10. See Madelon Gohlke,'"I Wooed Thee with my Sword": Shakespeare's Tragic Paradigms', in Lenz, Green and Neely, pp. 150–70.
11. See below pp. 31–2. The gaoler's daughter's bridle and the riding on a make-believe horse echo the accounts of charivari, the ritual social punishment of sexual offences, discussed by a number of historical anthropologists – see Natalie Zemon Davis (1975), 'Women On Top', Edward Thompson (1972) and Martin Ingram (1985), 166–97.
12. See John Willett (1964).
13. See Brecht, 'Study for the First scene of Shakespeare's *Coriolanus*', in Willett, pp. 252–66.

14. For a discussion of this and other productions, see John Webster, *The Duchess of Malfi*, ed Kathleen E. McLuskie (Bristol Classical Press, Bristol, forthcoming).

15. Brecht, 'Attempted Broadway Production of the Duchess of Malfi', reprinted in Manheim and Willet, pp. 424–5.

16. See Jeffrey Weeks, *Sexuality and Its Discontents* pp. 161–6.

17. See Tennenhouse, *Power on Display,* Goldberg, *James I and the Politics of Literature,* Belsey, *The Subject of Tragedy* and Bristol, *Carnival and Theatre.*

18. For an account of that process see Judith Fetterley, *The Resisting Reader.*

19. The sexual politics of academic and theatrical life are reflected in the fact that Culler's account of reading like a woman, like all the productions I have discussed, is offered by a man.

20. See Derek Longhurst, 'Not for All Time but for an Age', and Terence Hawkes, *That Shakespeherian Rag.*

CHAPTER TWO
'Locked up and beaten and flung about the room'

The competition over history and its continuous creative appropriation by directors and critics will not and should not be ended
by recourse to the 'facts' about any historical period. Nevertheless
history continues to be a point of leverage for interpretation of
texts. The question asked by historical critics is how far the
representation of women in early modern drama was a live issue at
the point of its original production: how far Shakespeare, or any
other dramatist, had indeed 'heard of Women's Lib'. One
feminist way of addressing this question is to investigate the 'real
lives' of early modern women. The aim would not be to pin down
historical 'truth' which could be opposed to the fictions of texts
but rather to investigate the material and ideological terms in
which women's lives were lived, and the extent to which these
terms inform or intersect with the material and ideological
conditions in which the drama was produced.

Such an investigation has been made more possible by recent
work in social history which attempts, through an elaborate
cross-referencing of diverse sources such as parish registers, tax
returns, court depositions and census findings, to reconstruct
historical communities,[1] elaborating in detail the economic and
social relationships which comprise early modern communities.
One of the most important effects of this kind of investigation is
the possibility it opens up of dealing with 'history from below'. By
focusing on particular, geographically limited, areas and paying
due attention to such material as court depositions in which men

27

and women speak for themselves, social historians can fill out the contexts for broader social phenomena such as changes in the rate of prenuptial pregnancy[2] or charges of witchcraft[3] or engagement in the conflicts of the Civil War.[4] Most crucially, these studies analyse the material circumstances in which early modern lives were lived, and discuss the relationship between those material circumstances and the processes of social life.

A central differentiation made by modern social historians is in their attention to the 'contrasting communities' of rural England.[5] The division of English communities between arable areas with nucleated villages and wood-pasture areas with more scattered settlements had, it seems, implications for more than agriculture. David Underdown has described how fears of a breakdown in family relations in the seventeenth century

> were particularly rife in wood-pasture areas. They may have been the product of a general sense of disorder caused by poverty and over-population. They may perhaps be related to the fact that in these places women often made greater contributions to household incomes (from spinning and marketing of dairy products) than was normally possible for the wives of open-field arable farmers, and have been more assertive in consequence. (Underdown 1985; p. 99)

A similar distinction has been applied with interesting results to patterns of prenuptial pregnancy: referring to Martin Ingram's research (1977), Margaret Spufford notes that

> in two parishes in the increasingly impoverished, populous and partly industrialised area of the county (of Wiltshire), 60% and 75% of the cases in which prenuptial pregnancy can be firmly deduced from the parish registers ended up by being presented in the ecclesiastical courts. But in another pair of parishes where population pressure was far less great, on the sheep corn uplands, either no cases or only 7% of cases of prenuptial pregnancy were presented. (Discussed in Spufford 1985; p. 42)

In each of these examples the historians are weighing explana-tions for differences in behaviour against the extent to which behaviour is sufficiently socially significant to warrant comment or action. The operations of patriarchy or the repressive apparatus of courts were, it seems, subject to considerable variation, a variation crucially affected by the material circumstances in which they operated. Those social historians who regard material and regional factors as most significant stress the evidence that the rural poor witnessed a crisis of subsistence in the 1590s. Margaret Spufford, for example, has shown that

> the wage labourer's wages brought him [sic] less food in 1597 than at any other point recorded between the 1260s when the records open and 1950 (Spufford 1985; p. 48)

while Keith Wrightson notes that

> the poor were no longer the destitute victims of misfortune or old age but a substantial proportion of the population, living in constant danger of destitution, many of them full time wage labourers. In both town and country a permanent proletariat had emerged, collectively designated the poor. (Wrightson 1982; p. 141)

Poverty had a particular effect on the women of rural communities since, as Margaret Spufford (1985) has shown, there was a strong correlation between population pressure, poverty and leywrite (bastardy) prosecutions. In a comparative study, Spufford has pointed out that the subsistence crisis of the 1590s had been paralleled in the late thirteenth century and there had been, in the earlier period of dearth, a similar rise in bastardy prosecutions. Spufford notes, however, that the earlier period did not experience a corresponding pressure from reformers of popular social behaviour. In both periods, she claims, it was the circumstances of poverty which made it impossible for poor women to raise the marriage portion which would have ensured their shift in status from unrespectable women to respectable ones.

Nevertheless, presentments to the church courts for bastardy, marital offences, defamation and scolding are also discussed by social historians in the context of a larger thesis of a 'crisis of order . . . in the sixty years before the civil war' (Underdown 1985b; p. 116). Both the descriptions and the explanations of these phenomena carefully balance material and ideological factors. Debate centres on the extent to which the perceived crisis of order is an epiphenomenon of other forms of economic change and the extent to which it was the result of a concerted effort by godly, 'middling sort of people' to impose moral and social control over the unruly, the vagrant, the bastard-bearing and the poor.[6] This 'repressive hypothesis' suggests that the period witnessed a concerted effort on the part of élite groups 'to establish firmer social and personal control over the body of the individual' (Ingram 1985a; p. 130). Katherine O'Donovan, for example, has suggested that the rise in presentments for bastardy can be seen as the result of firmer notions about the importance of public marriage officially sanctioned by the church as opposed to the informal social arrangements whereby an expressed intention to marry was sealed by the exchange of tokens before witnesses (O'Donovan 1982; p. 45). This view is supported by Houlbrook's findings that

> [I]n so far as it is possible to make the distinction 'social offences' were more strictly punished than 'church offences' in the arch deaconry courts. . . . Sexual delicts were the most thoroughly investigated and the most vigorously punished of all. (Houlbrook 1979; p. 47)

This repressive hypothesis is to some extent supported by the attitudes of offenders displayed in the depositions in the court cases. Houlbrook describes these depositions as 'a rich mine for the connoisseur of coarse stories' (Houlbrook 1979; p. 54) and it is certainly easy to gain from them an impression of rollicking freedom in all matters sexual. Catherine Jones of Keevil, for example, displayed a lack of proper respect for official procedures when she 'accused a married man of fathering her child in 1620' but nevertheless drank to 'all the merry conceits which had passed between them' (Ingram 1985a; pp. 151–2). However, presentments for bastardy as often displayed the differential power of men over women in scenes of rape or seduction of servant girls or poor women; the minority of women who were 'repeaters' present an image of social casualties

> often closely related to other bastard bearers, fathers of illegitimates or actual bastards, who produced more than one illegitimate child. Some of them clearly served as village whores. Elizabeth Long or Longynough, the daughter of a poor tiler of Wylye (Wiltshire) who was himself in trouble for sexual immorality, bore three illegitimate children between 1611 and 1620 (with fathers unknown in two cases) though she did claim to have married the father of her fourth child when she became pregnant in 1626. (Ingram 1985a; p. 152)

Élite groups may, then, have been at pains to control popular sexual behaviour through the enforcement of marriage but there seems to be little evidence for a systematic opposition to marriage on the part of the rural population. According to Houlbrook

> most of the matrimonial cases dealt with by the church courts were concerned with the validity of marriage . . . far rarer were suits in which individuals sought to escape their marriage partners, seeking sentences of annulment. (Houlbrook 1979; p. 54)

Susan Amussen (1985) and Jim Sharpe (1982) have shown, moreover, that in the numerous defamation cases brought before the church courts, the issue of chastity was most central to the popular sense of personal honour. Both men and women defended their reputations against accusations of fornication and women in particular

> were most concerned with their reputations for chastity, not for submissiveness, obedience, or being a good housewife. When Alice Fysher watched Olive Grymwood draw water from Fysher's well, and taunted 'You use it (the water) sluttishly and you wash your corrupt clowtes (clothes) in it' Grymwood did not complain; instead Fysher complained that Grymwood had responded by calling her 'a whore and an arrant whore and go play cock sodden again'. (Amussen 1985; p. 208)

Proper behaviour within marriage was, moreover, enforced not only by élite or official groups but also by the informal mechanisms of popular cultural forms. Women suspected of adultery or of domineering behaviour to their husbands were often punished by public humiliation: Martin Ingram quotes an account in which:

> [T]he twenty-second day of February, was Shrove Monday, at Charing Cross there was a man carried of four men, and afore him a bagpipe playing, a shawm and a drum playing, and twenty links burning about him, because his next neighbour's wife did beat her husband. (Ingram 1985b; p. 169)

This 'rough riding', also known as a 'skimmington', or charivari, was paralleled in numerous accounts of disorder and represented a way of drawing public attention to unacceptable private behaviour of married couples. Like the activities of official groups it enforced standards of neighbourly harmony and order but it was also more double-edged in its social impact. It was undoubtedly a frightening and shaming experience for the couple thus attacked and on some occasions it resulted in their departure, their effective expulsion from the communities. However, it was also a comic event. It often involved men dressing as women – a comic inversion rather than an attempt to deceive – and the noise of rough music and the beating of pots and pans expressed communal exuberance as well as social disapproval. When rough ridings got out of hand they too incurred the disapproval of élite groups (we might have no record of them otherwise), but the ultimate aims of the two groups in the enforcement of correct conjugal behaviour were not fundamentally at odds.

II

The debate among social historians about the relationship between the crisis of subsistence and the crisis of order, though it focuses frequently on the conduct of women, seems on the whole to bypass feminist concerns. In its setting up of an opposition between material and ideological explanations for the enforcement of marriage and acceptable social behaviour, it leaves the centrality of marriage as a focus for discussion unchallenged. In part this is a result of the evidence which, in parish registers, locates women at the point of transition into marriage or as the mothers of children born in or out of wedlock. The church courts were most concerned with marital offences and, as we have seen, scolding and quarrelling among women most often related to their sexual behaviour.

However, just as a feminist politics begins by insisting on the social construction of such institutions as marriage, so a feminist history might wish to question the way in which marriage was the sole route by which women could engage in the social lives of their communities. For regardless of women's feelings about marriage, it was undoubtedly an institution which exerted considerable influence in its power to transform the unrespectable to the respectable, the mortal sin of fornication to the conjugal duty of holy matrimony.[7]

Material and ideological explanations, however, can be seen as different sides of the same coin. The material circumstances which made it impossible for a bastard-bearer to raise a dowry may have made it essential for other women to marry and if, as the deposition material suggests, women accepted the status which marriage conferred, the effectiveness of ideological control is all the more evident. This is not to say that women were the passive victims of social transactions not of their making. The feminist historian Miranda Chaytor has investigated the more complex relations of whole kin groups in her study of family and kinship in the parish of Ryton in County Durham and has shown the finely tuned balance of economic and emotional relationships involved. Discussing the case of Agnes Smith, who chose to marry an elderly widower she 'liked not well', Chaytor makes the valuable point that women's emotional lives involved more than heterosexual passion.

> What women may have wanted from marriage, was often perfectly compatible with the interests of parents, kin and society as a whole. The love and attraction that they may have felt for a man, were not unconnected to other emotions, their need for honour, status and security. Women's sense of their sexual identity was constructed around their future function as wives and childbearers, their emotional and sexual needs were directed towards the roles which ensured their social prestige and economic security. (Chaytor 1980; p. 42)

This apparently easy fit between the needs of the individual and the needs of society is, however, no reason for sentimentality about early modern rural life: the pressure to marry, to fit emotional desires to social norms, was also a product of women's relative lack of power within that society. In her discussion of the frequent remarriage of widows even in circumstances which occasioned financial loss and social disapproval, Miranda Chaytor has shown how little autonomy women had to exercise their legal rights, to withstand pressure from a dead husband's remaining kin or to have access to her own resources in a society where the sexual division of labour militated against a single woman having control of the means of labour or participating in communally organised production (Clark, A. 1982; p. xxxvii).

This feminist focus on marriage as a locus of power relations removes the emphasis from the direct oppression which the institution and enforcement of marriage imposed on women. It allows for a more varied sense of the possibilities afforded by the structures in which most early modern women lived their lives. Vivien Brodsky Elliot, for example, in his study of patterns of marriage in London has noted that

> variables such as migratory status, socio-economic background, paternal mortality and the presence or absence of London kin affected the timing of their marriages and created considerable variation in their ages at first marriage. (Elliot 1981; p. 84)

The most significant variation noted by Elliot was between high and low status groups and this, in turn, was connected to how long a particular individual had lived in London. The London-born daughters of wealthy tradesmen, clergymen and gentry tended to marry young, entering arranged marriages with men older than themselves; lower status groups, in particular migrant single women, tended to marry later, of their own accord, men who were nearer their own age. This complex movement around status was different for men and women as is once again most evident in the case of widows. Elliot notes, for example, that

> Widows were at a high premium in the London marriage market, and for many a young journeyman without capital, marriage with a widow was a tempting means of gaining economic independence and freeing himself from subordinate status under a master.
> (Elliot 1981; pp. 83–4)

This release from subordinate status occasioned by a good marriage for men occasioned a concomitant decline in status for the women in question yet it may have been, as Miranda Chaytor suggests, that women were prepared to exchange sexual access and financial security for the social protection which marriage provided.

There is little direct evidence, of course, of women making this calculation in these terms: it is in the nature of ideology to make the institutions of society seem natural common sense, 'the pressures too self evident to be documented explicitly' (Chaytor 1980; p. 44). Nevertheless signs of strain did appear. Michael MacDonald (1981; p. 10), for example, has shown how many of the women who consulted the astrologer and physician Napier suffered from depression whose sources lay in the stresses of their roles as wives and mothers, where they were the focus of a wide network of kinship ties, sustaining their families and through them the social fabric itself.

Napier himself did not discuss the patients he saw in those terms. The language with which marriage and behaviour within marriage could be described was dominated by an official view, propagated in sermons and homilies and handbooks on marriage. These accounts of proper behaviour in marriage often set themselves against what they saw as changes in social behaviour but, according to Kathleen Davies (1977), the advice they offered and the view of matrimony they proposed had not changed from the medieval period on. The official defence of marriage proposed a humanised patriarchy in which power and status remained with men but under which women's subordination was mitigated by men's paternalistic concern for women's comfort and happiness:

> Is the Wife given unto her Husband by God? then must she resolve to giue herselfe wholly to him as her Owner, on whom God hath bestowed her, to whom he hath assigned her. . . . Neither is she to forsake him. For they are not to be sundered, nor seuered, whom God hath conjoyned and made one. . . .
> Lastly if a good Wife be such a special gift of God, then a good Husband is no lesse. For the Husband is as needful for the Wife as the Wife is for the Husband . . . and then will God undoubtedly with his blessing accompanie his gift to his owne glorie and their mutuall good. (Gataker 1624; pp. 22–4)

The turns of Gataker's rhetoric, like the rhetoric of many similar handbooks, indicate the abstract and theoretical character of his exhortations. Moreover, Gataker seems aware of this when he extends this advice in a further pamphlet, *A Wife in Deed,* in which he argues that a bad wife is no wife. As if alarmed by the implications, he then insists that nevertheless her unfortunate husband must bear with her: 'The bone thou must gnaw, that is fallen to thy Lot . . . either a Nurse to thee, or a Scourge' (Gataker 1624; p. 17).

This optimistic view of companionate marriage is accepted by such historians as Keith Wrightson (1982) and Alan MacFarlane (1970), for whom the paradigm case is offered by Ralph Josselin, the clergyman of Earls Colne, whose diary gives a vivid account of a man seeking to conduct his marriage, like all his affairs, according to the demands of the godly life. Josselin clearly cared deeply about his wife and his diary contains many touching notes of concern for his wife's health and safety, particularly when she bore their children. Jane, his wife, was blessed with health and vigour and a physical aptitude for easy childbirth and nursing. Marriage, moreover, offered her a considerable degree of autonomy and the possibility of important relations with other women, both neighbours and kin. As the couple grew older and the children more numerous, signs of strain appeared but Josselin made every effort to overcome them according to the ideals of godly wedlock:

> April 26 1646 . . . my dearest fayles somewhat in her household diligence, a wise woman builds her house. Lord thou hast made her so, still continue her so, give me a heart of love and care towards her continually. (MacFarlane 1976; p. 59)

Josselin's life as a clergyman and his intense concern for the health of his soul makes it hardly surprising that he sought to live his marriage according to the tenets of religious exhortation. Religion, moreover, sustained his position as head of the household and controller of his own life and those of others.

For a woman, however, even a devout woman, religious marriage would have been a rather different experience. A somewhat extreme version of this difference is powerfully dramatised in Philip Stubbes's hagiographic account of his brief married life with Katherine, whom he offers as *A Christal Glass for Christian Women*. Stubbes presents a view of marriage which fits suspiciously closely with the ideals of sermons and homilies. Katherine was obedient to her husband in all things and in her marriage cut herself off from all social contacts or alternative pleasures:

> She would verie seldome . . . go abroade with any, either to banquet or feast, to gossip or make merry, (as they tearme it) . . . there was not the dearest friend she had in the world that coulde get her abroad to dinner or supper, or to any other exercise whatsoever. (Stubbes 1591; sigs A2^v)

Katherine married Philip Stubbes at fifteen and was only .

nineteen when she died in childbirth, which suggests that her total subordination to her husband may have been a result of her immaturity. Moreover, what Stubbes glorified as 'true godliness' appears rather as a withdrawn and depressive character, obsessed with religion which provided her only comfort. When she became pregnant, the prospect of fulfilling the end of marriage gave her no joy:

> She would say to her husband, and many other her good neighbours and friends, not once, nor twice, but manie times, that she should never beare more children and that child woulde bee her death (Stubbes 1591; sig. A3ᵛ)

What Stubbes, and possibly Katherine herself, presented as prophecy, confirming God's joy in her life, could equally be read as a tragic indictment of a marriage which offered only travail and pain and ultimately death. After the birth of her child, Katherine fell ill with a quotidian ague (presumably some form of septicaemia) and suffered four days of delirium and hallucination in which she rehearsed the tenets of Protestant theology and in which there took place a 'wonderfull conflict between Sathan and her soule' (C3). Stubbes's account of her struggle is extremely moving as she did not pray for health but repeatedly cried 'why not nowe, O my good God; I am readie for thee, I am prepared' (Stubbes 1629; sig. A4).

Philip Stubbes was, of course, writing in the form of a saint's life death-bed story with the explicit intention 'to glorifie God and to edifie one another in the way of true godlinesse' (sig. A2). We might as a result be sceptical about his assurance that he 'set downe worde for worde as shee spake it, as neere as could be gathered' (Stubbes 1591; title page). Nevertheless this extraordinary text shows how the language of religion provided Stubbes with a way of making sense of the disastrous events of his marriage and conferred on Katherine a status which mere love and affection could never have rivalled. However grotesque it might seem to experience the anguish of death from septicaemia as a struggle with Satan, it does suggest the powerful effect of religion as the central reference point of Katherine's mind: and though Philip's admiration for her experience may seem callous, in the absence of more medically effective procedures it had a psychological and emotional fitness about it. For Philip and Katherine Stubbes marriage was only one locus of emotion and behaviour in a life conducted throughout in religious terms.

For many women, religion existed in rather more tense relation to marriage. Alice Thornton, for example, fell ill on her wedding-day and confided in her diary:

> I doe confesse I was very desirous to have delivered up my miserable life into the hands of my merciful redeemer who I feared I had offended by altering my resolve of a single life. (Thornton 1875; p. 83)

Alice Thornton's 'resolve of a single life' was informed by intense religious feelings, and she was one of the many women whom Sara Mendelson (1985; p. 195) has described as 'turning to the religious life to compensate for the inadequacies of wedlock'. Lady Margaret Hoby's diary provides additional evidence for this phenomenon. The name of Mr Rhodes, her chaplain, recurs almost every day. She prayed with him, heard him read and recorded conversations with him far more frequently than with her husband: he provides a constant source of interest in a pretty uneventful life.

For other women, religion provided the possibility of an involvement with public life. Rose Austen of Cranbrook in Kent, for example, left a number of bequests to neighbouring preachers, which suggested to Patrick Collinson that 'this widow woman was in the habit of "gadding to sermons"' and that she shared in the select society of the godly minded (Collinson 1965; p. 457). Accounts of radical religious groups all provide evidence of the significant involvement of women in their affairs:

> There were said to be more women than men in the first large body of English separatists, in London in 1568; and we know that later many left their husbands to go overseas to the Netherlands with Browne and Harrison. (Thomas 1965; p. 321)

Many of these women for whom commitment to radical religion meant a complete break from nation and kin as well as from husbands may have been among those who returned to England as preachers and prophets during the Civil War, contributing a strain of feminism to the radical ideas which that conflict threw up.[8] Women, moreover, seem to have been centrally involved in religious activism throughout the period:

> It was the women of London who occupied the front line in defence of their preachers. . . . The case of John Bartlett, the suspended lecturer of St Giles Cripplegate, was defended by sixty women who descended on [archbishop] Grindal in his own house. The bachelor bishop retreated before this monstrous imposition with the suggestion that they 'send half a dozen of their husbands, and with them I would talk'. (Collinson 1967; p. 93)

In Grindal's view, women had no right to talk independently of religious matters. The radical religious sects, however, offered the subversive possibility of a spiritual equality for men and women before God. As a result, the image of women preaching or even taking an active part in religious organisation suggested to some observers 'ambition and a desire to upset the established order'. (Thomas 1965; p. 331).

In the event that subversive potential was not fully realised: as Keith Thomas points out, it was contained by the idea of the separation of spiritual life from secular affairs:

> even the most radical sects became conservative as regards the organisation and discipline of the family. The Quakers were notoriously patriarchal and the Baptist churches continued to punish rebellious wives and servants. For the sects, as for the Presbyterians, spiritual equality was to remain strictly spiritual only. (Thomas 1965; pp. 334–5)

III

These somewhat random examples of women living within the institutions of religiously sanctioned marriage and working through the experience of both marriage and religion can provide a focus for examining the issues surrounding a feminist reading of the 'real lives' of early modern women. At the outset a distinction must be made between feminist history and a history of feminism. Feminist history is informed by the analytical and theoretical resources of modern feminism and seeks to explore the relations of power between men and women at particular historical moments. In the process it might find evidence of women's resistance to patriarchal institutions or of women's independent economic and social activity as well as evidence for women's subordination and oppression. It is tempting to see in this material about women working[9] or women petitioning Parliament[10] or women leading grain riots[11] evidence of a popular feminist groundswell. However, it is not in and of itself evidence of early modern feminist sentiments or activity. For a feminist politics involves more than discontent: it requires a movement directed towards fundamental change in the relations between men and women and the institutions which sustain them. As Buchanan Sharpe (1985) and John Walter (1980) have shown in their discussion of food riots and resistance to enclosures in early modern England, it is important in political analysis to maintain the distinction between dissatisfaction with local conditions and a movement directed by a sense that fundamental political change is both necessary and possible.

For most early modern women, relations between men and women took place within the family, which was the central institution within which they lived their lives. They may have combated misogyny and resisted oppression and asserted their independence within the family; nevertheless, activity which we might call feminist was restricted to those women for whom the contradictions between their claims to spiritual equality and their subordination within their families led to a choice which left this central institution behind. And as we have seen, even in those cases the institutions of the family and the state were able to accommodate even this fundamental challenge.

This sense that there was little in the conduct of early modern women which could properly be called feminist should not leave the impression that misogynist attitudes and patriarchal institutions went unchallenged. Relations between men and women provided an important locus for the discussion of the stability and organisation of power throughout society. They were the subject of intense debate in an outpouring of published material, from the Homilies of official culture to the jokes and merry tales which drew on and fed into popular culture. It is important not to hang too much historical weight on the existence of any of these texts, for the same text often points in different directions. The Homilies, for example, can variously be seen as the judicious rehearsal of accepted truths and the anxious reiteration of ideals under threat. The misogynist jokes and merry tales can set up similar echoes of the guffaws of confident male chauvinism or the nervous titters of henpecked husbands. All that can be firmly deduced at this historical distance is that these texts reiterated some of the ideas in circulation: they provided ways, in Mary Ellmann's phrase, of 'thinking about women'. Nevertheless, it is possible to feel in the narratives and the imagery and the inconsistencies of these texts the pressure-points which their stated 'attitudes', whether solemn or ribald, attempted to alleviate.

A significant body of writing which explicitly addressed questions of gender relations was the formal controversy regarding women in which writers praised and blamed women in essentialist terms with debating points culled from theological and classical sources.[12] It is worth stressing, as Linda Woodbridge (1984) does in detail, the literary traditions which informed this debate. The nature of women was a staple subject for rhetorical and poetic exercises, and the to and fro of the controversy often seemed self-generating, a manipulation of ideas rather than an entry into ideology.[13] For example, as Sandra Clark has pointed out:

> If we did not know, for instance, that Alexander Niccholes' *A Discourse of Marriage and Wiving* derives its cynical attitude from a long tradition of anti-feminist satire and its structure from a medieval parody of a religious poem on the sorrows of the Virgin Mary, we might think Niccholes both more misogynist as a man and more original as a writer than he deserves. (Clark 1983; p. 38)

Those who defamed women in this debate used the historical lore of wicked women combined with attacks on women's very natures; those who defended them simply reversed the arguments, with recourse to familiar legends of good women, questioning the decorum of attacking such weak and defenceless creatures. The formula for the defence is laid out in exemplary form in Ester Sowernam's preface to *Ester hath Hang'd Haman*, a response to Joseph Swetnam's notorious *Arraignment of Lewd, Idle, Froward and Unconstant Women:*

> I doe in the first part of it . . . plainely and resolutely deliver the
> worthiness and worth of women; both in respect of their Creation, as
> in the works of Redemption. Next I doe shew in examples out of both
> the Testaments: what blessed and happy choyse hath beene made of
> women, as gratious instruments to derive God's blessings and benefits
> to mankinde.
> In my second part I doe deliver of what estimate women have been
> valued in all ancient and moderne times, which I proove by
> authorities, customes and daily experiences. Lastly I do answer all
> materiall objections which have or can be alledged against our Sexe.
> (ed Ferguson 1985; p. 76)

At no point do the women writers question the terms of the
argument: imputations of vice against their sex constantly throw
them on to the defensive. Constantia Munda, another of
Swetnam's respondents, adopted a tone of moral indignation to
remind him that

> [a] private abuse of your own familiar doxies should not break out into
> open slanders of the religious matron together with the prostitute
> strumpet. (Munda 1617; C1^v–C2)

Women writers, in this as in other contexts, adopted a range of
views on the issue of their subordination and their social roles.
Outside the formal controversy, religious matrons instructed
their daughters not only in virtue but in subordination. Dorothy
Leigh, writing a handbook of advice for her children, sought

> to write them the right way that I had truly obserued out of the
> written Word of God, lest for want of warning they might fall where I
> stumbled (Leigh 1621); sig. A2^v)

In doing so, she places significant emphasis upon chastity, taking
ten pages to demonstrate

> that a woman that is truly chaste, is a great partaker of all other
> vertues; and contrariwise, that the woman that is not truly chaste,
> hath no vertue in her. (Leigh 1621; p. 30).

The main aim of her writing, however, is one of expiation. She
aims

> to encourage Women (who, I feare, will blush at my boldnesse) not to
> be ashamed to shew their infirmities, but to give men the first and

chiefe place: yet let us labour to come in the second; and because we must needes confesse that sinne entered by us into our posteritie; let us shew how carefull we are to seeke to Christ. (Leigh 1621; pp. 16–17)

The argument from origins was so firmly embedded as a rhetorical and argumentative mode in the period that a preoccupation with Original Sin recurs in both defences of and attacks upon women. Where Dorothy Leigh seems content to accept the burden of Original Sin and follow the theologically accurate procedure of seeking Christ, Aemilia Lanyer, in her long poem on the Passion of Christ, digresses in order to argue that the fault for the primal sin lay with the serpent and not Eve, who was in no position to know what she would lose:

> For, had she knowne of what we were bereau'd,
> To his request she had not condiscended.
> But she (poore soule) by cunning was deceau'd,
> No hurt therein her harmless Heart intended.
> (Lanyer 1611; sig. D)

Adam, she claims, should have used his superior experience to prevent the catastrophe: modern men, for their part, should not use Eve's fall against women in their own time:

> Then let us haue our Libertie againe,
> And challendge to your selues no Sou'raigntie;
> You came not in the world without our paine,
> Make that a barre against your crueltie;
> Your fault beeing greater, why should you disdaine
> Our beeing your equals, free from tyranny?
> If one weake woman simply did offend,
> This sinne of yours hath no excuse, nor end.
> (Lanyer 1611; sig. D2)

Lanyer's call for equality goes no further than freedom from tyranny and cruelty and, though it offers a more spirited defence of women than Dorothy Leigh's, it is nonetheless embedded in conventional rhetorical and theological terms.

Given the familiar and repetitive nature of these arguments, the interest of the material lies principally in the literary and rhetorical variations which can be played on the well-worn themes. One of the liveliest of the contributions is *Jane Anger her Protection for Women* (1589), which uses the familiar satiric technique of debunking classical figures in order to make a mockery of men who complain of their treatment at women's hands:

> But that Menalaus was served with such sauce it is a wonder: yet truely their Sex are so like to Buls, that it is no marvell though the Gods do metamorphose some of them, to give warning to the rest, if they could think so of it, for some of them will follow the smocke as Tom Bull will runne after a towne Cowe. (ed Ferguson 1985; p. 61)

Her description of Menelaus and other men as 'Smel-smocke' does more for the women's case than all the pious pleadings of women's conventional defenders. Anger is most effective in her impatience with the tedious repetitiveness of literary misogyny:

> If they have stretched their invention so hard on a last, as it is at a stand, there remaines but one help, which is, to write to us women. If they may once encroach so far into our presence, as they may but see the lyning of our outermost garment, they straight think that Apollo honours them, in yeelding so good a supply to refresh their sore overburdened heads, through studying for matters to indite off. And therfore that God may see how thankfully they receive his liberality, (their wits whetted, and their braines almost broken with botching his bountie) they fall straight to dispraising & slaundering our silly sex. (Anger 1589, ed Ferguson 1985; p. 59)

Anger's suggestion that the debate over women is an intellectual last resort was directed at the weary point-scoring which became its principal feature. It is easy to share her impatience. The puns of the opening sequence of Swetnam's *Arraignment,* for example, have the automatic twists of meaning of an oft-repeated comic routine:

> Moses describeth a woman thus: At the first beginning (saith he) a woman was made to be a helper unto man, and so they are indeed, for she helpeth to spend and consume that which man painfully getteth. (Swetnam 1615; sig. A3)

However, the repetitious terms and style of the debate were an indication not only of the longevity of the social concerns which it addressed but also of an impasse in the available ways of talking about them. Defenders of women could address such obvious abuses of male power, as their tyrannical and cruel behaviour, but the grievances which arose from differential power relations could not be addressed in the absence of more fully-articulated egalitarian discourses of sexual politics. Occasionally a defender of women will inveigh against the double standard of morality, as when Ester Sowernam denounces the different social attitudes to drunkenness and lust in men and women:

> So in all offences those which men commit, are made light and as nothing, slighted ouer; but those which women doe commit, those are made grievous and shamefull. (Sowernam 1617; p. 24. Quoted Woodbridge 1984; p. 97).

Sowernam, however, like many defenders of women since, was advocating a change in male behaviour rather than a change in the power relations which held the double standard in place.

Complex connections between gender relations, social relations and ways of speaking about them are comically revealed in one of Dekker's *Jests to Make you Merry:*

> A Water-bearer complaynd before a Justice, of his wife's misusing and over-maistring him: tis strange quoth the Justice, that you two should iarre, for I am told, that you (Sirra) are neuer seene to goe into an Alehouse but your wife is seene there too; you are never drunke but she is drunke too; you never quarrell with your neighbours but she quarrels too; I wonder that hauing quallities so alike you should no better agree. So do I and it please your Worship (sayd the Water-bearer) for my owne part I could agree with her if she were worse so she would be but better; I pray therefore let me have her bound, either to her good behaviour, or else to the peace. Seeke but out such a Scrivener (quoth the Justice) that can make such a bond, and thou shalt have my furtherance. (Dekker 1607; pp. 294–5)

The comic appeal of this story comes from a number of interlocking sources. The punch line is that no legal system can control women's insubordination, but the comic effects along the way are the display of a lower-class woman's insubordination and her water-bearer husband's confusion about what constitutes being better or worse for a woman. The issue of status here is all-important, for it allows the problem of women's insubordinate behaviour to be displaced on to a group who can be expected to be comically lawless, while displaying naïve faith in the ability of official culture to solve their problems by the mechanisms of the half-understood process of law. However, the comedy is also at the Justice's expense, for he admits the inability of the law to frame adequate controls over conjugal behaviour and by invoking a 'bond' quite explicitly indicates the particular inadequacy of the ideal of conjugal harmony proposed in the covenant ideal of Puritan handbooks on marriage.[14] The water-bearer and his wife had in fact solved the problems of conjugal harmony by abandoning the double standard and acting according to a rough-and-ready equality, but this was only permissible on the edges of the social order and even there was felt to go against some abstract ideal of correct social behaviour.

This perceived gap between an ideal of correct behaviour and the disordered reality of social relations made for an almost obsessive return to the subject of gender relations in popular literature. The treatment of women in ballads, for example, suggests complex connections between exemplary moral tales and the literary and social pleasures of a tall tale well told. The Hyder Rollins edition of the Pepys Collection of ballads includes a number of ballads about women who killed their husbands. They all take the form of a lamentation on the part of the repentant wife, followed by a fuller account of the circumstances of the crime. Anne Wallen's Lamentation, for example, explicitly warns:

> Then take heed wiues be to your husband's kinde,
> And beare this lesson truely in your minde,
> Let not your tongues oresway true reason's bounds,
> Which in your rage your utmost rancour sounds:
> A woman that is wise should seldome speake,
> Unless discreetly she her words repeat.
> (Rollins 1922; pp. 84–8)

These ballads partly dramatise appropriate womanly repentance; however, they are also cautionary: a reminder of the consequences of violent rebellion.

The *Warning for Wives By the example of one Katherine Francis (1629)* offers a further possibility. Its refrain asks

> Oh women,
> Murderous women,
> Whereon are your minds?
> (Rollins 1922; pp. 300–4)

which raises the central question of these narratives: the motivation of the murderous women. Anne Wallen was responding to her husband's drunken violence and Alice Davis killed her husband in a fight over money. Katherine Francis's motive is less immediately clear: she killed her husband when they were both drunk, and the balladeer simply announces:

> She long had thirsted for his blood,
> (Euen by her owne confession)
> And now her promise she made good,
> So heaven gaue permission
> To Satan, who then lent her power
> And strength to do't that bloody houre.
> (Rollins 1922; p. 302)

In the case of these ballads, motivation is not offered as justification. The framework of morality and expected conjugal relations is so firmly in place that there is no need to offer complex accounts of the women's feelings: they are evil, Satan gave his power, they repent all in accordance with the rightful order of things. However, since the described motives and circumstances cannot shake those foundations, they are not glossed over and they offer an interesting insight into the pressures of married life which might lead to murder.

Anne Wallen's contention with her husband was over work and leisure:

> My husband hauing beene about the towne,
> And comming home he on his bed lay down:
> To rest himself, which when I did espie,
> I fell to rayling most outragiously.

The angry tongue which Anne Wallen warns against in her speech of repentance seems in context a reasonable enough reaction. The story, moreover, goes on to make clear that her husband began the violence which led to his death.

In Alice Davis's case, her husband asked for some of her money. In spite of all the legal and ideological pressures to the contrary, she clearly felt that she had some right to refuse him:

> But words betwixt us then did passe
> As words to harsh I gaue,
> And as the Diuell would as then
> I did both sweare and raue.
> (Rollins 1922; p. 290)

Since the text does not endorse Alice Davis's behaviour it leaves her indignation to speak for itself. A similar effect is often created in texts ostensibly attacking women. Swetnam offers, as his example of a woman's outrageous railing, an impassioned speech on the indignities and injustices of women's oppression:

> She thundereth out a thousand iniuries that thou dost her, saying, My Corne he sendeth to the market, and my Catell to the fayre, and look what he openly findeth he taketh away by force, and what I hide secretly he priuely stealeth it away ... but now all this while she doth not forget to tell of her owne good huswifery, saying, I sit working all day at my needle or my distaff, and he like an unthrift and a whoremonger runneth at random. (Swetnam 1615; pp. 61–2. Quoted in Woodbridge 1984; p. 86)

Swetnam, along with misogynists who approved his sentiments, stands condemned out of his own mouth: but perhaps more significantly, the familiar matrimonial pressure-points of shared labour and resources are starkly revealed. These narratives provide evidence of power relations within marriage being hotly contested, through violent words and actions, by women who challenged the practices though not the ideals of subordination. As the structures of the narratives show, their actions did not seem to dislodge the ideology of patriarchal rights: the contradictions between ideology and action are simply left as contradictions.

IV

As well as being evidence of social dislocation, however, the disruptive behaviour of the women in these stories serves a literary function. If the women who figure in these ballads and debates were not disruptive, there would be no story and the contradictions which these stories enact would have no locus of action. For while recognising that ballads and merry tales and the more learned debates were the forms which mediated the experience of the relations of power between the sexes, we must also recognise the social pleasures which such material provided.

Ester Sowernam's contribution to the Swetnam controversy

begins with a vignette of the role which the debate about women might have played in the social life of London:

> upon my repaire to London this last Michaelmas Terme; being at supper amongst friends, where the number of each sexe were equal: As nothing is more usual for table-talke; there fell out a discourse concerning women, some defending, other objecting against our Sex: (Sowernam 1617; ed Ferguson, 1985; p. 75)

Ester Sowernam's presentation of the supper party is a delightful fiction but it is not inconceivable that such a scene might have provided the context in which the debate over women, or the latest joke from the lawcourts, was discussed. Ballads, moreover, as sung popular entertainment were as likely to be experienced in a social setting as read in private. Sowernam goes on to make a distinction between polite engagement in controversy and the 'scandalous and blasphemous' tones of Swetnam's railing but it is nevertheless clear that representations of relations between men and women in all the various forms they took were part of the currency of social exchange, as well as the object of official concern, and the lived experience of men and women.

This notion that the representation of gender relations was a form of social exchange may help to address the difficult problem of the comic treatment of male violence and oppression of women in such genres as 'gadding stories' and shrew-taming tales. An important initial gesture of feminist politics is the refusal of just such a social exchange by resisting misogynist jokes. Desdemona's dismissal of Iago's misogynist wit as 'Old fond paradoxes to make fools laugh i'th' alehouse' or the Duchess of Malfi's 'fie sir!' addressed to Ferdinand's joke about 'the lamprey that hath never a bone in it' may be examples of just such a resistance.[15] Nevertheless, resisting social approval of a joke does not deny that joke's comic structure, which needs to be analysed in order to understand its function in the construction of literary and ideological notions about men and women.

In his analysis of charivari, Martin Ingram has suggested that

> Deep in the heart of the organisers of the ridings lay the knowledge that women could never be dominated to the degree implied in the patriarchal ideal. For the ideal was only too plainly in conflict with the realities of everyday life. (Ingram 1985b; p. 176)

Ingram's opposition between the 'patriarchal ideal' and the 'realities of everyday life', however, obscures the fact that ideals have to be lived through the 'realities of everyday life', and one of the procedures which makes that possible is the resolution of that apparent opposition in fictional and cultural forms.

In both learned and popular renderings of the conflict between men and women, the uncompromisingly explicit ideological framework of the texts allowed considerable variety of treatment of characters and motivation, and therefore failed to close off the possibility of sympathetic engagement with the characters, even when their actions were condemned. In the ballads, the woman's crime can be set against her evident provocation by male inadequacy; in the merry tales, the comic treatment sets social disapproval of women's misbehaviour against the comic gusto with which it is conducted. In the 'gadding stories' women go out to drink and gossip, usually about men, with their neighbours. As Linda Woodbridge has shown, (1984; pp. 224–43) the comic energy lies with the witty women so that the familiar stories they produce about the sexual, economic and conjugal inadequacies of men in general and their husbands in particular are granted a powerful hearing.

In the shrew-taming stories, a similar tension exists between the comic power of violence, both by and against authority, and its ideological power. It is clear that violence towards wives was not condoned by official accounts of proper married relations, and indeed, explicit objections to wife-beating are presented as part of the strategy of humanising the extremes of patriarchy. The Homily on The State of Matrimony, for example, explicitly created a connection between violence and low social status, a division between 'common sort of men' and the more discriminating types which the Homily sought to construct:

> the common sort of men do judge that such moderation should not become a man: for they say that it is a token of womanish cowardness; and therefore they think that it is a man's part to fume in anger, to fight with fist and staff. (Homilies 1908; p. 537)

This effort to make a social division out of differences of behaviour has a complex effect in the shrew-taming stories, where the violent man's status as the hero has to be negotiated round the shocking effect of the violence itself. The men's aim in the story was mastery over women but it could be more sympathetically established by a combination of wit and violence than by violence alone.

This tension between violence, wit and comedy is evident in *The Merry Jest of a Shrewde wife lapped in Morelles Skin,*[16] in which a witty fellow marries a noted shrew, daughter of a noted shrew, and tames her by wrapping her bleeding, beaten body in the salted hide of his old horse. The story of how he gains control is presented as righting the topsy-turvy situation in which the bride's mother has henpecked her husband and could equally serve as a wishful alteration of the affairs of its assumed audience. However, the issue of violence is addressed in a number of different ways. The young man is presented sympathetically, but he clearly benefits financially from the marriage: the bride's economic value as a partner in a household is stressed and the bride's father pays the young man for removing his curst daughter; but her mother also pays 'an hundred pound in Golde' (423) as a guarantee that her husband will not try to beat her. The potential for violence in marriage is recognised, but violence is seen both as a desirable alternative to uxorious submission and as being connected in some way with the financial settlement which marriage involves.

Violence is also, however, connected to sexual domination. After the wedding night, the bride's mother visits her and is sent away, apparently so that the bride can feel unselfconscious about 'being in his arms heare all alone' (502). But the sex soon slides into violence:

> When that the mother departed was,
> They dallyed togither, and had good game;
> He hit her awry; she cryed, alas,
> What doe ye, man, hold up for shame . . .
> And they wrestled so long beforne,
> That this they had for their greate meade;
> Both shyrt and smock was all to-torne,
> That their uprysyng had no speede.
>
> (511–22)

This form of violent domination is presented as acceptable. The tone of the description is comic and the mother reassures the daughter that she need not be ashamed of what has happened:

> For this is honesty for thee and for us all.
> (563)

There is not the same sexual ambiguity about the violence which occurs at the end of the poem. The beating and wrapping in Morel's skin is a carefully calculated punishment for the wife's disobedience. Nevertheless, the way it is described emphasises the knockabout comedy of a physical fight rather than the suffering of the woman, or even the triumph of the man. A good deal of poetic energy goes into dramatising this conflict: the wife gives as good as she gets, abusing her husband both verbally and physically and reminding him of his dependence on her domestic work:

> Then he her met, and to her gan say:
> How sayest thou, wife, wilt thou be mayster yet?
> She sware by God's body and by that day,
> And sodaynly with her fyst she did him hit,
> And defyed him Dreuill at every worde,
> Saying precious horesone, what doest thou think?
> I set not by thee a stinking torde
> Thou shalt get of me neyther meate nor drinke.
> Then, quoth he, we must make a fraye,
> And with that her cloths he gan to teare
> Out upon thee horesone, than she did saye,
> Wylte thou robbe me of all my geare?
> It cost thee naught, thou arrant theefe;
> And quickly she gat hym by the heade,
> With that she sayde: God giue thee a mischiefe,
> And them that fed thee fyrst with breade.
> (927–34; 943–50)

This is not the oppression of a victim: it is presented as the necessary and only means to keep a shrew in order, and the comedy both softens and endorses the violence.

In part this violence is also endorsed because it is a response to the pressure-points of conjugal life which threaten a husband's power. The wife's shrewishness is presented as a direct response to the domestic work which marriage imposes, emerging quite suddenly when she has to feed not only her husband but the hired men on his farm:

He kepte both boye and also swayne,
That to the carte and plow did goe
And some kept neate, and some kept sheepe,
Some did one thing, some did another,
But when they came home to haue their meate,
The wife played the deuell then, like her mother.

With countenance grim and wordes smart
She gaue them meate, and bad them brast
The pore folke that come from plow and carte
Of her lewd wordes they were agast.
Saying eche to other: what dame is this?
The deuill I trow hath brought us here;
Our mayster shall know it, by heauens blisse,
That we will not serue him another yeare.

(599–614)

Within the expressed value system of the poem, the poor folks reaction makes it quite clear that the wife's behaviour is outrageous: within the poem's structure, on the other hand, it is a turning-point in the narrative and sets up not only suspense about how the husband will react but also the potential pleasure of witnessing a conflict.

However much a modern reader might be repelled by the violence of the story, seen in terms of a social exchange of ideas, the poem offered its contemporary audience not only the ultimate triumph of patriarchy, but a comic representation of the limits of that triumph and the arenas in which it is likely to be contested.

Even when there was no direct conflict between husbands and wives at stake, the image of the physically powerful woman offered a potential for comedy and excitement which made quite clear the boundaries of male control. The legendary tales which surrounded Long Meg of Westminster, for example, revel in her physical energy. She overthrows the carter who tries to over-charge her and the other women he has brought to London; she defends her honour and sorts out the tavern brawls in the inn where she finds a job. She even enlists in the wars with France to defend her country. She takes on, in short, all of the attributes of the popular hero but also provides the tales in which she appears with the additional edge of the comic and unexpected. In the end of course, she submits to her proper role as a wife:

The wars in France being ended, Meg came to her old residence at

Westminster and married a proper tall man, and a Soldier . . . yet
because he heard what she heretofore had done, and how manlike she
was . . . called her aside into a backchamber, and stripping her into
her petticoat, delivered her one staffe, and tooke himself another, and
told her that because he heard she was so manlike as to beat all she met
with, he would trie her manhood, and therefore bad her take which
cudgell she would. She replyed nothing but held down her head,
whereupon he gave her three or four blows, and she, in all
submission, fell down upon her knees, desiring him to hold his hands
and pardon her. Husband, quoth she, whatsoever I have done unto
others, it behoveth me to be obedient to you; and never shall it be said
though I can cudgell a knave that wrongs me, that Long Meg is her
husband's master; and therefore use me as you please! (sig B2ᵛ–B3)

The ideological point is clearly made but it is effected by a
witty reversal of the usual form of the anecdotes about Meg. Her
refusal to fight on this occasion is as surprising as the effective
combats throughout the story. The setting in a private room with
Meg in her petticoat further emphasises the sexual character of
the encounter for, just as she had defended her honour against all
comers, so, at the right moment, she accepts the necessity of
sexual submission to the right man.

In all these staples of the popular representation of relations
between men and women, the sexuality and the violence, the
reversals of expected roles and the endorsement of officially
accepted ones are symbolic counters in the construction of
narratives. They construct literary processes in which women are
variously the objects of ribaldry, pathos and sentimentality. Any
and all of these responses were no doubt part of women's
responses to the real situations in which they found themselves.
However, the popular literary versions of gender relations
organised these responses so that they were not in serious conflict
with the ideology of male supremacy. These narratives about the
subjection of women were the means by which statements about
the health of the culture could be made. For the writers of
homilies and conduct-books, women's disruptive behaviour had
to be borne in the interests of sustaining the institutions of godly
matrimony; for magistrates and the church courts it had to be
controlled in the interests of harmonious community; and for the
writers of merry tales or horrid crimes, its comic or pathetic
potential could be appreciated and enjoyed because it was

ultimately controlled both by the narrative framework and by the final assertion of patriarchal order. Virginia Woolf was right to observe that women *were* 'locked up and beaten and flung about the room'. But when that happened, stories were told about it in court depositions, in cautionary ballads and in merry tales. Oppression and subordination were the context in which women lived their lives, the stories which were told about that oppression provided the terms (language and structures) in which those lives could be endured.

Notes

1. See A. MacFarlane, *Reconstructing Historical Communities.*
2. See P. Laslett, *Family Life and Illicit Love in Earlier Generations* and M. J. Ingram, *Ecclesiastical Justice in Wiltshire, 1600–1640.* The historiography of sex and marriage is discussed in M. J. Ingram, 'The Reform of Popular Culture?' in B. Reay, *Popular Culture in Seventeenth Century England.*
3. See A. MacFarlane, *Witchcraft in Tudor and Stuart England.* For a full discussion of the historiography of witchcraft, see C. Larner, *Enemies of God*, Chapter 2.
4. See D. Underdown, *Revel, Riot and Rebellion. Popular Politics and Culture in England, 1603–1660.*
5. See M. Spufford, *Contrasting Communities. English Villages in the Sixteenth and Seventeenth Centuries.*
6. See M. J. Ingram, 'The Reform of Popular Culture?', and P. Collinson, *The Religion of Protestants*, Chapter 5. The question of the extent, efficacy and ideology of the reform of popular culture is central to all the essays in Reay, *Popular Culture in Seventeenth Century England,* though on the whole English social historians tend to resist monolithic theses of social change.
7. The influence of the thesis that women are a mode of exchange in early modern societies has been challenged by Susan Mosher Stuart. In 'The Annales School and Feminist History', she suggests that this model obscures the number of women who did not function within families in the period and begs the question as to why the currency of exchange should be women.
8. See C. Hill, *The World Turned Upside Down. Radical Ideas during the English Revolution*, Chapter 15, 'Base Impudent Kisses'.
9. The focus on women gaining independence through work is central to Alice Clark's classic of feminist history, *The Working Life of Women in the Seventeenth Century.* The connection between that focus and Alice Clark's own moment of feminist history is addressed

by Miranda Chaytor and Jane Lewis in the introduction to the 1982 edition.

10. See Patricia Higgins, 'The Reactions of Women, with Special Reference to Women Petitioners' in Brian Manning (ed.), *Politics, Religion and the English Civil War.*

11. Higgins also discusses (pp. 182–3) women's roles in protests against enclosure. The role of women in grain riots is discussed in John Walter, 'Grain riots and Popular Attitudes to the Law: Maldon and the Crisis of 1629' in John Brewer and John Styles, *An Ungovernable People, The English and their Law in the Seventeenth and Eighteenth Centuries.*

12. This context is laid out in Francis Lee Utley's pioneering work, *The Crooked Rib: An Analytical Index to the Argument about Women in English and Scots Literature to the End of the Year 1568.* L. Woodbridge, in *Women and the English Renaissance,* develops the discussion with a more detailed analysis of the rise and fall of the debate. She extends it beyond 1568 and takes the theatre into account. Some texts from the controversy are reprinted in M. Ferguson, *First Feminists: British Women Writers 1578–1799* and Henderson and McManus, *Half Humankind: Context and Texts of the Controversy about Women in England,* 1540–1640.

13. The problems of using written texts as evidence of historical processes is discussed in more particular detail in Chapter 3 below.

14. See James T. Johnson, 'The Covenant Idea and the Puritan View of Marriage'.

15. See Shakespeare, *Othello,* II. i. 138–9 and Webster, *The Duchess of Malfi,* I. i. 335–7.

16. ed. W. Carew Hazlitt, *Remains of the Early Popular Poetry of England,* volume IV. The poem is also discussed by Linda Woodbridge in 'New Light on *The Wife Lapped in Morel's Skin* and *The Proud Wife's Paternoster*'.

CHAPTER THREE

Women and Cultural
Production: The Case
of Witchcraft

If, as I concluded in the previous chapter, representations of
women are part of a cultural exchange, what procedures can the
feminist critic devise to analyse the relations between women in
the early modern period and their representation in its drama? It
is clearly inadequate simply to read off the conditions and
preoccupations of early modern women from their representation
in drama, however tempting such analogising might seem. A
telling warning against such procedures is offered in Barry
Smith's account of sexuality in Britain in the nineteenth century:

> This form of historical argument is common in literary circles. It
> consists of turning exegesis into historical evidence. The exposition
> begins by referring a literary text, the representativeness of which in
> time and place is unestablished, to an ideal type generalised from
> current fashions in literary interpretation. This happy conjunction
> itself becomes 'evidence' which 'proves' the historicity of the literary
> text and thereby transforms its fictional modes of thought and
> happenings into thoughts and events that actually occurred in the
> past. It is a superficially persuasive presentation, but it is not history.
> (Smith 1980; p. 185)

Nevertheless, the historicity of dramatic texts is undeniable in
that they were produced in the conditions and according to the
relations of early modern theatrical production. As such they can
be approached through a

criticism which would not be a commentary, which would be a
scientific analysis, adding an authentic knowledge to the speech of a
work without, meanwhile, denying its presence . . . a *positive criticism*
which would speak of the conditions for making a book. . . .
(Macherey 1978; p. 149)

Such a scientific criticism has been most effectively theorised
and put into practice in the work of Raymond Williams.
Discussing *The Country and the City* in an interview with Perry
Anderson, Williams declared that his aim was

to try to show simultaneously the literary conventions and the
historical relations to which they were a response – to see together the
means of production and the conditions of the means of production of
a particular set of literary texts. (Williams 1979)

The means of production of a theatrical text are the theatrical
conventions and the source material which enable it to take its
particular form while the conditions of the means of production
are the theatres and companies which produced it, together with
the surrounding historical circumstances which made its production viable.

One way of analysing the relationships between these theoretical abstractions and, in particular, their application to the question
of women would be to look at the treatment of witchcraft in two
plays, *The Witch of Edmonton* and *The Late Lancashire Witches*,
which dramatised actual cases, contemporary with the plays'
production. These cases offer particularly telling examples in that
as well as the plays' texts, we have available the source material
which the dramatists drew on, some evidence about the theatres
and companies in which the plays were performed and, through
the work of social historians of witchcraft, some sense of the
concerns which informed the contemporary preoccupations with
the phenomenon. We have, in other words, the product, the raw
material and the forms through which it was mediated.

Witchcraft, moreover, offers a particularly fertile ground for
feminism in that it seems to present an obvious case of the
systematic victimisation and oppression of women. Mary Daly,
for example, devotes a chapter of her *Gyn/Ecology* to an account
of the European witchcraze in which she rehearses the details of
torture and mass killings as examples of the concerted attacks

against women made by what she calls the 'Sado/Ritual State'. She inveighs against the conspiracy by powerful men to eliminate deviant and independent women in the interests of 'purifying the Body of Christ' and includes in her denunciation those historians who present other accounts of witchcraft:

> Hags [her appropriated term for powerful feminist women] are re-membering and therefore understanding not only the intent of the Sado-State – the torture, dis-memberment, and murder of deviant women – but also the fact that this intent is justified and shared by scholars and other professional perpetrators of this State. (Daly 1978; p. 185)

Mary Daly is explicitly opposed to the methods of what she regards as male scholarship and instead she uses the historical evidence concerning witchcraft as a kind of poetic imagery in the litany of fury with which she fuels her radical feminist politics. This poetic use of references to witches is evident in the poem with which she prefaces her chapter:

> Repeat the syllables
>   before the lesson hemorrhages through the brain:
> Margaret Barclay, crushed to death with stones, 1618.
> Mary Midgely, beaten to death, 1646.
> Peronette, seated on a hot iron as torture
>   and then burned alive, 1462.
> Sister Maria Renata Sanger, sub-prioress
>   of the Premonstratensian Convent of Unter-Zell,
>   accused of being a lesbian;
>   the document certifying her torture
>   is inscribed with the seal of the Jesuits,
>   and the words Ad Majorem Dei Gloriam –
> To the Greater Glory of God.
>
> What have they done to us?
>   (Robin Morgan, from 'The Network of the Imaginary
>   Mother, *Lady of the Beasts*' in Daly 1978; p. 179)

An assent to this view of witchcraft, a sense of unity with all oppressed women, is called forth by the humanist appeal for sympathy with any suffering, and a leap of political faith in the suggestion that the suffering of modern womanhood – 'what have they done to us?' – is analogous if not the same.

These powerful versions of the political connection between

witchcraft and feminism are also reflected in Caryl Churchill's play, *Vinegar Tom*, which makes a clear connection between sexual deviance and accusations of witchcraft. Churchill's witches, Alice, a marriage-refuser, Betty and a woman healer, are free sexual beings, uncontrolled by men. All are accused and found guilty by the witch-finder, Packer. However, the play is not restricted to the historical context. Inserted songs make clear the parallels with the situation of modern women, while a feminist ability to transcend this oppression is dramatised in the closing sequence in which Kramer and Sprenger, authors of the classic text of medieval witchcraft, the *Malleus Maleficarum*, are presented as a grotesquely comic double act. The scene demonstrates the deadly illogicality of misogynist theories of witchcraft by means of a simple rehearsal of its chop-logic theology.

These feminist versions of the witchcraze are obviously and explicitly inadequate as history. In presenting a monolithic explanation of the oppressive nature of the church and state and their oppression of women they make no distinctions of period or locality and pay scant attention to the material circumstances of accuser and accused. Nevertheless, they provide an interesting example of the process by which history is used as myth to inform political rhetoric, as well as an important reminder of the feminist dimension in the witchcraze which can easily disappear in less passionate analyses of its particular manifestations.

One historian who has paid careful and sympathetic attention to the feminist question is Christina Larner, whose work on Scottish witchcraft is a landmark in the field. Although Larner sees witchcraft primarily as an epiphenomenon of religious change and of attempts by the Calvinist state to impose a more systematic degree of religious orthodoxy, she also continually investigates the psychological and social factors which made women witches. She notes the long-lived stereotypes of women, the 'twin pillars of the Aristotelian view of women as imperfectly human – a failure of the process of conception – and the Judaeo-Christian view of women as the source of sin and the Fall of Man' (Larner 1981; p. 92). She argues, however, that

[t]he relationship between witch-hunting and women-hunting, is less direct. Witches are hunted in the first place as witches. The total evil

which they represented was not actually sex specific. Indeed the Devil himself was male. Witch hunting was directed for ideological reasons against the enemies of God, and the fact that eighty per cent or more of these were women was, though not accidental, one degree removed from an attack on women as such. (Larner 1981; p. 92)

Larner investigates the actual attraction of witchcraft for women and locates it in the differential power relations of the communities in which they lived, their scope for action, and, in the case of the poor, their sense of impotence:

In situations of domestic stress and tension in which men resort to violence, women use witchcraft. The female witches in the seventeenth century Scottish courts may be the equivalent of the males accused of slaughter and murder . . . women may turn to cursing to give vent to aggression or exercise power. They may fantasise about the Devil to bring colour to their lives. (Larner 1981; p.96)

Larner's sympathetic account of these powerless women presents the witch as far from the explicitly deviant political subversive of feminist myth. She describes her typical witch as 'a married, middle-aged woman of the lower peasant class' with 'a sharp tongue and filthy temper' (Larner 1981; p. 98). The witches' aims and aspirations were also not explicitly political in the sense of an alteration of power relations, but rather represented more limited attempts to transcend the material limitations of their lives. The Devil

told them, typically 'that they should never want'. . . . Bessie Wilson was told by the Devil "thee art a poor puddled (overworked) body. Will thee by my servant and I will give thee abundance and thee sall never want'. (Larner 1981; p. 95).

The absence of want was, moreover, not set at too high a cost. Even the devil's food at witches' meetings 'fell within the range of normal peasant fare: oatcakes and ale'. Sometimes it was 'the fare of the landed class: red wine, wheaten cake and meat'. (Ibid p. 96)

In the case of English witchcraft, the women accused were very similar in type to those revealed by the Scottish accounts (see Larner 1984; p. 73), but in England the incidence of witchcraft prosecutions was considerably lower. In England, moreover, unlike Scotland or Germany, the cases were more local and rarely multiple and the treatment of witches in local courts concentrated on the particular evil-doing (*maleficium*) of which the witch was accused rather than making theologically sophisticated accusations to do with the witch's soul, her pact with the Devil, and other forms of heresy. The third statute against witchcraft in England, passed in 1604, insisted more forcibly on the felonious nature of any contact with evil spirits, 'to or for any intent or purpose' regardless of the social consequences. In practice, however, most trial proceedings concentrated on 'alleged acts of damage against other persons' and 'seldom drew on allegations of devil worship' (Thomas 1971; p. 525). English law, moreover, included a number of lesser penalties for witchcraft, which resulted in a low ratio of those executed to those convicted, and convictions themselves were by no means automatic: half of all those indicted for witchcraft on the home circuit were found not guilty (MacFarlane 1970; p. 53).

Set against this experience of witchcraft at the popular level were the learned arguments of demonologists and theologians. Like the jurists who framed the 1604 statute, their concern was with the theological question of the possibility of the demonic pact. The debate lay between sceptics like Reginald Scot, who believed that 'God would not have allowed witches to exercise supernatural power', and those who 'regarded it as tantamount to atheism to deny the reality of spirits or the possibility of supernatural intervention in daily affairs' (Thomas 1971; p. 685). Even the latter group, however, found themselves in difficulties with particular cases faced with the difficulty of distinguishing between acts of *maleficium* instigated by a pact with the Devil and the frequent misfortunes which occurred from natural causes.

Evidence of a pact with the Devil had to come from the existence of a familiar, or the presence on a witch's body of teat-like marks or swellings which could be used to suckle such a Devil surrogate. It was, however, not beyond the imagination of some judges to recognise that 'the familiar might be a harmless domestic pet and the "mark" a natural excrescence' (Thomas 1971; p. 687).

These complex and competing ways of talking about witches

and women, the conflict between popular beliefs and the law all provide the raw material, the wide historical circumstances, which made plays about witchcraft feasible on the Jacobean stage. They were quite different from the specific and explicit conditions which led the Women's Press to publish Mary Daly or Monstrous Regiment to perform *Vinegar Tom*. However, both the Elizabethen and the modern writers were involved in a process of turning history into myth. For plays and other texts mediated the witch phenomenon and the complex of witch beliefs into a form which was readily accessible and which could be repeated through the conventions of drama available to the playwrights.

In the case of Dekker, Ford and Rowley's play, *The Witch of Edmonton*, there was an intervening stage between the particular case of Elizabeth Sawyer, executed as a witch at Tyburn in 1621, and the representation of her story by the Prince's Men on the stage of the Phoenix Theatre and at the Court of James I. It is impossible at this remove to get to the truth of what led to Elizabeth Sawyer's arrest and conviction,[1] but the outline of the story was known to the dramatists from a pamphlet written by Henry Goodcole, the visitor of Newgate Prison, entitled *The Wonderful Discovery of Elizabeth Sawyer*, which was published soon after her execution.

In his 'Apologie to the Christian Readers', Goodcole insists that he is not going to 'discusse or dipute of Witches or Witchcraft' (Goodcole 1621; sig. A3). Nonetheless, the greatest interest of his account derives from the way in which it reveals the conflicting ways of talking and thinking about witchcraft. In his examination of Elizabeth Sawyer, which takes the form of a catechising, Goodcole is at pains to stress the evil of cursing rather than to focus on the *maleficium* of which she was condemned. Elizabeth Sawyer was accused:

> That shee the said Elizabeth Sawyer, not having the feare of God
> before her eyes, but moued and seduced by the Diuell, by Diabollical
> helpe, did out of her malicious heart (because her neighbours where
> she dwelt, would not buy Broomes of her), would therefore thus
> revenge herselfe on them in this manner, namely, witch to death their
> Nurse Children and Cattel. (Goodcole 1621; sig. B1ᵛ)

It was further maintained that she

> by Diabollical helpe, and out of her malice afore-thought, did witch
> unto death Agnes Ratcleife, a neighbour of hers. (Goodcole 1621; sig.
> B1ᵛ)

There is a curious gap in these indictments between the notion
of 'Diabollical helpe' and the all-too-familiar details of rural
conflict. Goodcole seems anxious to close that gap by insisting on
the importance of human agency in calling up the Devil and
continuing an acquaintance with him through persistence in sin.

His first question presented the familiar, inescapable, double
bind of all such interrogations:

> By what meanes came you to have acquaintance with the Diuell?
> (Goodcole 1621; sig. C)

Elizabeth Sawyer's reply, that the Devil came when she was
cursing, was insisted upon both in her own repentant remarks
about her misuse of the tongue which is the glory of man and in a
marginal note in which, according to Goodcole, a bystander
repeated, and insisted on the significance of, her curses. When
asked why she had performed the *maleficium* of putting
Christians and beasts to death, Elizabeth Sawyer replied:

> the cause that moued mee to do it, was malice and enuy, for if any
> body had angred me in any manner, I would be so reuenged of them,
> and of their cattell. (Goodcole 1621; sig. C2)

She added that she *was* guilty of those deaths of which she had
been acquitted but denied 'the least hurt' against Agnes Ratcleife,
which suggests that Goodcole was less interested in the legal
verdicts than in the state of Elizabeth Sawyer's soul. The
remainder of the interrogation is taken up with trivia about the
truth of different assertions about her familiars, and reveals
incidentally that she had both a husband and children. The main
thrust is directed to Elizabeth's sins, which are reaffirmed in
Goodcole's conclusion:

> The Diuell rageth, and mallice reigneth in the hearts of many. O let it
> not doe so, for heere you may see the fruites thereof. (Goodcole 1621;
> sig. D3)

In the preamble to the catechising, Goodcole does describe the development of Elizabeth Sawyer's reputation as a witch. It followed the familiar pattern of a 'Great and long suspicion' held, rather unusually, by 'a worthy justice of the peace' which grew into 'great presumptions' at a number of unexplained misfortunes occurring in the rural community. Goodcole, however, seems a little torn between his evident belief that this is a case of witchcraft and the necessity for acknowledging the trivial ground on which the case was brought. Elizabeth Sawyer's neighbours tested her witchery by burning her thatch to see if she would come running and though Goodcole describes this as 'an old ridiculous custom', he nevertheless noted:

> This triall, though it was slight and ridiculous, yet it setled a
> resolution in those whom it concerned, to finde out by all meanes they
> could endeavour, her long and close carried Witchery, to explaine it to
> the world. (Goodcole 1621; sig. A4ᵛ)

For Goodcole, much more serious evidence was provided by the fact that after Elizabeth Sawyer was arrested, the Devil forsook her. The evidence lay in her pale face, her deformed body 'which so happened but a little before her apprehension' and, most tellingly, by the fact that the tongue which had cursed and blasphemed

> was not able to speake a sensible or ready word for her defense, but
> sends out. . . . many and most fearefull imprecations for destruction
> against her selfe then to happen, as heretofore she had wished and
> indeauoured to happen on diuers of her neighbours. (Goodcole 1621;
> sig. B)

What in the case of Scottish witchcraft was called 'smeddum', the ready ability to turn bad temper into voluble abuse, turned against Elizabeth Sawyer after her accusation and made her, fatally, accuse herself.

Elizabeth Sawyer's case followed familiar patterns and there seems little need for it to have been singled out for reproduction as a play. Goodcole's pamphlet, which provided key details, was obviously a deciding factor in that it produced the raw materials of the story in an accessible form. However, it did more than this: the 'Author's Apologie to the Christian Readers' makes clear that

Goodcole is also engaged in dispute over the tone and seriousness with which witchcraft is to be treated. He is anxious to assert the truth of his account:

> For my part I meddle heare with nothing but matter of fact, and to that ende produce the Testimony of the liuing and the dead, which I hope shall be Authenticall for the confirmation of this Narration, and free mee from all censorious mindes and mouthes. (Goodcole 1621; sig. A3)

Truth, it appeared,

> in some measure, hath received a wound already, by most base and false Ballets, which were sung at the time of our returning home from the Witches execution. In them I was ashamed to see and heare such ridiculous fictions of her bewitching Corne on the ground, of a Ferret and an Owle dayly sporting before her, of the bewitched woman brayning her selfe, of the Spirits attending in the Prison: all which I know to be fitter for an Ale-bench than for a relation of proceeding in Court of Justice. (Goodcole 1621; sig. A3ᵛ)

The judicial problem of trivial evidence for a serious offence and the fine demarcation between superstition and belief is evident here. However, the conflict between high and popular culture is also an important factor: Goodcole's painstaking seriousness put him clearly on the high side of that divide, but a similar conflict was equally marked in Dekker, Ford and Rowley's play. In the play, the story of Elizabeth Sawyer is one of three plots whose linking figure is less the witch herself than her familiar, the black dog. He appears to the bigamous Frank when he is trying to leave his second wife and, almost casually, edges his frustration and irritation into murder; he is also responsible for bewitching the morris and leading the morris leader, Cuddy Banks, into the ditch in pursuit of a spirit appearing as his lady love. The witch plot thus stands as a pivot between the poetic high seriousness of the story of bigamy and murder in Ford's part of the play and the comic romp of Cuddy and the morris which is thought to have been Rowley's contribution.[2]

With the story of Elizabeth Sawyer standing between two different styles it is not surprising to find conflict in the styles of presentation of the witch herself. She is introduced in a long speech in which she powerfully denounces the injustice of her situation and wishes that she could assume the power to effect revenge that witchcraft would give her:

> MOTHER. And why on me? Why should the envious world
> Throw all their scandalous malice upon me?
> Cause I am poor, deform'd and ignorant,
> And like a bow buckl'd and bent together
> By some more strong in mischiefs than myself?
> Must I for that be made a common sink
> For all the filth and rubbish of men's tongues
> To fall and run into? Some call me witch,
> And being ig orant of myself, they go
> About to teach me how to be one; urging
> That my bad tongue, by their bad usage made so,
> Forespeaks their cattle, doth betwitch their corn.
> Themselves, their servants, and their babes at nurse.
> This they enforce upon me, and in part
> Make me to credit it.
>
> (II. i. 1–13)

In writing the speech, Dekker was able to draw on the tradition of such angry revengers as Hieronimo and Shylock, turning the 'smeddum' of real witches into a powerful statement of individualism, an assertion of individual rights against injustice rather than the 'malice and envy' which Goodcole found in the case. This powerful introduction lessens the potential for comedy in the business with the black dog. Dekker further heightens the seriousness by picking up on the figurative potential of the dog; Elizabeth Sawyer describes her enemy, Banks, as

> . . . this black cur
> That barks and bites and sucks the very blood
> Of me and of my credit.
>
> (II.i. 114–16)

In a remarkable sentence which echoes modern analysis of the process of becoming a witch, she declares:

> . . . 'tis all one
> To be a witch as to be counted one.
> Vengeance, shame, ruin light upon that canker.
>
> (II.i. 116–18)

As she curses, the dog appears and, in the exact words cited by Elizabeth Sawyer to Goodcole, triumphantly announces:

Ho! Have I found thee cursing? Now thou art
Mine own.

(II.i. 118–19)

In this introduction, theatrical tradition, popular ballad
material and the evidence from the Goodcole pamphlet merge.
The ballad tradition which Goodcole was at pains to repudiate
informs the references to corn bewitched and the witch's
statement that

... old beldams
Talk of familiars in the shape of mice,
Rats, ferrets, weasels, and I wot not what
(II. i. 100–2)

but the dramatists place this information at one remove from the
actual events of the play. They use the theatrical tradition to turn
Elizabeth Sawyer into a more heroic revenger and exploit the
proven theatrical potential of magic by introducing Faustian
'*Thunder and Lightning*' (SD II. i. 144) and sealing the pact with
blood from the witch's arm. However, they also locate the play
firmly in a rural context by introducing the picturesque business
of the preparations for the morris in the middle of the scene. For
the purpose of the play was not to dispute of witches and
witchcraft but to entertain an urban audience with images of
country life.

In this play the intellectual disputes about witches and
witchcraft are filtered through the literary traditions for representing the country. These involved conflicting versions of
pastoral in which the country was both locus of simple virtue,
opposed to urban and courtly corruption, and a comic source of
clownish, low humour, a foil to the knowing sophistication of the
urban élite. The Edmonton scene and the Frank Thorney plot,
are introduced by the deal between Old Thorney and Old Carter
in which Frank, already married to Winifred, is betrothed to
Susan. Old Thorney refers to Old Carter as a 'gentleman' and
receives this crusty answer:

No gentleman I, Mr Thorney. Spare the mastership; call me by my
name, John Carter. 'Master' is a title my father nor his before him
were acquainted with, honest Hertfordshire yeomen. Such an one am
I; my word and my deed shall be proved one at all times. I mean to

give you no security for the marriage money. . . . Bonds and bills are but terriers to catch fools and keep lazy knaves busy; my security shall be present payment. And we here about Edmonton hold present payment as sure as an alderman's bond in London, Mr Thorney. (I. ii. 3–8, 14–17)

This is the world of realist pastoral celebrated in the wedding scene and the morris where the worst a witch can do is to trick Cuddy Banks into falling into a stream or comically silence the fiddler at the morris entertainment (III. iv). The power of the play lies the way it shows this same simplicity turning vicious in its superstitious violence towards Mother Sawyer. In the scene in which Mother Sawyer's witchcraft is revealed, various yokels, including Old Banks, her principal accuser, lament the effects of Mother Sawyer's witchcraft on their behaviour:

BANKS.   My horse this morning runs most piteously of the glanders, whose nose yesternight was as clean as any man's here now coming from the barber's; and this, I'll take my death upon't, is long of this jadish witch, Mother Sawyer.
1. I took my wife and a serving-man in our town of Edmonton, thrashing in my barn together such corn as country wenches carry to market; and, examining my polecat why she did so, she swore in her conscience she was bewitch'd. And what witch have we about us but Mother Sawyer?
2. Rid the town of her, else all our wives will do nothing else but dance about other country maypoles.
3. Our cattle fall, our wives fall, our daughters fall, and maid-servants fall; and we ourselves shall not be able to stand if this beast be suffered to graze amongst us.
(IV. i. 1–14)

Banks, who appeared in the earlier scene of accusation, is presented as an unpleasant figure, but the other country fellows with their bawdy humour are from the stock of comic clowns. As a result, the scene edges uneasily between violence and humour. This rural comedy is, moreover, placed by the arrival of *Sir Arthur Clarington and a Justice* (SD IV. i. 28), who condemn the country folks' lawlessness and rescue Mother Sawyer. Their intervention shifts the discussion on to the difficult area, discussed by Goodcole, of the relationship in the eyes of the law between trivial superstition and a serious offence. The conflict is revealed in the confrontation between Old Banks and the Justice:

JUSTICE.	You must not threaten her; 'tis against the law. Go on.
BANKS.	So, sir, ever since, having a dun cow tied up in my back-side, let me go thither or but cast mine eye at her, and if I should me hang'd, I cannot choose, though it be ten times in an hour, but run to the cow and taking up her tail, kiss – saving your worship's reverence – my cow behind, that the whole town of Edmonton has been ready to bepiss themselves with laughing me to scorn.
JUSTICE.	And this is long of her?
BANKS.	Who the devil else? For is any man such an ass to be such a baby, if he were not bewitched?
SIR ARTHUR.	Nay if she be witch, and the harm she does ends in such sports, she may scape burning.
JUSTICE.	Go, go. Pray vex her not. She is a subject And you must not be judges of the law To strike her as you please.

(IV. i. 52–67)

The serious issue, for Banks, of his status within the community, cannot be handled_by the play, for that kind of analysis of rural society is outside the boundaries of the theatrical traditions of pastoral. The scene is more concerned to establish the impartiality and sanctity of the law, which is not mocked, and only intervenes when the case of Ann Ratcliffe makes the witch's action more serious and more clearly indictable. The Justice is only moved to intervene when Mother Sawyer's curses take the more dangerous form of an attack on the society which he upholds. As he questions the witch, her language changes from the curses of the theatrical revenger to those of the theatrical satirist.

JUSTICE.	You are too saucy and bitter
MOTHER.	Saucy? By what commission can he send my soul On the devil's errand more than I can his? Is he a landlord for my soul, to thrust it When he list out of the door?
JUSTICE.	Know whom you speak to.
MOTHER.	A man. Perhaps no man. Men in gay clothes, Whose backs are laden with titles and honours, Are within far more crooked than I am, And if I be a witch, more witchlike.

(IV. i. 82–91)

This shift into the language of satire is in part a product of the theatrical tradition in which satiric commonplace forms the ready material for diatribe. When Anne Ratcliffe runs mad, her mad monologue takes the familiar form of wild satiric fantasy:

ANNE.   Hoyda! A pox of the devil's false hopper! All the golden meal runs into the rich knaves' purses, and the poor have nothing but bran. Hey derry down! Are not you Mother Sawyer?
MOTHER.   No, I am a lawyer.
ANNE.   Art thou? I prithee let me scratch thy face, for thy pen has flay'd off a great many men's skins. You'll have brave doings in the vacation, for knaves and fools are at variance in every village. I'll sue Mother Sawyer, and her own sow shall give in evidence against her.

(IV. i. 180–88)

However, it has an interesting effect on the focus of the play and its implications for the representation of witchcraft and women.

Like the witches discussed by Christina Larner, Mother Sawyer, in this play is hunted by Banks as a witch and not as a woman. There is nothing explicitly sexual in the denunciations of her, and she is not presented primarily as a gendered figure. However, in the plots with Cuddy Banks and Frank Thorney, the connections between witchcraft and ways of discussing women overlap considerably. When Cuddy Banks comes to Elizabeth Sawyer to ask her help in wooing Katherine Carter, he says that he has been bewitched already by Katherine herself:

Bewitch'd me, *hisce auribus*! I saw a little devil fly out of her eye like a burbolt, which sticks at this hour up to the feathers in my heart.

(II. i. 217–19)

The context of his requests gives the commonplace metaphor of love as witchery a striking resonance. The same metaphor is further developed in Mother Sawyer's satiric diatribe which contrasts the rural witchcraft of *maleficium* and comic disorder with the urban and courtly witchcraft of lust and corruption:

What are your painted things in prince's courts
Upon whose eyelids lust sits, blowing fires
To burn men's souls in sensual hot desires,
Upon whose naked paps a lecher's thought
Acts sin in fouler shapes than can be wrought?
. . . These by enchantments can whole lordships change

> To trunks of rich attire, turn ploughs and teams
> To Flanders mares and coaches, and huge trains
> Of servitors to a French butterfly.
> Have you not city witches who can turn
> Their husband's wares, whole standing shops of wares,
> To sumptuous tables, gardens of stol'n sin,
> In one year wasting what scarce twenty win?
> Are these not witches?
>
> (IV. i. 105–19)

This language comes directly from the literary traditions of complaint and satire[3] and is in no sense authentically Mother Sawyer's. However, the witchery of courtly corruption is located in women, the instigators of lust and corruption and the profligacy of conspicuous consumption by which women waste the hard-working citizen.

The witchcraft material, which seems in danger of subverting established views of witchcraft by its sympathetic treatment of Mother Sawyer, is thus located in familiar ideological and linguistic terms of misogynist satire and pastoral treatment of rural life. The comic treatment of rural superstition undermines the belief in witches but it replaces that belief with the tradition of misogynist satire which locates the evil of witchcraft in the evil of women. When witches cease to be hunted as witches, the traditions of their theatrical representation give greater scope for them to be hunted as women.

The contradictions between these different dramatic modes, which give the play its power, are in part a result of the special circumstances of its production. The works of Rowley, Dekker and Ford, who collaborated in writing the play, span the spectrum of popular to élite drama, and the Prince's Men who performed the play were at that brief moment in their history when they moved from the popular end of the market, when they had performed mainly in the provinces, to their period at the Phoenix, which was a fashionable indoor theatre catering for a richer and more theatrically experienced audience. The play's vindication of the law, its exoneration of the gentlemen accused of Susan Carter's death, and its modulation of superstition into comedy would have offered no threat to that audience's view of the world. Any threat which the Elizabeth Sawyer case might have offered to the stability of the rural order is contained by the dramatic form in which it is presented. It constructs its audience as sceptical, upholders of the law, sympathetic to the victims, both women and men, while at the same time entertaining them with images of country life, picturesque and exotic low-life characters whose critique of urban society is deflected onto its women.

It is unlikely that the authors of this play had any such clearly defined ideological project. The play's misogyny is no more coherent than its individualism. The speed of the play's composition necessitated recourse to the familiar and well-turned dramatic structures. Nevertheless, as Raymond Williams has suggested.

> What in the history of thought may be seen as a confusion or an overlapping is often the precise moment of the dramatic impulse: since it is because the meanings and experiences are uncertain and complex that the dramatic mode is more powerful, includes more than could any narrative or exposition. (Williams 1980; p. 72)

In the *Witch of Edmonton*, Elizabeth Sawyer's individualism, the poetic power of her satire and her denunciation of conventional society provide an oppositional resonance and a potential connection with feminism which could only be more fully developed in its after-life in twentieth-century productions.[4]

II

This overlap between a comic treatment of rural superstition and an uneasy engagement with misogynist themes is evident, in a rather different form, in the later treatment of a specific case of witchcraft, Heywood and Brome's *The Late Lancashire Witches*. This case of witchcraft accusation in Pendle has also been left virtually unexplored by modern social historians and it is difficult to arrive at a full understanding of the circumstances in which it took place. Rather unusually for an English witch case, seventeen women were accused of holding a witches' sabbath, and were arrested and held in Lancaster castle. Seven of the accused were remitted for examination by Bishop Bridgeman of Chester, who was sceptical about the evidence and, after four of them had died in prison, sent the remaining three to London for further examination. Almost all the evidence rested on the testimony of a child, Edmund Robinson, who produced an extraordinary story of a fight with a boy who turned out to have a cloven foot, of following a strange light and finding it carried by Loynd's wife, one of the accused (Webster 1677). The boy claimed to have seen the witches pulling on bell ropes which produced food, to have found two greyhounds in a bush and seen one of them turn into a white horse which carried him along with the witch 'to a place called Horestones in Pendle Forest, where he saw a number of persons gathered together who gave [him] meat' (Calendar of State Papers Domestic (CSPD) Charles I, 1634–5; p. 141).

Young Edmund Robinson's story seems a classic case of literary witchcraft being used as part of popular superstition. Indeed, when he later rescinded his story, he claimed that he was recounting tales which had been part of the country's folklore from the time of the earlier, famous, witchcraft case in the same area in 1612. The examinations of the witches themselves reveals again the familiar story of the mixture of self-accusation and transferred reputation which informed so many successful prosecutions. In his recantation Edmund Robinson said that

> he framed those tales concerning the persons aforesaid, because he heard the neighbours repute them for witches. He heard Edmund Stevenson say that he was much troubled with the said Dicconson's wife in the time of his sickness, and that he suspected her, and he heard Robert Smith say that his wife, lying upon her death bed accused Jennet Hargraves to be the cause of her death; and he heard William Nutter's wife say that Jennet Devys and William Devys had bewitched her; and it was generally spoken that Beawse's wife, who went a-begging, was a witch, and he had heard Sharpee Smith say that the wife of John Loynd laid her hand upon a cow of his, after which she never rose. (CSPD Charles I, 16 July 1634; p. 152)

One of the examined witches, Margaret Johnson, accepted the accusation and elaborated on it with an exciting tale:

> About that time, walking in the highway in Marsden in Whalley, there appeared to her a man in black attire, with black points, who said to

her, if she would give him her soul, she should want nothing, but should have power to hurt whom she would. She refused and he vanished. In this manner he ofttimes resorted to her, till at last she yielded, and he gave into her hand gold and silver; but it vanished soon again, and she was ever bare and poor, though he oft gave her the like. He called himself Mamilion, and most commonly at his coming had the use of her body; after this he appeared in the shape of a brown-coloured dog, a white cat, and a hare, and in those shapes sucked her blood in a manner described. (CSPD Charles I, 13 June 1634; p. 78)

Mary Spencer, on the other hand, denied the accusation, though she recognised that it had been levelled because 'Her father and mother were condemned last assizes for witches, and are since dead and buried' (CSPD Charles I, 1634–5; p. 79).

When the witches were brought to London, they were examined by the King's physician who made arrangements for 'choice of midwives to inspect and search the bodies of these women' (CSPD Charles I, 1634–5; p. 98). The witches were pardoned by Charles though they were still taken back to Lancaster castle where they may have remained until their deaths (Clark, 1958; p. 124).

The circumstances of the Lancaster witch case and the various accounts in which it was recorded reveal, once again, that witchcraft was the site of conflict within popular culture and exerted considerable power over people's view of the world and of themselves. One of the most extended accounts of the case is provided in Webster's *Displaying of Supposed Witchcraft*, which was published in 1677, during the decline of belief in witchcraft. Webster shows a thorough scepticism about witchcraft, which may have been why he included the extraordinary Lancashire case, and his account is couched in pseudo-academic rhetoric. He begins his story of the Lancashire witches

About the year 1634 (for having lost our notes of the same, we cannot be so exact as we should). . . . (Webster 1677; p. 276)

suggesting a concern for historical accuracy which his text cannot fulfil. He attempts, however, to establish a clear distinction between his own learned care and the credulity of those who were taken in by the superstitious tales. He describes his attempts to question Robinson at the time when he was in charge of a church.

Robinson was apparently accompanied by two men as well as his father and

> did make a practice to go from Church to Church that the Boy might reveal and discover witches. (Webster 1677; p. 277)

Faced with Webster's insistent questioning, the boy's minders refused to allow any further questions. In particular they resented the imputation that Robinson had acted under pressure, insisting that no such suggestion had been made by any of the authorities.

Webster's suggestion that Robinson 'was taught and suborned to devise and feign those things against them' (Webster 1677; p. 277) is, of course, too pat an explanation of the phenomenon. The boy's accusations could have carried no weight without a structure of belief and pressures in the community. Moreover, the behaviour of the authorities, the continued questioning and the examination by midwives suggests that scepticism was only just emerging as the dominant element in official procedures. Witchcraft seemed to be emerging from the firmly held centre of a belief system to the material for tall tales, the province of specifically popular, rural superstition. The dramatisation of those tales was part of that procedure.

Heywood and Brome's play was quick to pick up the dramatic potential of the material. The witches' arrival in London seems to have occasioned some public interest if Webster's account of 'great sums gotten at the Fleet to show them, and publick Plays acted thereupon' can be believed. Certainly the Prince's Men had to relicense an old play, *Doctor Lambe and the Witches*, because of adding some new scenes, and the King's Men petitioned the Revels Office to prevent other companies using material about witchcraft in old plays (Potter *et al.* 1982; p. 170). Brome and Heywood's play was performed before the final judgment on the witches had been pronounced, as the epilogue makes clear:

> Now while the Witches must expect their due
> By lawfull Iustice, we appeale to you
> For favourable censure; what their crime
> May bring upon 'em, ripeness yet of time
> Has not reveal'd.
>
> (Hewood 1964; p. 262)

The verdict in the case was irrelevant for the story could be treated according to the needs of the theatre and had no impliction for the guilt or innocence of the parties involved. As the prologue says, it filled a gap in the theatrical market rather than being an intervention in a serious concern:

> Corrantoes failing, and no foot post late
> Possessing us with Newes of forraine State,
> No accidents abroad worthy relation
> Arriving here, we are forc'd from our owne Nation
> To ground the Scene that's now in agitation.
>   (Heywood 1964; p. 188)

The prologues's mocking reference to 'These Witches the fat Iaylor brought' is borne out in the play's comic tone and style. It is brimming with material, much of it taken from the trial proceedings, which are presented as a series of set pieces, either presented on the stage or, where the demands on theatrical resources would have been too great, described in poetic monologues. Unlike Dekker, Ford and Rowley's play, this does not deal with the making of a witch. The witches are accepted as such from their first entrance when, in a scene reminiscent of the Hecate scenes in *Macbeth*, they call to their familiars to 'Come away, and take thy duggy' (II. i) and plan their mischief, a conventional mixture of *maleficium* and practical jokes. The appearance of 'Spirits' in the scene gives some scope for theatrical inventiveness but the tone throughout is comic rather than sinister. The witches laugh as they contemplate mischief achieved and in prospect,

> which shall beget
> Wonder and sorrow 'mongst our foes,
> Whilst we make laughter of their woes.
>   (II. i. 188)

The witches present themselves as both the performers of this mischief and the audience for it. The spirits are instructed to 'fly about the taske, that we projected in our Maske' and Mawd, the chief witch, says that she will fly 'O' th' Steeple top'; there, she says, 'Ile sit and see you play'. The audience in the theatre are invited to take a similarly distanced view of the witchcraft by the tone and style of its presentation. A central scene depicts the wedding between two servants, which is bewitched. The familiar images of rural festivity with music and feasting are turned upside down. A spirit snatches the wedding-cake and '*poures down bran*' SD II. i. p. 205); the plate of Mutton is presented as 'hornes' and when the pie is opened, birds fly out of it. Later in the wedding scene, the fiddlers play out of tune so that the dance cannot continue and, in the following scene, the witches feast on 'the cheare that was prepared to grace the wedding feast'. The imagery of thwarted festivity and disharmony offers plausible evidence for a symbolic reading of the scene in which witchcraft is seen as both evidence and cause of the disruption of harmonious social relations. However, the comic effect of the scene suggests that this serious subtext has become an automatic and dead metaphor, creating a thematic unity in the play but neutralising any serious satiric implications. The world is turned upside down by witchcraft rather than because of any more fundamental instability.

Other scenes of magic are primarily excuses for comic display. During her examination, Mary Spencer of Burneley had confessed that

> [w]hen she was a young girl, and went to the well for water, she used to tumble or trundle the collock, or peal, down the hill, and she would run after it to overtake it, and did overye (overhie) it sometimes, and then might call it to come to her, but utterly denies that she ever could make it come to her by any witchcraft. (CSPD Charles I, 1634; p. 79)

The episode, nevertheless, is incorporated into the play when Mall, master Generous's servant, who performs magical feats of fetching wine from London, riding a horse through the air, is able to magic her pail to her. It is an entertaining theatrical trick, but it presents no real threat to the social order. After the wedding magic, one of the characters says that 'these Hags had power to make the wedding cheare a *Deceptio Visus*' (III. i. p. 208). The theatrical form of the play turns most of the magic into just that. It is conjuring rather than heresy, it is comic reversal rather than serious social satire.

The forms of this magic are what might be expected of these dramatists in this theatrical context. By the 1630s the trenchant satire of the turn-of-the-century city comedies has been flattened into permitted and automatic comic reversal.[5] Certain satiric attitudes had hardened into comedy; the set-piece forms in which they are dramatised prevent any fresh exploration of a complex social reality. In this play, the social forms of marriage and inheritance are addressed, but such critique as is offered is formalised into a show. In one of the bewitching scenes, Whetstone takes his revenge on the gallants who have called him a bastard. He asks if any of them would like to see his own father and, when they ask to do so, presents them with dancing images of a Pedant, a Taylor and a Groom, each of whom could, circumstantially, have committed adultery with the gallants' mothers. The form is comic, though the laughter dies away as each of the men is attacked in turn. It is a bawdy joke in theatrical form and though it obviously touches at the heart of social assumptions about inheritance and social status its implications are localised, unexplored in the remainder of the action. Their location as set pieces, moreover, distances the jokes even further. The audience is not invited to laugh at a bawdy joke enacted in the narrative but to be entertained by the effect the joke has on others. The audience cannot simply share Whetstone's point of view since in the remainder of the action he is first a fool and then a witch. It can thus remain aloof from the action, wiser and more sophisticated than both the perpetrator and the butt of the joke.

A similar set of theatrical procedures seems to be at work in the principal scenes, in which the effect of witchcraft is to turn the ordered world of patriarchy and degree upside down. Once again the effect is primarily comic, as the characters describe

> All in such rare disorder, that in some
> As it breeds pitty, and in others wonder,
> So in the most part laughter.
>
> (I. ii)

The younger generation of the Seely household have taken to ordering their parents about; the servants, in turn, show no respect for them. This provides obvious comic turns in the broad country speech of the servants and such obvious inversions as Gregory's complaint that his father 'was at the Ale Club but tother day, and spent a foure penny' (I. i. p. 182).

Nevertheless the question of Gregory's inheritance is rather more fully developed in the action and the motif of disorder in the household allows for an extended focus on the potential for disruption in marriage. In a temporary return to normal, the servants Parnell and Lawrence are married and, as we have seen, their wedding festivities are disrupted by the witches and their spirits. At the wedding, Lawrence is presented with a codpiece point by Mall, one of the witches, and a few scenes later the couple are threatened with a skimmington because Parnell has beaten him. Before the skimmington arrives, the couple are examined by Doughty, one of the spokesmen for moderation, who finds that Lawrence has unexpectedly turned out to be impotent. This allows for a good deal of bawdy comedy as Lawrence protests his former prowess and Parnell expresses comic dismay at the failure of her expectations. She makes it clear that as far as she is concerned the consummation of marriage is the crucial factor in the reputation for honesty:

> Marry sir, and beat him will I into his grave or backe to the Priest, and be unwaddes agone, for a I wonot bee baund to lig with him and live with him, the laife of an honest woman for aw the layves good in Loncoshire.
>
> (III. i. p. 232–3)

It is this reputation which the skimmington is presumably out to challenge but when it does appear, it acts much more as an entertainment than as a force for social control. Doughty's companions insist on his staying to see 'the shew' and the stage direction suggests fairly extended entertainment:

> *Enter drum (beating before) a Skimington, and his wife on a horse; Divers country rusticks (as they passe) Par. puls Skimington of the horse: and Law. Skimingtons wife: they beat em. Drum beats alar. horse comes away: the hoydens at first oppose the Gentlemen: who draw: the clownes vaile bonnet, make a ring Par and Skim fight.* (SD p. 234)

The entertainment value of this rural festivity for both Doughty and the audience in the theatre is evident when, after the show, Doughty concludes the action and pays the participants with beer money. His condescending distance from the ritual and its significance could certainly be paralleled by the real behaviour of country gentlemen towards popular culture,[6] but the audience in the theatre, paying clients too, are invited to share it.

Whatever the actual character of the Globe audience at this play, they are being invited to see themselves as urban and élite, distanced from the pressures of rural existence where sexual and marital problems are the province of comic country folk. The general representations of witchcraft in the play are seen as venial and comic, however unpleasant they may be for those on the receiving end of the witches' malice. The tall tales of Robinson's deposition and the traditions of comic theatre combine to represent witchcraft as a strange and exciting phenomenon but not one which presents a fundamental challenge to the way in which the characters see the world.

Nevertheless, as we have seen, when witches are not feared as witches they may still be feared as women, and in the case of Mistress Generous, the witch whose situation is given more plot time than most of the others, this seems to be the case. Mistress Generous's behaviour is first presented as simply suspicious. Robin, the groom, reports to her husband that she has asked for his horse to be saddled without his permission and has paid him to keep silent about the matter. Robin's comic servant routine, in which he answers his master in the most roundabout way possible, suggests the beginnings of a familiar adultery plot, but Mr Generous's response moves the action to an altogether different way of speaking of marital relations. He described his wife as a paradigm of godly wifehood:

> ... a good woman and well bred
> Of an unquestioned carriage, well reputed
> Amongst her neighbours, reckon'd with the best
> And ore me most indulgent.
>
> (II. i. p. 192)

The play provides no space to develop the tensions which might have led this paragon to witchcraft, and Generous's discovery of her involvement takes place in a way which makes the tone of the action very difficult to establish. He exits to bridle a strange horse which has magically conveyed Robin to London and re-enters with his wife who has apparently been the horse in question. His astonishment, however, is far from comic and is expressed in a rhetoric which comes from high tragedy:

My blood is turned to ice, and my all vitals
Have ceased their working! dull stupidity
Surpriseth me at once, and hath arrested
That vigorous agitation . . .

(IV. i. p. 225)

His horror at finding that his wife is a witch implicates him in her
sin. He confesses that in spite of his continuous efforts to resist
the devil

that Serpent twin'd me so about,
That I must lie so often and so long
With a Divell in my bosom.

(IV. i. p. 226)

Mrs Generous's offence is seen as a sin against matrimony as
much as against God, and the scene develops into one of
passionate reconciliation as she asks pardon not only from heaven
but also from her husband.

The passion, however, is dislocated by Robin's continued
comic cheerfulness, as he punningly jokes about the idea of
transformation:

What cheere sir, show yourself a man, though she appeared so late a
Beast; Mistresse confesse all, better here than in a worse place, out
with it.

(IV. i. p. 227)

The uneasy mixture of comedy and passion is a product of the
literary traditions which were at the dramatists' disposal in
writing the scene. The conventional comic servant remains
unchanged throughout, while the rhetoric used by the husband
is drawn from familiar portrayals of the man wronged in
marriage. The offence is witchcraft but the only available
dramatic language for dealing with erring women is that of
domestic melodrama. The play can find no consistent style in
which to hunt women as witches, and in moments of high passion
it reverts to the familiar denunciation of women for their failings as
wives.

In the event, Mrs Generous, in spite of her repentance, returns
to witchcraft. She is discovered a second time when the hand
which one of the witches' victims has cut off matches her wrist.
Once again Mr Generous takes the offence personally and finally

gives up his interest in his wife, determined that his 'house no more be made a Hell'. The metaphoric language of the husband wronged by adultery is made literal by the witchcraft plot and it is impossible to say if the effect is tragically or comically grotesque.

The sexual dimension of witchcraft, so seldom present in English cases, is fully exploited here. Margaret Johnson's deposition (see above p. 88) had provided the material for such a presentation, and the official scepticism about her testimony is absent in the dramatisation. One of the witches, Peg, confesses, as Margaret Johnson had, to coupling with the Devil. However, her confession is met only with mocking asides from her interlocutors. The opportunity for misogynist denunciation is not taken up and Peg's pleasure at that 'sweet coupling' is no more remarked on than Parnell's lament that her husband cannot satisfy her sexually.

These curious shifts of tone and material in the play's presentation of witchcraft complicate the problem of how to read the play as a cultural document. David Underdown (1985), in his analysis of the control of women in the early modern period, refers to the play as further evidence of the 'gender crisis' which he locates in the period generally. He is right to do so, in that the terms of the drama restate the commonplaces about women's subordination and the violation of patriarchal harmony caused by women acting as free agents, either by correcting their husbands, as Parnell attempts, or by gadding about in secret, like Mrs Generous. Nevertheless, such an account says nothing of the forms and effects of this particular manifestation of the 'gender crisis'. This play seems to me rather to allay anxieties about a real crisis of gender relations through the knowing quality of the dramatists' treatment. For them, the problems of rural hierarchy, and the disruption occasioned by witchcraft accusations, are safely enclosed in stories which can be reproduced for the entertainment of an urban audience. This development is hardly surprising, since as well as being a dramatist Heywood was a tireless collector and anthologiser of stories. His *Guneikeon* (1620) is a massive compilation of stories about women and includes sections of (mainly classical) lore on witchcraft. None of this material is used directly in *The Late Lancashire Witches*, but

Heywood's biographer, Arthur Clark, suggests that Brome, faced with dramatising the material, may have approached him as a 'famous witch-lorist' to assist in the task (Clark 1958; p. 121).

The reaction of at least one gentleman who saw the play at the Globe is available to us in the form of a remarkable document discovered by Herbert Berry in the Phelips papers in the Somerset Record Office. A letter from Nathaniel Tomkyns records how he visited the Globe on the third day of a three day run of the play and

> found a greater apparance of fine folke gentmen and gentweomen then I thought had bin in town in the vacation. (Berry 1984; p. 212)

The letter provides an unusually detailed account of 'the slights and passages done or supposed to be done by these witches', which suggests that the details of performance are well recorded in the text. Tomkyns concludes the letter with a critical assesment of the play:

> And though there be not in it (to my understanding) any poeticall Genius, or art, or language, or judgement to state or tenet of witches (which I expected) or application to vertue but full of ribaldrie and of things improbable and impossible; yet in respect of the newnessness of ye subject (the witches being still visible and in prison here) and in regard it consisteth from the beginning to the ende of odd passages and fopperies to provoke laughter, and it is mixed with divers songs and dances, it passeth for a merrie and excellent new play. (Berry 1984, p. 213)

The interest of this document is in Tomkyns's expectation that the play would discuss the 'tenet of witches' and his recognition that this issue was denied by the form and the theatrical pleasures that it offered. Witchcraft clearly was seen as a live intellectual issue (Tomkyns expresses no similar interest in the role of women) but a 'merrie and excellent new play' on the subject did not need to engage with it on any but the most general terms.

This process of turning experience into stories is a primary function of the drama in the culture of a particular society. It serves both to rehearse the beliefs and attitudes of that society and at the same time to distance them, to make them more manageable. Discussing Lenin's critique of Tolstoy, Pierre Macherey describes how

[t]he text constructs a determinate image of the ideological, revealing it as an object rather than living it from within as though it were an inner conscience. (Macherey 1978; p. 132)

A similar process seems to be at work in this text. The belief in witchcraft, and the role of women within it, is revealed as an object both for wonder and mirth, and those for whom it is part of an inner conscience are variously mocked and pitied. Nevertheless the inner conscience of the role of women and their potential for disruption is left unexamined, taken as the necessary framework which makes the rest of the play make sense.

Martin Butler has made out a powerful case for Brome as a systematic and revolutionary critic of the Caroline social and political order. He convincingly argues that Brome's play *The Antipodes*, which also features a world turned upside down, is

brilliantly successful in its combination of popular satiric devices and sophisticated dramatic technique in the interests of a comprehensive political statement. (Butler 1984; p. 219)

In that play, however, the tighter framework of the play-within-the-play, and the greater precision of the political references, permit a close fit between the expectations of the audience in the theatre and the events on the stage. In the earlier, witchcraft play, written perhaps under greater pressure of time, the rag-bag of material and styles shows both witchcraft and popular misogyny declining into the stuff of jestbooks and easy theatrical ribaldry from which Goodcole, for example, had been at such pains to rescue them.

Keith Thomas has argued that laughter is a way of relieving the uncomfortable pressures on social life. However, there also comes a point when a joke is automatically comic simply through familiar rehearsal and no longer touches a raw nerve. It may be that by the 1630s witchcraft had become just such a phenomenon for urban audiences and that theatrical misogyny was taking the same route.

Notes

1. I am deeply grateful to Andrew Butcher, whose exhaustive search through all the relevant witchcraft records failed to find the deposition material relating to Elizabeth Sawyer's case.
2. For a discussion of this play in the context of dramatic collaborations, see Lois Potter *et al., The Revels History of Drama in English, Volume IV, 1613–1660.*
3. See Peter, *Complaint and Satire in Early English Literature* and Tourneur, *The Revenger's Tragedy,* III. v. 61–98, discussed below pp. 124–6
4. See in particular the 1981 RSC production, directed by Barry Kyle, discussed in Simon Trussler's introduction to the play.
5. See Potter *et al., The Revels History of Drama in English, volume IV* 1613–1660, pp. 229–34.
6. See David Underdown, *Revel, Riot and Rebellion,* p. 67.

CHAPTER FOUR
'What should chaste ears do at a play?'

In analysing the connections between the 'tenet of witchcraft' and its representation in the structures of particular plays, I have ignored that most difficult issue in feminist criticism: the differential relationship which men and women have to the culture of their time. In modern criticism, women's responses to literature and drama can be arrrived at either by the publication of criticism by particular women or by the sociological methods of the readership survey such as Janice Radway (1984) provides for women reading the romance. For the early modern period such procedures are frustrated by the almost complete absence of evidence. Barry Reay has noted that 'Women were excluded from many of the points of contact for popular culture' (Reay 1985; p. 10), participating primarily as spectators in the male-oriented festivities and leisure activities of the period. They were excluded, too, due to the lower levels of literacy, from written culture: 'the coming of writing ... merely added to the list of cultural items which women did not share' (Reay 1985; p. 11).

On the rare occasions when women did express an opinion about what they had read or seen, it was clear that they had firm opinions about it. As we have seen, the women contributors to the debate over women were as ready to criticise the style as the opinions of their opponents. Moreover, it seems that metropolitan debates in criticism could inform the views of even such an occasional critic as Lady Southwell, who sent her views on the moral importance of poetry in a letter to her friend Lady

Ridgway.[1] A similar moral concern informed one woman's critical comment on the theatre, Constantia Munda's swipe at Swetnam, which denounces the way that

> Every satiricke poetaster which thinkes he hath lickt the remit of his Coripheus and can but patch a hobling verse together, will strive to present unseemly figments imputed to our sex (as a pleasing theme to the vulgar) or the publique Theatre's teaching the worser sort that are more prone to luxurie, a compentious way to warne to be sinful.
> (Munda 1617; sig. A2)

These rare and scattered expressions of critical opinion fit easily into the broader outlines of Elizabethan criticism and, like them, fail to provide any firm evidence about the ways in which Elizabethan women saw themselves represented on the stage. Nevertheless, as with other areas of social life, women's attendance at the theatre was much observed and written about and that evidence can provide some understanding of the cultural significance of women as an audience for Elizabethan drama.

Women certainly did attend performances of plays.[2] Humphrey Mildmay's account book notes in 1632; 'Expences att a playe with my wife'. It notes also that in 1635, on 11 December, 'To dynner came Sr Chr: Abdy and wente to the Newe playe wth my wife', and that in 1638 he went 'To a play with Mrs James' (Bentley 1941, vol. II; pp. 675–7). Lady Anne Clifford saw a performance of Fletcher's *The Mad Lover* at court in 1635 and in 1632, when Captain Essex and Lord Thurles fell to brawling at Blackfriars Theatre, the Captain was 'attending and accompanying my Lady of Essex in a boxe in the playhouse at the Blackfryers' (Gurr 1987; p. 240).

Nevertheless, all the evidence about women as audiences, beyond the baldest and most inconsequential references, is fraught with difficulties of interpretation. Neither 'women' nor 'plays' are unproblematic categories for modern analysis and they were even less so for the Elizabethan observer. The presence of women at a play often seemed to require some special comment. John Chamberlain, writing about the wild success of Middleton's *A Game at Chesse*, a scandalous satire on Spain, notes:

> the Lady Smith would have gon yf she could have persuaded me to go

with her. I am not so sowre or severe but that I wold willingly have
attended her, but I could not sit so long. . . . (Gurr 1987; p. 235)

Was Chamberlain's sourness at visiting the play at all or at
accompanying a lady to it?

A more neutral observation, such as that of Duke Philip Julius
of Stettin Pomerania, still regards women in the audience as a
special category. Describing the Blackfriars Theatre in 1602 he
observes:

> there are always a good many people present, many respectable
> women as well, because useful argumenta, and many good doctrines,
> as were told, are brought forward there. (Harbage 1941; p. 51)

References to women in contemporary accounts of the theatre
audience are to a category rather than to an observed social group.
That is to say, the notion of 'women' was part of an argument
about the nature of the theatre as a social and intellectual
phenomenon rather than neutral social observation. As we have
seen, those who approved of the theatre said that women were
there for the 'useful argumenta and many good doctrines': those
who felt differently repeated the age-old claim that the theatre,
like any public assembly, was dangerous to women's morals.
Gosson describes how in this 'generall Market of Baudrie'

> you shall see suche heauing, and shoouing, suche ytching and
> shouldring, too sitte by women, suche care for their garments that
> they bee not trode on: Suche eyes to their lappes, that no chippes light
> in them: such pillowes to ther backes, that they take no hurte . . .
> suche tickling, such toying, such smiling, such winking, and such
> manning them home, when the sportes are ended, that it is a right
> Comedie, to marke their behaviour. (Gosson 1579; sig. C^v)

The accuracy of Gosson's observation is open to question when
we find Stubbes describing the same 'comedie' in almost the same
words in his *Anatomy of Abuses*.[3] For both Stubbes and Gosson,
and the other polemicists against the stage, the presence of
women in the audience was proof of the licentiousness of plays
and Gosson explicitly warned the 'gentlewomen citizens of
London' against the tainting effect of being seen at plays even
when their motives in attending them were above reproach:

> I have seene many of you which were wont to sporte your selues at
> Theatres, when you perceiued the abuse of those places, schoole your
> selues, and of your own acord abhorre Plays. (Gosson 1579; sig. F2)

Those who argued about the effects of drama on morals often confused the behaviour of characters with the behaviour of audiences:

> Some citizens wives, upon whom the Lord for ensample to others
> hath laide his hands, have even on their deathbeds with teares
> confessed, that they have received at those spectacles such filthie
> infections, as have turned their minds from chast cogitations, and
> made them of honest women light huswives. . . .
>   Whosoever shal visit the chappel of Satan, I meane the Theater,
> shal finde there no want of yong ruffins, – nor lacke of harlots, utterlie
> past al shame: who presse to the fore-front of the scaffoldes, to the
> end to showe their impudencie, and to be as an object to al mens eies.
> (Anon [Anthony Munday], *A third blast of retrait from plaies and
> Theaters* 1580; pp. 125, 139. In Gurr 1987; p. 206)

For the open, public nature of the theatre meant that women in the audience were as much part of the spectacle to be commented on as women on the stage. Dekker's anecdote from *Jests to Make You Merry* describes

> A Wench having a good face, a good body, and good clothes on, but of
> bad conditions, sitting one day in the two-penny roome of a
> play-house, & a number of yong Gentlemen about her, against all
> whom she maintaind talke, One that sat over the stage, sayd to his
> friend: doe you not thinke that yonder flesh will stincke anon, having
> so many flyes blowing upon it. Oh (quoth his friend) I thinke it
> stinckes already, for I never saw so many crowes together but there
> was some carion not far off.
> (Dekker, *Jests to Make You Merry* 1963; p. 292)

The presence of women in the audience was felt by opponents of the stage to be directly connected to the immorality of the drama itself: John Lane claimed that if plays were more chaste

> Then light-taylde huswives which like *Syrens* sing,
> And like to *Circes* with their drugs enchant,
> Would not unto the Banke-sides round house fling,
> In open sight themselves to show and vaunt:
> Then, then I say they would not marked goe,

Though unseene to see those they faine would know.
(John Lane, *Tom Tell-Troths Message, and His Pens Complaint*; sig. F3.   In Gurr 1987; p. 215)

In part, Gosson's objection to women attending plays was part of a general disapproval of any pleasure that did not focus on the matrimonial home, and plays are one of a list of public diversions which women should avoid. Nevertheless, in the context of discussions of theatre the references to women play a more particular role. The dangers to their chastity presented by gadding in public provided a usefully concrete example of the immorality of plays, which was otherwise somewhat hard to pin down. Defenders of the theatre could counter arguments about the licentious subject-matter of the plays themselves, but they follow a different route in their discussion of the conduct of the audience. Given the public nature of the theatre they constantly seek to divide up the audience, addressing themselves to the discerning, the richer and the more fashionable sections. The defenders of the private theatre assured its clientele of its own exclusive character[4] and Dekker explained that, even within the public, open-air theatres, the once-fashionable boxes had fallen from favour owing to 'the iniquity of custom, conspiracy of waiting-women and Gentelmen-Ushers that there sweat together' (Dekker 1963; p. 247). Ben Jonson, of course, was contemptuous of the audience even at the private theatres; in his commendatory verses to Fletcher's *The Faithful Shepherdess*, his poetically satiric list of the types in the audience goes down in social stages, with the women some way down. It was, he says,

> Compos'd of *Gamester, Captaine, Knight, Knight's Man,*
> *Lady*, or *Pusil*, that weares maske, or fan,
> *Velvet* or *Taffeta* cap.
>   (Bowers ed. vol. III 1976; p. 492)

What these comments have in common is that they are all responses to a new cultural phenomenon which radically altered the relationship between an audience and the plays they saw. With the establishment of professional, permanent theatre companies in London, working out of purpose-built theatres, plays ceased to be an aristocratic pastime or an occasional popular treat like a travelling fair, and instead became part of commercially available leisure. The theatre had a role in the London economy and in the structure of its audience's lives. The playing companies kept part of the old form of patronage; they were named after the titles of their nominal patrons and after the accession of James I came under the patronage of the crown. However, this patronage played only a minor part in their economic survival, which depended much more on their paying audience – patrons in the modern sense of the word. Aristocratic and royal patronage could be invoked when the companies needed support against the city authorities but this was the last vestige of a residual form of organisation and was directed towards giving them a stronger economic base.[5]

This shift in the relations of production of theatre caused no little anxiety and it affected men and women in different ways. The anxiety is evident in contemporary writers' awareness of the levelling effect of this transformation of drama into a commodity purchaseable by anyone who had the money:

> the place is so free in entertainment, allowing a stoole as well to the Farmer's sonne as to your Templar: that your Stinkard has the self-same libertie to be there in his Taobacco Fumes which your sweet courtier hath; and that your car man and Tinker claime as strong a voice in their suffrage, and sit to give judgement on the plaies life and death, as well as the prowdest Momus among the tribe of Criticks. (Dekker 1609; p. 49)

Given the relative expense of plays and the fact that they were performed in the afternoons during working hours, it is unlikely that any audience contained the range of social types that Dekker described.[6] However, what is clear is Dekker's disapproval of this change and its implications for artists, the primary producers of the theatre's raw materials. For what was now available to the paying audience was not just an afternoon's entertainment but other formerly aristocratic privileges of learning and wit: Dekker ironically dedicated *The Gulls Hornbook* to those who

> haunting theatres . . . sit there like a popinjay, only to learn play-speeches which afterwards may furnish the necessity of his bare knowledge to maintain him in table talk. (Dekker 1609; p. 9–10).

A gallant, he suggests, could literally dine out on his knowledge of theatre and he advises his would-be fashionable gull to

> hoard up the finest play scraps you can get; upon which your lean wit
> may most savourly feed for want of other stuff when the Arcadian and
> Euphuized gentlewomen hath their tongues sharpened to set upon
> you. (Dekker 1609; p. 55)

Dekker's opposition between the foolish young man who has his
learning from plays and sharp-tongued gentlewomen who have
theirs from Lyly's *Euphues* or Sidney's *Arcadia* suggests that
women were not thought of as the primary consumers of this new
form of leisure. In the world of commercial leisure, plays were
seen as part of a quartet of fashionable diversions.[7] As Thomas
Nashe describes:

> men that are their own masters . . . do wholly bestow themselves upon
> pleasure, and that pleasure they divide . . . either into gaming,
> following of harlots, drinking or seeing a play. (Nashe 1972; p. 112)

For within the language and associations of satire and polemic,
women were not consumers but part of what was consumed –
either explicitly in brothels or in the supposed assignations which
the theatre made possible:

> By sitting on the stage, if you be a knight, you may happily get you a
> mistress; if a mere Fleet-street gentleman, a wife. (Dekker 1609;
> p. 51)

These observations were not, of course, objective sociological
analysis but they formed the associations about the theatre in
contemporary writing. Men were not the only consumers of
theatre but they were (to use the language of modern consumption) the targeted audience in both play texts and discussions of
theatrical activity.

For women, playgoing appears in a different context of
pleasures. Lady Mildmay, an exemplary stay-at-home wife,
described how during her visits to London

> Some great personages, ladies of my acquaintance, would persuade
> me to go with them to the Court to feasts, marryages, and plays,
> saying it was a pity my youth should be swallowed up without all
> pleasure or delight in the world. (Meads 1930; p. 52)

Plays in this extract are seen, not as publicly consumed commercially available pleasures and pastimes, but as part of a network of social relations in which women might be involved. It is perhaps for this reason, as much as the dominance of men's memoirs, that we most frequently find women accompanying men to the playhouse. Lady Mildmay apparently went with her husband 'and company' to Blackfriars in 1635: after the play her husband 'wente abroad by myself to worse places alone' (Bentley vol. II 1941; p. 677). The particular social and financial implications of going to the theatre are evident in Lady Anne Halkett's account of her theatre visits:

> so scrupulous I was of giving any occasion to speake of mee, as I know they did of others, that though I loved well to see plays and to walke in the Spring Garden sometimes (before itt grew something scandalous by ye abuse of some), yett I cannot remember 3 times that ever I wentt with any man besides my brothers; and if I did, my sisters or others better than myselfe was with mee. And I was the first that proposed and practised itt for 3 or 4 of us going together withoutt any man, and every one paying for themselves by giving the mony to the footman who waited on us, and he gave itt to the play-house. And this I did first upon hearing some gentlemen telling what ladys they had waited on to plays, and how much itt had cost them; upon which I resolved none should say the same of mee. (Gurr 1987; p. 195)

Clearly women could defy convention and attend even the public amphitheatres. Chamberlain tried twice to see Ann Carleton's sister, Elizabeth Williams; he found that 'the first time she was at a neighbour's house at Cards and the next she was gone to the new Globe to a play' (Gurr 1987; p. 204). However, contemporary accounts of women at the theatre constantly construct them either as objects of 'pleasure' to be 'consumed' or as linked to the residual forms of patronage which remained in court masques and aristocratic theatre.

David Bergeron's account of women as patrons of drama shows that aristocratic women were the dedicatees of plays primarily intended for amateur performance, including Sidney's *Lady of the May*, dedicated to his sister Lady Herbert or the production of Jonson's *Cynthia's Revels*, addressed to Lucy Russell, Countess of Bedford. For these aristocratic women, an interest in plays was part of a general intellectual involvement with poetry and men of letters, rather than with the world of commercial theatre. Women seem to have attended plays as occasional treats and were strongly discouraged from the public consumption of leisure which might compromise their virtue. The way the theatre was presented, its role in the public culture of urban life, militated against women having direct access to it.

In spite of their marginal importance in the economics and culture of London theatre, women were frequently appealed to in the texts of plays. The notion that women made special requirements as an audience is evident in dedications addressed to women or prologues which appeal to their presumed taste. In Wilmot's dedication of *Tancred and Gismunda* to Lady Mary Peter and Lady Anne Grey, the ladies are asked to vouch for 'the sweetness of voice and liveliness of action' which graced the Inner Templars' production at court, suggesting that the ladies were as good a judge as any of dramatic performance. However, the poet goes on to question how suitable 'a discourse of two lovers' is to be presented to ladies whose 'wisdoms' require 'the knowledge of wise, grave and worthy matters tending to the good instructions of youths of whom you are mothers' (ed Dodsley 1964; vol. 7 p. 10).

The notion that women exercise special artistic demands on the theatre is also evident in the epilogue to Shakespeare's *Henry VIII*, performed at the Globe in 1613. It claims that the play's only virtue lies in the praise it will gain from

> The merciful construction of good women,
> For such a one we show'd 'em: if they smile
> And say 'twill do, I know within a while
> All the best men are ours; for 'tis ill hap
> If they hold when their ladies bid 'em clap.
> (10–14)

In the face of this evidence for a special role for women as an audience, Linda Woodbridge has taken literally this deference to women's taste. She asserts that 'for a few years [women] were strong enough and assertive enough to influence the drama's image of womankind' (Woodbridge 1984; p. 266). However, her delightful image of 'pistol packing London dames' does not match the kind of women appealed to in these epilogues, and it is unlikely that the shift from misogyny to a more positive image of

women could be affected by direct pressure from women in the
audience. Prologues which explicitly set the tastes of men and
women against each other often extended the comic sex war
beyond the action of the plays into the world of the audience. In
the Epilogue to *As You Like It* Rosalind plays on the double role
of boy and girl she had acted in the play and is as impudent to the
men and women in the audience as she had been to Orlando in the
action:

> I charge you, O women, for the love you bear to men, to like as much
> of this play as please you; and I charge you, O men, for the love you
> bear to women – as I perceive by your simpring none of you hates
> them – that between you and the women the play may please.
>
> (14–21)

The ironic tone of Rosalind's Epilogue is an extension of the tone
of the play; when plays took up the sex war more fiercely, the tone
of the address to women altered accordingly. The Prologue to
Swetnam the Woman Hater, the sub-plot of which deals directly
with the trial and conviction of the famous misogynist, marks the
division between men and women more bitterly:

> The women are all welcome; for the men
> They will be welcome; our care's not for them.
> 'Tis we, poore women, that must stand the brunt
> Of this dayes tryall . . .
> The men, I know, will laugh, when they shall heare
> Us rayl'd at, and abused; and say 'tis well,
> We all deserve as much.

One way of drawing particular attention to the separateness of
women and men in both the audience and the action was to insist
on how special it was for a woman to speak in the theatre at all.
Rosalind asserts that 'it is not the fashion to see the lady the
epilogue', and the Prologue to *Every Woman in her Humour* –
another 'misogyny' play – announces that 'a she prologue is as rare
as a Usurer's Almes . . . and the rather I come woman, because
men are apt to take kindelye any kinde thing at a womans hand'
(Prologue, 5–6). The double bluff, of course, is that in all of
these prologues women were played by boys: the direct address to
the audience is still held fast in the fictive world of theatrical
convention.

In one of the most extended versions of that joke, Ben Jonson inserted a series of 'intermeans' between the acts of *The Staple of News*, in which women – supposedly from the audience – comment on the performances and on playgoing in general. Unlike the Grocer's wife in Beaumont's *Knight of the Burning Pestle*, who 'was nere at one of these playes as they say before', these ladies are self-confident and experienced playgoers. They argue with the Prologue and assert their right as women to sit on the stage with the best. When the Prologue asks

> What will the Noblemen thinke, or the grave Wits here, to see you seated on the bench thus?

Gossip Mirth retorts

> Why, what should they thinke, but that they had Mothers, as we had, and those Mothers had Gossips (if their children were christned) as we are, and such as had a longing to see Playes, and sit upon them, as wee doe, and arraign both them, and their Poets?
>
> Induction, 15–21)

The ladies' taste tends to the old-fashioned. In the first intermean Tattle longs to see the Fool, and the objection to the play the ladies are watching is that it does not include the expected types. In the second intermean they complain that the play does not fit the familiar Morality Play conventions, for

> here is never a Fiend to carry him away. Besides, he has never a wooden dagger! I'd not give a rush for a Vice, that has not a wooden dagger to snap at everybody he meetes.
>
> (II, Intermean, 10–13)

Mirth, the most sophisticated of them, understands that Vices do exist in the play 'But now they are attir'd like men and women o' the time, the Vices male and female! (II, Intermean, 16–17)'.

The conversations of the gossips and the energy with which they discuss the issues of the play give them a certain realism and make it tempting to see them as portraits of the women in the audience whom Linda Woodbridge fancies influenced the playwright's representations of women. However, they are rather too carefully integrated both into the themes of the play and into Jonson's recurring anxieties about his audience. They present an entertaining account in the third intermean of the way in which they spread news abroad:

> I have had better newes from the bake-house, by ten thousand parts, in a morning: or the conduicts in Westminster! all the newes of Tutle street and both the Alm'ries! the two Sanctuaries! long, and round Wool-staple! with King's-street and Channon row to boot! . . . my gossip Tattle knew what fine slips grew in Gardines-lane; who kist the Butchers wife with the Cowes breath; what matches were made in the bowling-Alley, and what bettes wonne and lost; how much griest went to the Mill, and what besides!
>
> (III, Intermean, 18–28)

The breathless tone of this account of London gossip, authenticated by the use of real street names, is nevertheless a device to give greater realism to the main action. The gossip's discussion and explanation of the play is also Jonson's half-mocking attempt to ensure that the audience understands the action, while at the same time flattering those of the audience who do understand by contrasting them with the gossips on stage. For Jonson, opinionated, old-fashioned, middle-aged women were the antithesis of the audience he desired.[7] How far they were represented in the audience he actually received is impossible to tell.

The gossips of Jonson's intermeans are also made up of the stereotypes found in other contemporary accounts. Gossip Censure's simpering attraction to one of the play's characters is an expression of the 'female audience as groupie':

> I protest, I was in love with Master Fitton. He did weare all he had, from the hat-band to the shooe tye, so politically, and would stoop, and leere.
>
> (IV, Induction, 32–4)

In part the gossips are showing their inability to go beyond the most literal and direct appreciation of the action, missing completely the allegory Jonson had provided for the reader of the play. However, this portrayal of the gossip as groupie is in the tradition of the witty stories told of women falling in love with and making assignations with the actors in character. Among many ribald anecdotes about women, Manningham's diary records how

upon a tyme when Burbidge played Rich(ard) 3 there was a Citizen
grewe soe farr in liking with him, that before shee went from the play
shee appointed him to come that night unto hir by the name of
Rich(ard) 3. (Manningham 1976; p. 75)

Shakespeare took Burbage's place and when Burbage arrived at
the assignation, told his servant to tell him that William the
Conqueror came before Richard the Third.

It is extremely unlikely that this story is true, but it indicates
the ways in which jokes could be generated in the gap between
real life and theatrical life, particularly when the issue of sex
connected the two. It is impossible at this distance in time to
know how women saw themselves on stage or what pleasures they
gained from the theatre. All that we can observe is the powerful
images and the scope for both laughter and moral anxiety which
was produced by the explosive intertwining of the discourses of
theatre and the discourses of sex.

Notes

1. See Jean C. Cavanaugh, 'Lady Southwell's Defence of Poetry'.
2. See Gurr, *Playgoing in Shakespeare's London*, Appendix 1 *passim*.
3. See Stubbes, *Anatomy of Abuses* (sigs. L8–L8^v).
4. See below, Chapter 8.
5. See Wickham, *Early English Stages*, Chapters 4 and 5; also Agnew,
   Worlds Apart, pp. 1–16.
6. On the debate over the social composition of the audience, see
   Harbage, *Shakespeare's Audience*, Cook, *The Privileged Playgoers of
   Shakespeare's London*, Butler, *Theatre and Crisis* and Gurr,
   Playgoing in Shakespeare's London.
7. See below, Chapter 7.

CHAPTER FIVE
'To represent such a lady'

This constant, witty play around the sexuality of men and women on and off the stage creates even more complex resonances through the use of boy actors to play all women's roles. This practice calls into question the relationship between the actor and his role, the nature and limits of theatrical representation and the connection between the theatre and the world beyond. Of necessity it stands in the way of a simple correlation between the theatrical representation of women and their treatment either in social formations or in other forms of ideological construction. Among both Elizabethan commentators and theatre historians the discussion of boy actresses circles around the dividing point between the theatre and the world, either locking them into the world of representation or seeking to generalise from them about the nature of male and female sexuality. The two positions are seen as mutually exclusive. Jensen, for example, firmly asserts:

> Like any convention in any art form, the use of boy actors in female roles was a practice that audiences accepted without confusion or feelings of sexual ambivalence. (Jensen 1975, p. 6)

In this view, theatrical convention is seen as a form of translation in which the reality of the narrative is reproduced on the stage – in such a way as to close off or suppress any irrelevant thoughts about the actors or the nature of their activity on the stage. 'Convention' is seen as a stable controller of meaning, mediating between a stable text and a stable reality.

The opposite point of view sees theatrical representation as open to a knowing awareness of its own activity and is seen at its most extreme in Lisa Jardine's claim (Jardine 1983; pp. 9–36) that homosexual attraction towards the boy players was a primary pleasure for Elizabethan theatre-goers. This interpretation sees performance as paramount, suppresses entirely the narrative which is being enacted and focuses exclusively on the relationship between performer and audience. Boys dressed as women acting out a narrative are seen as the same as boys dressed as women in a tavern or on the street.

Part of the difficulty and confusion which attends these discussions is a product of Elizabethan confusions in a similar discussion. The boy actresses could not be 'like any convention in any art form' for theatrical representation in general and boy players in particular were, for the Elizabethans, a source of anxiety and heated debate. The whole business of theatrical representation violated notions of decorum and degree and in particular the practice of boys playing women transgressed the primary boundary between male and female. Moreover, there was biblical authority for objection to that practice in the injunction against cross-dressing, so the question recurs with wearisome regularity in all the contemporary discussions of the anti-theatrical prejudice.[1]

Like the modern discussions, the arguments of the anti-theatrical polemicists wilfully confused the requirements for putting a narrative on stage with behaviour in real life. The defenders of theatre were quick to point out the distinction:

> nor do I hold it lawfull to beguile the eyes of the world in confounding the shapes of either sex, as to keepe any youth in the habit of a virgin, or any virgin in the shape of a lad, to shroud them from the eyes of their fathers, tutors, or protectors, or to any other sinister intent whatsoever. But to see our youths attired in the habit of a woman, who knowes not what their intents be? Who cannot distinguish them by their names, assuredly knowing they are but to represent such a Lady at such a time appoynted. (Heywood 1610; sig. C3ᵛ)

Heywood sought to protect the theatre by insisting on the limits of its specificity and the purity of its intentions. He distinguishes between the dangerous cross-dressing for nefarious purposes in the real world and the stable representations of women fixed by the boundaries of narrative and the stage.

Heywood's position and that of the 'convention' critics clearly has a good deal of common-sense support. The fictions of Elizabethan drama would have been rendered nonsensical if at every appearance of a female character – say Ursula the pig woman or the Duchess of Malfi – their gender was called into question. Nevertheless the conditions in which that stability prevailed and the process by which it was sustained bear some investigation.

The clearest sexual indicators which could 'represent such a Lady at such a time appoynted' were voice and costume. The boy players had unbroken voices and the examples of women's costumes from Henslowe's inventory suggest that considerable trouble and expense went into providing appropriate costumes for those playing women's parts.[2] These indicators seem to have been sufficient in themselves and not merely aids to the boy player's suitability for representing a woman. Flute the bellows mender in *A Midsummer Night's Dream* is, after all, told that his incipient beard is no bar to an adequate representation of 'the lady that Pyramus must love':

> That's all one: you shall play it in a mask;
> and you may speak as small as you will.
> (I. ii. 45–6)

Pictorial representations of scenes from Elizabethan drama, moreover, portrayed women characters as women without any hint of sexual ambiguity. As R. A. Foakes's collection of illustrations has shown, the representation of women in pictures of the Elizabethan stage drew on contemporary iconographic traditions. Arethusa in the title page to *Philaster* is shown with fully exposed breasts, and Zenocrate in the woodcut in the third edition of *Tamburlaine* depicts 'a conventional representation of a richly dressed women' (Foakes 1985; p. 88). The theatre, like other modes of signification, drew on familiar signifiers of sexuality as it did for those of class or profession or royalty. These signifiers drew on the real world or the permanent attributes of the actors who bore them only in so far as those elements in the real world themselves depended upon familiar systems of signification.

In plays where representation of fictional characters is produced by emblem and symbol, where the acting style evidently proceeds by a set of formal encounters, the difficulty of incorporating a stable representation of women was not great. The signification of 'woman' is entirely contained within the text and in no way depends on the personality or gender of the actor in question. If we return to *A Midsummer Night's Dream* we can see that Quince and his fellows are dealing with just such stable categories. Bottom asks 'What is Pyramus? A lover, or a tyrant?' and is confident that he could play either: it is a simple extension of his confidence for him to feel that 'An I may hide my face, let me play Thisbe too. I'll speak in a monstrous little voice' (I. ii. 46). Bottom's self-confidence is based on his perception of the fixed relationship between character, action and narrative which had been created by the literary and dramatic traditions which the Elizabethan dramatists inherited.

When dramatic narrative moves away from these simple oppositions, however, the players' roles require a different kind of dramatic control, as Bottom and his mechanicals find out when they try to control the difficult and shifting relationship between the representation of a narrative and the perceptions of the audience. They debate how to control the limits of their fiction so as not to affright the ladies with their lion and invoke the real phases of the moon to overcome the technical difficulties of stage lighting. The range of solutions that they suggest spans the spectrum of representation from the static emblem which requires a special gloss – 'this lanthorn doth the horned moon present' (V. i. 230) – to the channelling of the world outside the fiction:

> You may leave a casement of the great chamber window where we play open; and the moon may shine in at the casement.
> (III. i. 52–4)

A good deal of the humour of the mechanical's play in *A Midsummer Night's Dream* depends upon the recognition that their fixed and conventional notions of representation are becoming out of date. Indeed the effect of the play within the play is to ensure the greater reality – of the main action. Their style of acting, associated with earlier emblematic and rhetorical drama, came to be an object of mockery in contrast to the apparently spontaneous, internally constructed notions of character and action developed in later plays.

But this spontaneous, internally constructed notion of character was itself the result of careful dramatic control – particularly in the case of women characters. In Shakespeare's romantic comedies, for example, the discussions of femininity, and the role of cross-dressing in the plots seem always to be inviting and at the same time denying a metatheatrical awareness of the true identity of the actor playing the woman's part. The 'realishness' of the boy players' femininity was asserted not only by the self-enclosed, self-referential visual and verbal indicators but by its contrast with what it was not. The cross-dressing of Shakepeare's romantic heroines is thus used partly as a means of resolving plot but also as a means of asserting their true femininity. Their characters as women are seen as something essential and internal and not a simple result of their clothes. In *The Two Gentlemen of Verona*, for example, when Julia plans her pursuit of her true-love, she has this exchange with her maid:

LUCETTA.   But in what habit will you go along?
JULIA.   Not like a woman, for I would prevent
           The loose encounters of lascivious men;
           Gentle Lucetta, fit me with such weeds
           As may beseem some well reputed page.
LUCETTA.   Why then your ladyship must cut your hair.
JULIA.   No, girl; I'll knit it up in silken strings
           With twenty odd conceited true-love knots –
           To be fantastic may become a youth
           Of greater time than I shall show to be.
LUCETTA.   What fashion, madam, shall I make your breeches?
JULIA.   That fits as well as 'Tell me, good my lord,
           What compass will you wear your farthingale?'
           Why even what fashion thou best likes Lucetta.
LUCETTA.   You must needs have them with a codpiece madam.
JULIA.   Out, out, Lucetta, that will be ill favour'd.
LUCETTA.   A round hose, madam, now's not worth a pin
           Unless you have a codpiece to stick pins in.
JULIA.   Lucetta, as thou lov'st me, let me have
           What thou think'st meet and is most mannerly.
                                          (II. vii. 40–58)

Part of the wit of this complicated exchange depends upon the realisation that Julia and Lucetta are both played by 'fantastic youths' in costume; however, it also plays on the inappropriateness of male dress for a female heroine – 'that fits as well as "Tell me, good my lord, what compass will you wear your farthingale?"' Moreover, the joke about the empty codpiece may have a satiric resonance at the expense of gallants in the audience, but it also clearly indicates that, within the fiction, Julia lacks the primary sexual signifier. The overall effect of the sequence, like Rosalind's frequent references in *As You Like It* to the woman's heart which lies beneath her doublet and hose, is to insist on the true and essential character of Julia's femininity, a fictional identity which transcends her clothes.

Bawdy jokes about the connection between clothes and sexual identity are developed into a complete scene in *The Roaring Girl* when Moll Cutpurse is fitted for breeches by a tailor:

TAILOR.	I forgot to take measure on you for your new breeches.
MOLL.	What fiddling's here? would not the old pattern have served your turn?
TAILOR.	You change the fashion, you say you'll have the great Dutch slop, Mistress Mary.
MOLL.	Why sir, I say so still.
TAILOR.	Your breeches then will take up a yard more.
MOLL.	Well, pray look it be put in then.
TAILOR.	It shall stand round and full, I warrant you.
MOLL.	Pray make 'em easy enough.
TAILOR.	I know my fault now, t'other was somewhat stiff between the legs, I'll make these open enough, I warrant you.

(II. ii. 73–87)

These instances could be seen merely as the necessary development of a convention but for the fact that transvestite heroines almost all appear in plays where questions of sexual identity are only one point on a spectrum of questions about identity, action and representation. In *The Two Gentlemen of Verona*, Valentine's character as a lover is determined by the list of special marks which his servant mockingly itemises:

... first you have learn'd, like Sir Proteus, to wreath your arms like a malcontent; to relish a love song, like a robin red-breast; to walk

> alone, like one that had the pestilence; to sigh like a schoolboy that
> had lost his ABC; to weep like a young wench that had buried her
> grandam; to fast like one that takes a diet; to watch, like one that fears
> robbing; to speak puling, like a beggar at Hallowmas.
>
> (II. i. 17–25)

Speed's list of similes shows that each attribute is precisely *not*
like a lover's. It is only when taken together that they produce the
correct diagnosis: the representation of a lover or a tyrant or a
woman is part of a system of representation rather than the result
of a single conventional attribute.

The situation is even more complicated when the category
woman is part of a system of representation rather than the result of
Sylvia, which causes Julia to question how far the differences
between them are the product of 'true' distinctions or simply
differences of representation:

> Here is her picture; let me see, I think
> If I had such a tire, this face of mine
> Were full as lovely as is this of hers;
> And yet the painter flatter'd her a little,
> Unless I flatter with myself too much.
> Her hair is auburn, mine is perfect yellow;
> If that be all the difference in his love,
> I'll get me such a colour'd periwig.
> Her eyes are grey as glass, and so are mine;
> Ay but her forehead's low and mine's as high.
> What should it be that he respects in her
> But I can make respective in myself,
> If this fond love were not a blinded god?
> Come shadow, come, and take this shadow up,
> For 'tis thy rival.
>
> (IV. iv. 180–93)

Julia does not compare herself to Sylvia but to Sylvia's picture:
the realities are irrelevant, the representations are all. At that
moment the shadow of Julia, disguised as a page can only
compare unfavourably with the flattered shadow of Sylvia,
dressed in the tires of formal portraiture.

The fact that there is a further, extra-diegetic, reality, in which
Julia is not a lady at all but a boy, need not enter into the
awareness at this point: it does not do so, for example, in modern
productions in which Julia is played by a woman. Indeed, to

introduce the ambiguities of gender at this point would muddy an elegant opposition.

II

Questions of role playing and acting need not lead beyond the narrative to a notion of metatheatre; they can be used to privilege the act or role played by the narrative hero or heroine as the one that has 'that within which passes show'. The convention helps to hold the action of the play within the narrative so that the boy player – or any other player – will only 'represent such a Lady at such a time appoynted.

Nevertheless, the implications of these discussions of acting and playing are further complicated by their use in literary descriptions of 'real life'. The list of women's parts which Heywood gives in the prefatory verses to *An Apology of Actors* makes no concession to the fact that these women would be played by boys. They are simply part of a pre-existing moral typology:

> She a chaste Lady acteth all her life
> A wanton courtezan another plays.
> This covets marriage loue, that, nuptial strife
> Both in continual action spend their days.

The moral typology not only provides character but determines narrative, and notions of decorum determine the relationship between the two.

Behind all such discussions lay the trope of the *theatrum mundi*,[3] the notion that there was a vital, if ill-defined, connection between the theatre and the world. In the Induction to *Antonio and Mellida* this question is addressed with precise reference to the roles of lover, tyrant and woman:

FELICHE. Why, what must you play?
ANTONIO. Faith, I know not what, an hermaphrodite, two parts in one; my true person being Antonio son to the Duke of Genoa, though for the love of Mellida, Piero's daughter, I take this feigned presence of an Amazon, calling myself Florizel and I know not what. I a voice to play a lady! I shall ne'er do it.

ALBERTO.   O, an Amazon should have such a voice, virago-like.
             Not play two parts in one? away, away; 'tis common
             fashion. Nay, if you cannot bear two subtle fronts under
             one hood, idiot go by, go by, off this world's stage. O
             time's impurity!

ANTONIO.   Ay, but when use hath taught me action to hit the
             right point of a lady's part, I shall grow ignorant, when
             I must turn young prince again, how but to truss my
             hose.

FELICHE.   Tush, never put them off; for women wear breeches
             still.

                                        (Induction, 67–80)

Alberto's comments reassure Antonio that he has only to look to
the world in order to see how to play a part. However, the world
beyond the play which he invokes is not the real world of variety
and inconsequentiality but the constructed world of satiric
commonplace. As in other examples of the *theatrum mundi*, the
comparison is not between acting and truth so much as between
competing fictions. Since the world can only be defined in terms
of its significations, the actor has to turn to those signifying
systems in order to represent the truth of the fiction he enacts.

   This is seen even more clearly in the Induction to *The Taming
of the Shrew*, where the comedy plays on the limits of competing
fictions. The Lord's page plays the woman's part in the elaborate
deception worked on Sly but he soon has to establish the limits of
his role. Sly responds to the news that he has a wife by claiming
his conjugal rights. The page's only self-protection – short of
exposing the fiction completely and destroying the joke – is to
retreat hurriedly into a further elaboration of the fiction to save
his/her honour:

   Thrice noble lord, let me entreat of you
   To pardon me yet for a night or two,
   Or if not so, until the sun be set,
   For your physicians have expressly charged,
   In peril to incur your former malady
   That I should yet absent me from your bed.
   I hope this reason stands for my excuse.
                          (Induction 2, 116–22)

Yet Sly was convinced of the page's femininity less because of the
boy actor's truth to life than because they both inhabit the same

fictional world. The Lord who is directing the show instructs his servants in the most effective and convincing presentation of their fiction:

> Sirrah go you to Barthol'mew my page
> And see him dressed in all suits like a lady.
> That done, conduct him to the drunkard's chamber,
> And call him 'madam', do him obeisance.
> Tell him from me – as he will win my love –
> He bear himself with honourable action,
> Such as he hath observed in noble ladies
> Unto their lords, by them accomplished.
> Such duty to the drunkard let him do,
> With soft low tongue and lowly courtesy,
> And say 'What is't your honour will command
> Wherein your lady and your humble wife
> May show her duty and make known her love?'
> And then with kind embracements, tempting kisses,
> And with declining head into his bosom,
> Bid him shed tears, as being overjoyed
> To see her noble lord restored to health,
> Who for this seven years hath esteemed him
> No better than a poor and loathsome beggar . . .
>   (Induction 1, 102–20)

The page's woman's part will be achieved by the appropriateness of his costume and the other servants' behaviour towards him but, most importantly, it will be effected by his dialogue and gestures. The more difficult matter of his tears, however, will require a technical trick:

> And if the boy have not a woman's gift
> To rain a shower of commanded tears,
> An onion will do well for such a shift,
> Which in a napkin, being close conveyed,
> Shall in despite enforce a watery eye.
>   (Induction 2, 121–5)

Paradoxically, the Lord's description of the trick draws the most explicit analogy with the supposed 'real' world, but his sense of 'woman's gift' is itself entirely literary. The young boy actor has none of the stereotyped attributes of a 'real life' woman so he must resort to the techniques of duplicitous women rendered familiar by such fabliaux tales as Dunbar's *Twa Merrit Wemen and the Wedo*[4] or by the woman in 'The Boke of Mayd Emlyn' who, after

she had pushed her husband down a well, attended his funeral
where

> A reed onyon wolde she kepe
> To make her eyes wepe
> In her kerchers.
>   Hazlitt 1866; p. 93)

The key to effective mimesis lay not in close observation of the
real world but in imitating fictional antecedents.

The distinction between men and women on stage and off
consisted of a series of related and intertwined distinctions, all
governed by and informing convention. They ranged from a
simple unquestioned statement – 'this is a man', this is 'such a
Lady at such a time' – to a complex set of moral categories. In
social life the distinction between maleness and femaleness is
paramount and in narrative or fictional life it carries the same
central importance. But it cannot be known with certainty. The
primary, physiological, distinction could not, of course, be
represented on the stage.

In plays where the difference between a man and a woman is of
crucial narrative importance, the distinction is either simply
effected by *fiat*,[5] or by a displaced revelation, the removal of a hat
or a wig. However, these narrative questions of maleness and
femaleness can only provide the initiative or the resolution of a
plot. For a woman character to be adequately represented on the
stage, the category of woman must be disintegrated into the
components of the moral typology – chaste lady, courtesan,
married love, nuptial strife – which equally depend upon systems
of signification.

More complete frustration with the system of signification is
evident in *Much Ado About Nothing*. Claudio, having rejected
Hero on their wedding day, attempts to justify his action by
interpreting the signs for the assembled company. He asserts:

> She's but the sign and semblance of her honour.
> Behold how like a maid she blushes here.
> O what authority and show of truth
> Can cunning sin cover itself withal!
> Comes not that blood as modest evidence
> To witness simple virtue? Would you not swear,
> All you that see her, that she were a maid

By these exterior shows? But she is none:
She knows the heat of a luxurious bed;
Her blush is guiltiness, not modesty.
(IV. i. 32–41)

No blush at all need have come from the boy player; within the drama he is merely an emblem to be read according to different models of reality. Claudio's model of reality is based on the imagery and typology of misogynist satire with its talk of 'pamper'd animals that rage in savage sensuality' and is a discourse shared by misogynists throughout the drama; its value and power depended on the status of the man who used it. Knowledge of the 'true' gender of the boy player may complicate but it cannot simply deny the complexity of these questions of significance. The frustrated critic may wish, like the puppet in *Bartholomew Fair*, simply to lift the skirts and expose the reality behind the signification but the result, as in Jonson's play, would simply be be a disconcerted silence. For the question of the theatrical representation of femininity cannot be restricted to the physical; gender has never been coterminous with biological sex. When dramatists tried to complicate 'the woman's part', they took on board the moral and social definitions which in their fixity could always be challenged by the flux of action both fictional and real.

III

These conclusions about how gender and sexuality were represented in Elizabethan drama cannot, nevertheless, provide any clear guidance as to how players were perceived by their contemporary audience. It may be, as the moralists asserted, that the boys were subject to homosexual exploitation by the adult players[6] or were the object of their audience's homosexual lust. If that was the case it is remarkable that no specific charge of homosexuality was ever brought against an actor or a boy player. Even the scandal over the abduction of Henry Clifton's son[7] involved only the social difference between a chorister in the Chapel Royal and 'the base trade of a mercynary enterlude player'. Moreover, the clamour of antitheatrical attack is not the only, or even the most reliable, sound of response to the

Elizabethan theatre: the institution was defended by the highest in the land, and even municipal attempts at control are delivered in the more measured tones of a concern for public order, with apparently little anxiety about sexual mores or the nature of representation.[8]

Nevertheless, the boy actresses do seem to have generated a disproportionate amount of fuss, a fuss which cannot be accounted for simply as misguided prejudice or a failure to understand the nature of representation. In its fervour and its language, the attacks on the boy players echoed attacks on other forms of social change, providing an example of what Stuart Clark has described as 'the periodic social need to relocate moral and cultural boundaries by means of accusations of deviance' (Clark 1970; p. 99).

In their attack on the boy players, however, the moralists had chosen the most difficult and most shifting of moral and cultural boundaries – the relationship of clothes to sex. At its most extreme, the case was simple: as Philip Stubbes wrote:

> Our apparell was given as a signe distinctive, to discern betwixt sexe and sexe, and therefore one to weare the apparell of an other sex, is to participate with the same and to adulterate the veritie of his owne kinde. (Stubbes 1583; p. 38)

Clothes, as Stubbes acknowledged, were signs. They were signs, Stubbes and others were sure, of a natural and unchangeable phenomenon: sex was 'the veritie of his own kind'. However, as in the theatre, these 'verities' could not extend very far. Stubbes had to go on to make a further distinction in kind; not between male and female but between needful and excessive modes of dress:

> when they have all these goodly robes upon them, women seeme to be the smallest part of themselves, not natural women, but artificiall women, not women of fleshe and bloud, but rather Puppits, or Mawmets consistyng of ragges and cloutes compact together . . . . (Stubbes 1583; p. 39)

Stubbes's slide into metaphor indicates the impossibility of talking about clothes without invoking pre-existing moral categories, the most influential of which is the distinction between the natural and unnatural.

A similar confusion pervades the 'Homily Against Excess of Apparell'. It begins generously enough by accepting that God 'alloweth us apparell not only for necessity's sake but also for an honest comliness'. However, 'honest comliness' is soon having to be set against 'fine bravery' which will be an inducement to 'wanton, lewd and unchaste behaviour' and distinguished further from the necessary adornment appropriate to high degree (Homilies 1908; p. 325). For women the case was even more complicated, for in moral and metaphoric terms it seems they needed no clothes at all:

> Let women be subject to their husbands and they are sufficiently attired. . . . (Homilies 1908; p. 330)

What was clearly most important of all was the 'difference in apparel between an honest matron and a common strumpet' (Homilies 1908; p. 328). As in the discourses of satire, the distinction between male and female in fact mattered less than the moral and social distinction between chaste and unchaste, noble and common. In spite of the evidently serious and didactic purpose of the Homily, its conviction that it was addressing real social ills, it cannot escape from the rhetoric of complaint and the categories of decorum:

> many a one doubtless should be compelled to wear a russet coat which now ruffleth in silks and velvets, spending more by the year in superfluous apparell than their fathers received for the whole revenue of their lands. . . . (Homilies 1908; pp. 334–5)

The signs of morality, since they were established by custom and not by nature, were notoriously unstable. They were, moreover, under pressure from a different tradition in which nature is best seen stripped of all customary embellishment. The reductive logic and static oppositions of this kind of writing could easily be overturned by the common-sense wit of the new generation of satirists such as Henry Fitzgeffrey:

Socraticke Doctors, Catoes most austeer
Roule up the Records of Antiquity,
To frame Abridgements for youth's Liberty.
Accuse Wit's folly, Time's strange alterations;
The vaine expence of cloth consuming fashions
When their allowance was (themselves can tell)
At least unto a Codpiece halfe an Ell
. . .
As if a Frounced, pounced Pate coo'd not,
As much Braine couer, as a Stoike cut.
Or practicke Vertue, might not lodge as soone
Under a Silken, as a Cynicke gowne.
                    (Fitzgeffrey 1617, sigs B4^v, C2)

A pair of pamphlets responding to the androgynous fashions of
the turn of the century conducted the debate in familiar terms.
Hic Mulier took the line from decorum, calling on 'the powerfull
Statute of apparell' to:

lift up his Battle Axe, and crush the offenders in pieces, so as every
one may be knowne by the true badge of their bloud or Fortune.
(Anon 1620; sig. C^v)

The defensive reply, *Haec Vir*, challenged the simple fit between
sartorial signifier and moral signified and asked

. . . because I stand not with my hands on my belly like a baby at
Bartholomew Fayre, that moue not my whole body when I should,
but onely stirre my head like Iacke of the Clocke house which hath no
ioynts, that am not dumbe when wantons court me, or because I weep
not when iniury gripes me, like a worried Deere in the fangs of many
Curres, am I therefore barbarous and shameless? (Anon, 1620;
sig. B3)

However, before we can take these iconoclastic inversions as true
statements of youthful defiance or feminist self-assertion, we have
to note that they merely involve choosing a different set of
oppositions and metaphors with which to score debating points in
a contest which repeats itself throughout the period. It was a
contest, moreover, which embodied anxiety about the sexual and
social definition but which could only reveal its elusive and
contradictory nature.

IV

In subsuming questions of gender into the moral and social typologies of sumptuary regulation Elizabethan commentators on the stage and on social mores were able to avoid direct confrontation with questions of sex and gender. Nevertheless, on a few occasions, the gender ambiguity which the convention of boys playing women allowed was given the literary and theatrical space to tease out more complex ways of seeing the boundaries of gender and sexuality. One of the best known of these is Shakespeare's sonnet 20, which celebrates the 'Master Mistress of my passion' and dramatises the problem of male and female signification in the fullest possible way.

In the opening lines the gender of the beloved addressed is not entirely clear:

> A woman's face, with Nature's own hand painted
> Hast thou, the Master Mistress of my passion.

Nevertheless she/he is defined through an opposition to conventional female moral categories: she/he has

> A woman's gentle heart, but not acquainted
> With shifting change, as is false woman's fashion;
> An eye more bright than their's, less false in rolling
> Gliding the object whereupon it gazeth.

A figure with the opposite to women's attributes has to have something male about him, and indeed is

> A man in hue, all hues in his controlling
> Which steals men's hearts and women's souls amazeth.

The force of that *moral* opposition between men and women is, however, complicated by the third quatrain. In spite of the unfeminine virtues which the beloved possesses.

> For a woman wert thou first created
> Till Nature as she wrought thee fell adoting
> And by addition me of thee defeated
> By adding one thing to my purpose nothing.

The sonnet turns on the difference between the beloved's feminine beauty, which can be verbally but not physically distinguished from the false beauty of other women. Since the

lover's face is 'with Nature's own hand painted', by implication
'false woman's fashion' is not natural but social. The logic of
Nature's painting is thwarted by the addition of the primary
sexual signifier: 'one thing to my purpose nothing'. This
'addition' is the only difference between a young man and a
woman but it is sufficient to change not only the young man's
gender but all the moral signification that goes with it. However,
by the end of the sonnet the poet realises that the only purpose of
maleness is the relationship, both natural and social, of sex:

> But since she prick'd thee out for women's pleasure,
> Mine be thy love, and thy love's use their treasure.

The truth at the heart of the beloved's beauty is 'one thing to my
purpose nothing'. The categories of sexuality are artificially
constructed but they carry nevertheless the most serious social
taboos. Once again the emphasis is on familiar moral categories
but the poem shows an awareness that men and women might be
created out of an overlapping system of differences and, more
dangerously, that these physical attributes might inspire love
regardless of their ascription to a particular gender.

That rather more threatening possibility of physical passion
which is not appropriately directed is raised, albeit lightheartedly,
in *The Maid's Metamorphosis*, performed by the children of Pauls
in 1600. The play combines the story of Ascanius' thwarted love
for Eurymine, and her adventures in the forest where she has fled
from her murderers, with a conflict between Juno and Iris, played
out on the fates of the unfortunate lovers. This combination of
different styles and ways of resolving the action allows strange
clashes which raise interesting questions about the literary and
theatrical conventions governing combinations of the sexes.
Having escaped from death, Eurymine takes up a pastoral
existence, keeping sheep in the forest, where she encounters
Apollo. He tries at first to seduce Eurymine to be his lover and,
when she refuses, attempts 'with proffered force a silly Mayd to
touch' (III. ii. 188; ed Bond 1902). In order to prevent the rape,
Eurymine asks Apollo to show his power by transforming her into
a man. Apollo grants her request but, out of spite, says that he
will change only her body and not her desires:

> I graunt thy wish, thou art become a man:

I speake no more then well performe I can,
And though thou walke in chaunged bodie now,
This pennance shall be added to thy vow:
Thy selfe a man, shalt loue a man, in vaine:
And louing, wish to be a maide againe.

(III. ii. 223–7)

Apollo's spite is caused by his own thwarted passion for the boy Hyacinth and raises questions about the relationship between sexuality, gender and sexual desire. It seems to support the essentialist view that since Eurymine is a woman she can only love men. However, since she will be a man when she does so, it is clearly not impossible for men to love men. Sexual desire is thus located both in the essential characteristics of one gender and in the contingent desirability of the beloved.

The situation is further complicated when Ascanius comes to the forest in search of his beloved. He is dismayed to find that she has been transformed into a man. He is outraged by the suggestion that he might be 'haunted with such lunacie' (IV. i. 153) as to love a boy, but his comic page, Ioculo, tries to resolve the difficulty by suggesting that the problem is a metaphorical one:

Women weare breetches, petticoates are deare.
And that's his meaning, on my life it is.

(IV.i. 118–19)

However, this simple retreat into the metaphors of misogynist satire is explicitly prevented by the action of the play. It uses the *fact* of Eurymine's transformation to investigate further the connections between homosexual friendship and heterosexual desire, playing on the ambiguous use of the word 'love' and the familiar opposition between true identity and 'habit' in both the social and the sartorial senses:

EURYMINE.   How gladly would I be thy lady still,
            If earnest vowes might answere to my will?
ASCANIUS.   And is thy fancie altered with thy guise?
EURYMINE.   My kinde, but not my minde in any wise.
ASCANIUS.   What though thy habit differe from thy kind:
            Thou mayest retain thy wonted louing mind.
EURYMINE.   And so I doo.
ASCANIUS.   Then why art thou so strange?
            Or wherefore doth thy plighted fancie chaunge?

EURYMINE.   *Ascanio*, my heart doth honor thee.
ASCANIO.   And yet continuest stil so strange to me?
EURYMINE.   Not strange, so far as kind will give me leave . . .
                                              (V. i. 17–26)

The dialogue continues to turn on friend and love and sex until
Ascanius reluctantly concludes 'Then haue I lost a wife' and
Eurymine confronts him:

But found a friend, whose dearest blood and life,
Shal be as readie as thine owne for thee:
In place of wife, such friend thou hast of mee.
                                              V. i. 47–50)

The possibility of resolving these difficulties by a homosexual
attachment is not allowed within the scope of this story, and the
problem is eventually solved by Apollo relenting and declaring
baldly 'she is a maide again'. In the same process, he reveals that
Eurymine is in truth the long-lost daughter of Aramanthus and so
the social bar to her marriage with Ascanius is removed to ensure
the final happy ending.

In one sense this comic circling around questions of gender and
sexual identity is a displacement of the real barrier to the lovers'
union, Eurymine's obscure birth. Identity in this play is bound
up not only with gender but also with status, but these are
presented as narrative rather than social problems. The lovers'
problems are merely the narrative framework on which the other
dramatic pleasures of the play, the songs and the comic turns of
the witty pages, are grafted. The lovers' despair can be treated as
another comic episode precisely because they inhabit a magical
story world in which gender identity or social status are dramatic
counters available for the dramatist to play with in making his
play. As a social idea the notion of gender instability is at least
unnerving and at most subversive: in dramatic play it enables wit
and bawdy and turns of plot which finally can be held in place and
restored to safety by narrative closure. When in *Twelfth Night*
Viola finds herself loving a man who thinks she is a boy and being
beloved by a woman, she can sigh 'O time, thou must untangle
this, not I/It is too hard a knot for me t'untie', we know that Time
is in the hands of the dramatist, who will restore rightful sexual
relations when the full dramatic potential has been fulfilled.

Sexual identity was available for 'play' of this kind partly because of the tradition of tales of metamorphosis. Heywood in his *Guneikeon* tells the story of Iphis, whose female sex was concealed by her mother to save her from her father's vow to murder any girl children. There was no difficulty in disguising her sex, for

> The habit of a Boy she wore
> And it had such a face,
> As whether she were Boy or Gyrle,
> It either Sex would grace.
> (Heywood, 1620; p. 366)

When she/he came to marriageable age a bride was chosen for her who was in every way suitable:

> they were bred together, brought up and schooled together, and as they had like instructions, so they had like affections, they were paralleld in love but not in hopes. (Heywood 1620; p. 366)

The mother prays to Jupiter, who intervenes directly and saves the situation by turning Iphis into a man as he leaves the marriage ceremony.

In retailing the finale of the story, Heywood moves from prose narrative to verse, claiming to quote from 'Ovid my maister'. The transformation he describes lists the signifiers of masculinity: the longer strides, the darker complexion, the broader shoulders and even shorter hair. Though the necessary, fundamental physiological change also occurs, it is included in 'she feeles about her something grow' which could equally extend to all the other physical changes. As a tall tale of divine intervention the story is deftly enough handled, but Heywood tries to claim some historical authenticity for it with accounts of parallel modern stories. He refers to accounts of children who 'have been mistaken for daughters, and so continued some yeeres' until the truth is dicovered at 'the age of twelve, or thereabouts' when male sexual organs appear. Heywood, however, does not see the transformation as one of physiological development. For him the change is occasioned by the child's becoming 'able to distinguish of good or evil (being capable of passions, and subject to affections) whether Loue or Time have produced these strange effects I am not certaine' (Heywood 1620; p. 367). Love and Time as modes of causation fit well into narrative patterns of tales of metamorphosis on or off the stage: they fulfil the literary pleasures of suspense and surprise and hold at bay the moral and social panic which ensued on the rare occasions when real cases of homosexuality or transexuality appeared to challenge these familiar ways of talking about sexual identity before the courts of early modern Europe.[9]

The ambiguities around sexual identity may have seemed particularly pointed in the reign of a homosexual king. David Seville (1986) has suggested that Day's *Isle of Gulls* was a direct commentary on the sexual intrigues of the Jacobean court. The comic movements of the plot certainly turn on sex and disguise and involve the hero, Lysander, disguising himself as an Amazon so that he can court his beloved Violetta. The Duchess falls in love with the Amazon and suggests that s/he might pretend to be a man but still enjoy the behaviour open to women:

> Seeme coy, look nice and, as we woemen use
> Be mild and proud, imbrace and yet refuse.
> (Day 19; p. 252)

To complicate the action, the Duke falls in love with the Amazon too and the action consists of a series of complicated encounters until the rightful sexes are appropriately paired off.

Given the prevalence of the comic conventions which the play uses, it seems unnecessary to insist on a particular satiric application. It consists of a series of satiric set pieces in which the pages are constantly employed to mock the action and call the seriousness of the whole endeavour into question. It is probably most appropriate to place the play in the genre of parodic comedy produced by boy players in the early years of the century.[10] Nevertheless it indicates the theatre did provide a number of conventions through which even potentially dangerous matters to do with the sex could be explored.

These ways of talking about sex intertwine in an even more complex way with the image of the theatre in Francis Osborne's observations of the King's unseemly conduct towards his favourites at court:

> the love the King shewed was as amourously conveyed as if he had mistaken their sex, and thought them ladies; which I have seene Sommerset and Buckingham labour to resemble in the effeminateness of their dressings ... [James] ... kissing them after so lascivious a

mode in publicke, and upon the theatre, as it were, of the world . . .
prompted many to imagine some things done in the tyring house that
exceed my expressions. . . . (In Goldberg 1983; p. 143)

The connection between behaviour in the theatre and the
tiring-house which Osborne suggests, may reflect the actual
behaviour of actors and their young apprentices. However, it also
provides an elegant and witty image with which we could both
mask and expose the scandal of the King's behaviour. The King's
conduct is an 'act' in the theatre of the world which may or may
not represent a reality in the off-stage world of the tiring-house.
Moreover, the reality which it may have represented could not be
named: it is enough that the sexuality is lascivious; the young
men to whom it is directed are suitable objects because they are
effeminate and are effeminate because they are suitable objects for
a man's lust.

Similarly, in the world of the commercial theatre the meaning
of boys playing women had to be negotiated in every case. It was
not fixed as a 'fact' or a 'convention' but was part of a system of
representation which perhaps had to be clearly articulated, and
explicitly produced because of the contradictions of the poetic
and satiric traditions on which it drew. The signs which
connected clothes and sex and gender were shifting and ambiguous: writers for the theatre exploited that ambiguity for witty
and comic and often disconcerting effect.

Notes

1. See Jonas Barish, *The Antitheatrical Prejudice*, Chapter 4, 'Puritans
   and Proteans'.
2. See Henslowe's inventories of costume in R. A. Foakes and R. T.
   Rickert, *Henslowe's Diary*, pp. 291–4, 319–20, 321–3. A sugges-
   tive modern reconstruction of the role of the boy player is provided
   by David Gentleman's cartoon showing the transformation of a boy
   into a woman by the addition of petticoat, corset, bumroll, dress,
   ruff, wig, fan and jewels in John Russel Brown, *Shakespeare and his
   Theatre*, pp. 26–7.
3. The Shakespearean *locus classicus* in *As You Like It*, II. vii.
   139–66, 'All the world's a stage', is a case in point. The Seven Ages
   of Man is a literary construction, listing types much as Heywood's

poem does. The evident discrepancy between that conventional representation and the characters of Orlando and Adam validates the greater 'realishness' of the fictional characters.

4. William Dunbar's widow is equipped with 'a watter spunge ... within my wyde clokis/Than wring I it full wylely and wetis my chekis'. See *The Poems of William Dunbar*, ed W. Mackay Mackenzie (London, 1932), p. 95.

5. Examples include Beaumont and Fletcher, *Philaster*, Ford, *The Lover's Melancholy*, Ben Jonson, *Epicoene*, Anon., *The Maid's Metamorphosis*.

6. This charge was brought most explicitly by Stubbes and Prynne. For a full discussion of the evidence see W. Robertson Davies, *Shakespeare's Boy Actors*, pp. 10–15, and Lisa Jardine, *Still Harping on Daughters*, Chapter 2.

7. See G. E. Bentley, *The Jacobean and Caroline Stage*, vol. II, pp. 43–5.

8. On attempts to control the theatre see Glynne Wickam, *Early English Stages*, vol. III, Chapters 3 and 4.

9. See, for example, the case of the French transexual Marin de Merci, discussed in Stephen Greenblatt, *Shakespearean Negotiations* Chapter 3.

10. See R. A. Foakes, 'Tragedy of the Children's Theatres after 1600'.

CHAPTER SIX

'Devis'd and play'd to take spectators': Women in Dramatic Structures

So far I have been suggesting that the representation of women in Elizabethan culture depended upon a constant negotiation around a number of ways of speaking about women. In social life the patriarchal family provided a locus in which women could not only lead their lives but also sustain the definitions which made those lives meaningful. Evidence that the patriarchal family was not, in the end, effective in these functions was dealt with by the structures of popular culture which either mocked or warned against challenges to this central institution and provided the compensating pleasures of communal laughter or pathos.

Representation of women in theatre involved a similar procedure of negotiation between the narrative function of women's roles and the social implications which can be drawn from them. However, I would argue that in the case of theatre, the direct link between cultural forms and social forms is broken by the particular characteristics of the theatre as a mode of cultural production. In the emergent commercial institution, images and ideas were part of a financial exchange and offered none of the participatory qualities of the popular culture of rural communities.[1] As such the material of the theatre, as we saw in the case of the witchcraft plays, was part of a stock which was recycled and reproduced as much with regard to its saleable theatrical potential as in response to the direct pressures of particular cultural needs. The cultural meaning of 'women' on the Elizabethan stage cannot, as a result, be inferred by direct recourse to social or ideological pressure since it was constantly mediated by the form of the drama and the demands of the theatrical institutions which it sustained. Women characters in plays can, therefore, be seen as part of the stock; a means of providing dramatic comedy and pathos, suspense and surprise as well as the manipulation of socially determined ideas. Elizabethan dramatists inherited not only a set of ideological assumptions about relations of men and women but also the dramatic structures within which these were enacted. One of the most powerful and fascinating aspects of Elizabethan drama is its tendency to play these off one against another. For example, in *The Revenger's Tragedy*, the revenger hero, Vindice, addresses the skull of his dead mistress thus:

> Does the silk worm expend her yellow labours
> For thee? For thee does she undo herself?
> Are lordships sold to maintain ladyships
> For the poor benefit of a bewitching minute?
> Why does yon fellow falsify high ways
> And put his life between the judge's lips
> To refine such a thing, keeps horse and men
> To beat their valours for her? . . .
> Does every proud and self affecting dame
> Camphor her face for this, and grieve her Maker
> In sinful baths of milk, – when many an infant starves
> For her superfluous outside – all for this?
>
> (III. v. 72–87)

The commonplace misogyny of the *memento mori* formula is here given poetic energy by the particularity of the references, and the speech stands as one of the most memorable versions of that trope. Moreover, the commonplace emblem is given considerable impact by the presence on stage of the skull of Vindice's mistress dressed 'in tires' as a court lady awaiting an assignation with her lover. The scene is also enlivened by the grotesque comedy in the situation, rendered both more grotesque and more comic in the ensuing scene in which the lustful Duke makes love to the skull and finds that he has been killed by the poison which Vindice has applied to its face.

The scene overflows with meaning. It enacts the *memento mori*; it enforces the connection between lust and death; and since lust in these plays is directed at women, it places women at the centre of all this symbolism, an emblem of corruptibility and the source of corruption. In the Duke's death-throes, Vindice acts as a grotesque parody of the spiritual advisor, reminding him of the inevitability of his death and the already advanced state of his physical decay.

The dramatic dynamic of the play, however, does not allow the scene to stay still as a moral emblem. It is complicated, theatrically if not morally, by Vindice's and Hippolito's knowing manipulation of the emblem as part of their triumph over the Duke: 'the quaintness' as Hippolito puts it, 'of thy malice above thought (III. v. 108). The moral emblems of the *memento mori* or satiric misogyny, the material of preachers and moralists, had become, in the hands of dramatists, a source of knowing 'play', a means of varying and intensifying the horror and the humour, the theatrical pleasures which were their stock in trade.

In the sub-plot, in which Vindice agrees to seduce his sister Castiza for the courtier Lussurioso, we find a similar 'play', not only with moral concepts but with familiar scenic shapes. As a court pander Vindice does a very convincing job, and though he is angrily rejected by Castiza, he is able to seduce her mother by invoking the 'angels' of a courtier's gold. In the event this plot leads nowhere, Castiza remains unseduced and the action is completely forgotten in the finale. However, it provides a witty variation on the action: the mother is violently forced into repentance by her sons, then appalled to find that Castiza seems to have accepted the arguments of lust, then relieved to find that she is only being tested and that the chaste heroine and the loving mother can be reunited. The dynamics of this action consist of taking two moral types, the chaste heroine and the loving mother, overturning them in action and then restoring them to the *status quo ante*. It is a narrative pattern which is repeated again and again throughout the drama and it forms a kind of *lazzo*, as in the *commedia dell'arte*, in which the characters have a particular narrative potential – she who is to be seduced, she who will/will not pander her daughter – that provides them with a range of language and situation which the dramatists could exploit at will.

The additional variation is the connection between love and money, which had also been played through in the play on 'angels' and 'devils' in the scene from *The Revenger's Tragedy*. Gratiana had insisted that

> the riches of the world cannot hire
> A mother to such a most unnatural task.

But Vindice assures her:

> No but a thousand angels can,
> Men have no power, angels must work you to't .
> (II. i. 85–8)

It was a familiar pun which encapsulated satirical views about the transfer of values into commodities. Nevertheless, when the idea is given dramatic currency it can be enacted in a variety of different ways with particular resonances in its application to women.

The Biblical proverb, 'the price of a good woman is above rubies' is collapsed into the simpler metaphor in which virginity is seen as a jewel, though with the important difference that

> Jewels being lost are found again, this never;
> 'Tis lost but once, and once lost, lost forever.
> (Marlowe, *Hero and Leander*, ii, 85–6)

The rhetorical implications of the irretrievability of virginity can, moreover, go in two directions, as Vindice makes clear when he importunes Castiza:

> Lose but a pearl, we search and cannot brook it,
> But that once gone, who is so mad to look it.
> (II. i. 234–5)

The double edge of this metaphorical and moral connection provides it with effective resonances in the dramatic situation in which it occurs. When Brachiano makes love to Vittoria in Webster's *The White Devil*, the property jewels which each of them wears are invested with sexual and symbolic charges by the embedded reference to the trope:

> BRACHIANO.   What value is this jewel?
> VITTORIA.   'Tis the ornament
> Of a weak fortune.
> BRACHIANO.   In sooth, I'll have it; nay I will but change

	My jewel for your jewel.
FLAMINEO.	Excellent,
	His jewel for her jewel, – well put in, duke.
BRACHIANO.	Nay, let me see you wear it.
VITTORIA.	Here, sir.
BRACHIANO.	Nay lower, you shall wear my jewel lower.
FLAMINEO.	That's better; she must wear his jewel lower.

(I.ii.227–8)

In this scene Flamineo delightedly draws the audience's attention to the ironic play with the metaphor of virginity as a jewel. In other contexts it is the character's unselfconscious use of the metaphor which renders the irony more telling. In the sub-plot of Heywood's *A Woman Killed with Kindness* Mountford finds himself in financial difficulties and insists that he cannot sell his house, declaring that

> I now the last will end and keep this house
> This virgin title never yet deflower'd
> By any unthrift of the Mountfords' line.
> (vii. 22–4)

Nevertheless, when he finds that Acton, his creditor, loves his sister, Susan, he is content to see her virginity deflowered in order to keep the virgin title of his honour intact:

> O sister! only this one way,
> With that rich jewel you my debts may pay.
> (xiv. 47–8)

Mountford is, of course, disapproved of for his attempts to prostitute his sister but the opposition between his virgin honour and the jewel with which Susan can save him is further complicated when Acton repents his lust and agrees to marry Susan. For Susan's virginity is like jewels in the market which are useless unless they are traded. Female chastity is important for ensuring the honour of men in the certainty of their estate and the easy passage of inheritance, but it exists only to be traded. The concern is that the trading should take place on the most advantageous terms.

The potential in this combination of metaphor and dramatic structure is realised most powerfully in Middleton's *Women Beware Women*. Leantio uses the lapidary metaphors throughout, describing his beloved Bianca as a 'most unvaluedest purchase' (I. i. 12) and her virtues as 'jewels kept in cabinets' (I. i. 56). In spite of his care for her, Leantio's jewel is stolen by characters who are provided with a much wittier sense of the real relations involved in sexual exchange. When Fabritio introduces his daughter Isabella, who is to be married to the idiot ward, he jokes 'She's a dear child to me . . . dear to my purse I mean' (III. ii. 107–9), warding off with mirth the deadly earnest sense in which Isabella is being offered for sale. The reality of that transaction becomes more evident in the scene where the ward comes to look her over and asks to see her teeth and how she walks, as if he were buying a horse. The satiric point is evident and telling but its dramatic realisation, once again, makes it more complex. For this scene is comic as well as satiric and the laughter is at the ward's expense. He is mocked, not because he treats a human relationship in financial terms – Fabritio and Livia both do the same – but because he does so without wit and is quite unable to deal with the paradoxes and contradictions involved.

Later in the play Isabella laments that 'men buy their slaves but women buy their masters'. However, her willing acquiescence in an adulterous, and as it happens incestuous, affair with her uncle Hippolito makes her statement less tragically poignant, if no less true. Her lament at the commerce behind relationships between men and women is made possible and activated by a particular application of the extended metaphors of chastity as a jewel. The whole play is concerned with the buying and selling, the keeping and stealing, of sexuality, but the characters' theatrical power depends on their ability to deal with this commerce rather than simply to deplore it.

In giving such statements of social observation or ideological assertion to their characters, dramatists are at one remove from the statements themselves. The ideology of virginity, love and marriage is embedded in the language and dramatic structures which they employ to construct narratives, make jokes, exploit ironies and otherwise vary the theatrical pleasures which they offer an audience.

II

These complex dramatic uses of the connections between women, sex and money illustrate the ways in which social ideas can be transformed into witty theatrical effects. The narrative functions of women characters could be employed in a similar way, generating scenes which could be varied to alter and develop the structure of the plays in which they occur. For example, the narratives of romantic comedy often conclude with marriage and many of them, as a result, involve 'choosing scenes' early on in the action. In *The Two Gentlemen of Verona*, for example, Lucetta, the waiting maid, discusses all Julia's suitors, beginning with 'What thinkst thou of the fair Sir Eglamour?' Apart from the hero, Proteus, none of the suitors named ever appears in the play whose action turns out to offer Julia little choice of lover. The scene serves simply to introduce the heroine and offers the pleasures of a double act between mistress and servant, as each of the alternative suitors is dismissed with a witty quip. This kind of scene, like a *commedia dell'arte lazzo*, was elastic in form as the number of suitors could be varied for different effects. In *The Merchant of Venice*, for example, Shakespeare varied the basic structure: in Act 2, Scene 1, Portia, like Julia, is offered a list of suitors to be discussed and dismissed but this basic situation is then integrated into the casket plot. The verbal dismissal of lovers in a dialogue is expanded into two comic scenes in which Morocco and the Prince of Aragon display their unsuitability showing both that Bassanio is the true lover, and that the leaden casket must win the lady fair.

The choosing scene is a useful device for it introduces a woman character in a way which makes her narrative function clear while, at the same time, leaving open the possibility for variation and suspense. The action of the play depends upon the woman finding a partner before the plot is concluded. The discussion of choice offers the illusion that they will be active in that process but that it also serves as a theatrical endorsement of the choice that the narrative has already imposed.

The expectations set up by the 'Sir Eglamour' scenic structure can have complex implications when it is used in contexts where there is no straightforward fit between the choosing woman and the chosen hero. In *'Tis Pity She's a Whore*, Ford varied the familiar scenic structure to startling effect. Annabella is introduced discussing the merits of her suitors with Putana and Ford's

economic handling of the scene uses it to provide information
about Soranzo's past and to characterise Putana by her enthusiastic appreciation of the suitors' physical attributes. Nevertheless
the structure of lovers rejected and a lover chosen leads the
audience to accept Annabella's choice in spite of the startling
danger of incest which emerges when the lover turns out to be her
brother Giovanni. Annabella's choice is further ratified by the
physical organisation of the scene. Her dialogue with Putana takes
place on the upper acting level which means that the suitors, as
well as being discussed, can be observed below. It opens
excitingly with a duel between rival suitors and a discussion of the
context for Annabella's marriage. After the initial dialogue,
Bergetto and Poggio appear and the grotesque comedy of their
appearance is then contrasted with the arrival of Giovanni.
Giovanni is given a slow-motion dumb show in which to make his
value and his presence felt, not only by Annabella but also by the
audience:

ANNABELLA.	But see, Putana, see! what blessed shape
	Of some celestial creature now appears!
	What man is he, that with such sad aspect
	Walks careless of himself? . . .
PUTANA.	'Tis your brother
ANNABELLA.	Sure 'tis not he; this is some woeful thing
	Wrapped up in grief, some shadow of a man.
	Alas he beats his breast and wipes his eyes,
	Drowned all in tears; methinks I hear him sigh.

(I. ii. 126–38)

Structurally, the scene introduces Giovanni as a lover, both in the
symbolism of his action and in the fact that he occupies the
position of contrast to the unsuitable lovers dismissed in the
dialogue between Annabella and Putana. The play does not fully
endorse the lovers view of the special character of their love, the
sense that it erases 'that rigour/which would in other incests be
abhorred' (V. v. 72–3). However, the dramatic structure in
which the love affair is introduced goes some way to making that
point of view seem possible.

III

Both the choosing scenes of love stories and the satiric connection between women, sex and money arise out of the tendency to locate women dramatically in the arena of heterosexual relations. However even when the main narrative was not focused primarily on love, sex and marriage, women characters could be introduced to vary and intensify the action. In Kyd's *The Spanish Tragedy*, for example, the presence of the women characters permits a contrast between the framing revenge action for Andrea's death in battle and the main narrative of Hieronimo's need to revenge the death of Horatio, his son. The framing action provides a technical and mechanical need for revenge, whereas the action involving women sets up the more pressing emotions of sympathy, pathos and the dramatic irony of violence interrupting love.

In the scene before Horatio is murdered he has an assignation with Bel-Imperia in an arbour:

HORATIO.	Hark, madam, how the birds record by night,
	For joy that Bel-Imperia sits in sight
BEL-IMPERIA.	No, Cupid counterfeits the nightingale
	To frame sweet music to Horatio's tale.
HORATIO.	If Cupid sing, then Venus is not far:
	Ay, thou art Venus or some fairer star.
BEL-IMPERIA.	If I be Venus thou must needs be Mars,
	And where Mars reigneth there must needs be wars.

(II. iv. 28–35)

The formality of this scene of love making presents the contrast between love and war in the imagery of Mars and Venus but also offers a moment of beautiful calm which serves as an ironic prelude to the violence. The question of Bel-Imperia's motives in passing her love from the dead Andrea to his friend Horatio, carries no dramatic weight, for her symbolic function in creating the mood of the scene is far more important.

Isabella, too, though she has no determining role in the narrative, provides an important focus for pathos which engages the audience in concern for the completion of the action. As the revenge is delayed and the action stalls, Isabella goes mad and cuts down the arbour in which her son was killed, cursing it with eternal barrenness:

> An eastern wind commixed with noisome airs
> Shall blast the plants and the young saplings;
> The earth with serpents shall be pestered,
> And passangers, for fear to be infect,
> Shall stand aloof, and looking at it tell
> 'There, murdered, died the son of Isabel.'
>
> (IV. ii. 17–22)

The pathos of madness and suffering is available in Hieronimo's scenes of frustrated supplication to the King or his laments over vengeance unfulfilled; however, by using a woman character the dramatist can extend the resonances of the tragic events by playing on the imagery of barrenness and death which has particular application to a bereaved mother. Isabella's speech makes the analogy explicit:

> And as I curse this tree from further fruit
> So shall my womb be cursed for his sake;
> And with this weapon will I wound the breast,
>
> *(she stabs herself)*
>
> The hapless breast that gave Horatio suck.
>
> (IV.iii. 35–8)

Like the arbour itself, or the bloody handkerchief which Hieronimo retains throughout the action, Isabella is part of the emblematic structure of the play, sustaining the coherence of emotion and motivation throughout. Her role contributes to making revenge an emotional as well as a plot necessity, adding to the play's dramatic power.

This functional aspect of women's roles in drama is used by dramatists, even when the characters who perform that function are more fully developed in the remainder of the actions in which they appear. Ophelia's mad scene in *Hamlet*, for example, seems to arise out of her character and situation but, like Isabella's mad scene in *The Spanish Tragedy*, it occurs when the hopes for the consummation of revenge seem lost and a new emotional drive is needed to carry the play to its conclusion. The pathos of Ophelia's distribution of flowers, moreover, depends upon connections between women and nature similar to those invoked in Isabella's destruction of the bower; the difference is that the formal rhetoric of Isabella's curse of general barrenness is transformed into the inconsequential snatches of bawdy, indicating the loss of Ophelia's particular hopes of more fruitful wedlock with the distracted prince.

Subsequent reworking of women's mad scenes combines the elements in different ways, but the effect of pathos generated by presenting women in a deformed relationship with nature remains a constant. Webster's treatment of Cornelia's madness in *The White Devil* for example, explicitly echoes Ophelia in 'there's rosemary for you, and rue for you' (V. vi. 73). The traditions of acting women and madness seem, by the time of this play, to be clearly enough established for Webster to leave the action to his boy player with the simple direction: '*Cornelia does this in several forms of distraction*', constructing the shape for her mad scene out of the familiar elements of natural imagery and the pathetic irony of an old woman preparing her winding-sheet for a lost son.

In a play which constantly parodies and distances its emotional moments in dumb shows and satiric commentary, Cornelia's mad scene is quite explicitly presented as a set piece. Flamineo insists that he must see his mother winding Marcello's corpse and Francisco '*draws a traverse*' to 'discover their superstitious howling'. Nevertheless this image of woman in her most iconic role, grieving over her fallen son, is the one moment in the play which cannot be ironised. Even the cynical, sophisticated Flamineo finds:

> I have a strange thing in me, to the which
> I cannot give a name without it be
> Compassion.
>
> (V. iv. 110–12)

His reaction to his mother's grief is in part owing to his own involvement in his brother's death but, more significantly, it is a reaction to the theatrical power of women as bearers of emotional meaning through a tradition of iconic representation.

IV

This iconic representation of women on the Elizabethan stage, the single visual image viewed by audience and characters alike, is an important groundbase for the representation of women in the structures of the drama as a whole. One of the most common forms in which women appear is as the static figure commented on, described and judged.

In the final scene of Heywood's *A Woman Killed with Kindness*, Anne, the repentant adulterous heroine is presented '*in her bed*'. She is dying: her husband has shown his gentle spirit by not punishing her adultery with death, but her repentant sense of her own sin has killed her. As the simple image *Anne in her bed* she is the focus for emotional sympathy – her maid Sisley cries 'What shall I do for my poor mistress'. However, that emotional sympathy has to be mediated through an awareness of the reality of her repentance. She asks

> Blush I not, brother Acton? Blush I not Sir Charles?
> Can you not read my fault writ in my cheek?
> (xvii. 57–7)

and they assure her that the sickness which her repentance has brought on has also removed the signs of sin:

> Alas good mistress, sickness hath not left you
> Blood in your face enough to make you blush.
> (xvii. 58–9)

Drained of the blood of her sin, Anne is now fit for a reconciliation with her husband, which is effected once again in the static image of their final embrace:

> Pardon'd on earth, soul, thou in Heaven art free;
> Once more thy wife, dies thus embracing thee.
> (xvii. 121–2)

The pathos of the final reconciliation is made possible by its being placed within the frame as a static symbolic image closing off any complicating memory of Anne's adulterous feelings for Wendoll, her lover, or of the marriage which made the adultery possible.

One of the interesting aspects of this play is its lack of

complicating emotional encounters, in particular its complete failure to explore the motivation or the process of the relationship between Wendoll and Anne. Their adultery is presented as given, an unaccountable deformation of the conjugal happiness with which the play begins. As a result it can be dramatised as a series of static images viewed and read by other characters in the action and, through them, by the audience in the theatre. The single scene in which Wendoll seduces Anne ends with an embrace which is held so that it can be viewed by Nicholas the servant, who will report their sin to his master. When Frankford surprises them in bed the action, once again, takes on a dumb-show slow-motion form as

> Enter Wendoll, running over the stage in his night gown, he
> [Frankford] after him with his sword drawn: the Maid in her smock
> stays his hand and clasps hold on him. He pauses a while.
>
> (SD xiii. 65)

Anne's adulterous state is also dramatised in symbolic form by her appearance

> in her smock, night gown and night attire
> (SD xiii. 77)

In part these images can be seen as part of the text's realism: Anne is in her smock because she has just risen from bed. However, they also make a pattern of telling visual images which the dramatist exploits for their symbolic meaning and the emotional power which they will generate.[2]

In a later scene, when Anne has been banished from the conjugal home, Frankford searches for the last of her possessions which will remind him of her existence and sends after her a lute which she has left behind. Nicholas, the faithful servant, catches up with her and returns it. Anne takes the lute from him and plays on it, commenting on the symbolic significance of her action:

> We both are out of tune, both out of time
> (xvi. 19)

The dramatic action then stops so that she can once more be presented as a static symbolic image. She plays on the lute and Wendoll enters behind her to comment on the emotional and moral significance of her action. By being placed in this symbolic frame, Anne ceases to be the individual idiosyncratic figure, involved in an action through her own motive and volition, and becomes a symbolic focus of pity, an archetype of the sorrowful and repentant woman

> Making their flinty hearts with grief to rise
> And draw down rivers from their rocky eyes
>   (xvi. 56–7)

V

In *A Woman Killed with Kindness* Anne Frankford's part fulfils both mimetic and symbolic functions within the narrative. She is, on the one hand a figure in a particular story of adultery and repentance and, on the other, a paradigm case of the adulteress and repentant wife. The movement between the two kinds of role is partly effected by the theatrical organisation discussed above, but it is also made explicit when Anne appeals directly to the women in the audience:

> O women, women, you that have yet kept
> Your holy matrimonial vow unstain'd,
> Make me your instance: when you tread awry,
> Your sins like mine will on your conscience lie.
>   (xiii. 141–4)

This movement between the mimetic and the emblematic was a legacy from earlier morality drama in which moral abstractions were represented by figures on the stage. However, in the case of women characters it was particularly long-lived and exerted considerable dramatic influence because of the prevalence of iconography which drew on essentialist definitions of women's social roles and limited her dramatic ones accordingly. One of the most important of these definitions is contained in the image of woman as mother which carried associations of natural relations together with the memory of the icon of Charity, often presented as accompanied by children (Warner 1985; p. 250). The story of Patient Grissil, dramatised first by John Phillip and then by Dekker, presents a paradigm case of the dramatic potential of motherhood as a source of emotional power. In this story, taken from the last book of Boccacio's *Decameron*, a Marquis marries a poor girl and then tries her patience and submission by first removing her children from her, then returning her to her father and finally calling her to celebrate his marriage to another woman. In the final sequence the other woman is revealed as the lost daughter and Grissil's continued patience is rewarded by her being reinstated as wife, mother and worthy consort to her aristocratic lord.

The emotional centre of the play occurs in the testing sequence in which first Grissil's daughter and then her son are taken from her. Phillip's version presents a potential conflict between the emblematic and mimetic methods of characterisation. In order to arouse the full pathos from the image, Grissil has to be presented missing her children:

Grissil, my Ladie and wife,
With whom in Love and feare I have lead my life;
Farther thou knowest my Daughter which shee doth nourish,
And with the Mylke of her brestes foster and cherishe ...
                                                            (1020–2)

In fact, in keeping with her aristocratic status, Grissil's babes have been given to a wet nurse. In both child-killing scenes it is the nurse rather than Grissil herself who resists the Marquis's servant, arguing for the natural affinity between creatures and their young as shown by even lions, tigers and bears. Nevertheless, the bereft mother offers an unproblematic focus for pathos, as Grissil appeals directly to women in the audience:

My Daughter reft from tender Paps, alas my wofull paine,
And Causleslie by Tyrants fearce, with bloodie sword thus slaine
Farewell swet Childe thy Mother now, shall se thy face no more,
Help spoused Dames, help Grissil now, hir fate with teares to plore,
Gushe forth your Brinie streames, let tricklinge abound
The earth and fyrmament aboue, fyll with your mournfull sownd.
                                                            (1199–1204)

In Dekker's version of the play, the essentialist view of womanhood is invoked by the Marquis's complacent certainty:

Tush, tush, it cannot be but sheele returne,
I know her bosome beares no marble heart
I knowe a tender Mother cannot part,

With such a patient soule, from such sweet soules.

                              (IV. i. 78–81)

When Grissil returns for a last look at her babies, she asserts not
her rights as a mother but her almost involuntary capacity for
nurture, presenting herself as an emblem of overflowing plenty:

> See heer's fountaine,
> Which heaven into this Alablaster bowles,
> Instil'd to nourish them . . .
> My angrie breasts will swell, and as mine eyes
> Let fall salt drops, with these white Necter teares
> They will be mixt: this sweet will then be brine,
> Theyle crie, Ile chide and say the sinne is thine.

                              (IV. i. 123–35)

Dekker's Grissil makes no direct appeal to mothers in the
audience but the scene's pathos depends upon notions of what is
appropriate to womanhood transformed by the symbolism of the
involuntary lactation into an icon of great moral and dramatic
power.

    However, in spite of the continuing power of essentialist
images of women, some features of the characterisation of
Griselda did change in the 50 years between Phillip's version of
the play and Dekker's. Both plays chart the Marquis's power over
Griselda in the imagery of the clothes he gives her when they
marry. In Phillips's version, after Gautier had reassured Grissil's
father that his intentions are honourable, Grissil is taken off by
Ladies to be dressed as fits her new status. When she returns,
richly dressed, the dialogue reinforces the symbolic significance of
the change:

> GRISSIL.   O noble Lord, these costlye Robes, unfitly
>   seeme to bee:
>   My ragged weed much more then this, doubtles
>   contented mee.
> GAUTIER.   These garmentes nowe to thine estate belong,
>   my Lady deare,
>   Disdaine them not, but for my sake refuse
>   them not to weare.

                              (822–5)

When Gautier sends Grissil back to her father, however, he insists
that she return as she came, stripped of her finery. Grissil meekly
agrees

Take here these Robes and ornaments costly,
Take here these things and Iuellus sumptuous,
Take here the Ringe wher with we ioyned Matrimonie,
Which daie was solomnysed and to all men ioyus,
Bestow them where it shall please thee, my Lord most bountuous
For all that euer I receiued of thee, I yeld thee againe,
Beinge well contented in my former state to remaine.
(G iii. 1624–30)

In order to avoid leaving the actor naked on stage (and incidentally revealing the boy beneath) Grissil is allowed to retain her smock; however, even that theatrical necessity is, by the imagery, turned into part of the symbolic exchange between Grissil and her lord:

A symple Smocke to hide and couer my nakednes,
Be it never so simple I besech your goodnes,
Which I craue, to recompence my virginitie,
The which I brought but cary not a waie with me . . .
(G ii. 1649–52)

When the play was reworked by Dekker, the dramatic style allowed some complication in the audience's view of events. Dekker retains the verbal and visual contrast between Grissil's poverty, emblematised by her clothes and the finery she receives from her lord, but the question of how this is to be seen is complicated by the accompanying text.

In the opening sequence, Grissil must be seen by the Marquis but before he arrives she questions the morality of appearing in public at all:

Father me thinkes it doth not fit a maide,
By sitting thus in view, to draw men's eyes
To stare upon her.
(I. ii. 25–7)

Her father tries to reassure her by making a rather fine distinction between 'wantons' whose 'loose eyes tell/That in their bosoms wantonness does dwell' and Grissil, whose obvious virtue consists partly in her personal integrity, partly in her clothes, and partly, it would seem, in her lack of personal attraction:

thy sun
Is but a Starre, thy Starre, a sparke of fire
Which hath no power t'inflame doting desire:

Thy silkes are thrid-bare russets: all thy portion
Is but an honest name.

(I. ii. 45–9)

The confusion of these lines is a result of the author becoming tangled about the theatrical implications of a notion of personal integrity which transcends clothes and social status. If Grissil's honesty is symbolised by her 'thrid-bare russets', she will be compromised rather than elevated by accepting the Marquis's finery, so Dekker omits the dressing scene after Grissil has accepted the Marquis's suit. Indeed Babulo, Ianicle's comic servant, expresses his suspicion at the whole transaction with the view that 'It's hard for this motley Ierkin to find friendship with this fine doublet'. When, as in Phillip's version, the Marquis insists upon the emblematic importance of clothes, hanging up Grissil's russets as mocking 'monuments of thy nobilitie', his action seems not only cruel but lacking in moral sophistication. Grissil for her part is unmoved by the reminder of her poverty. She sees her new clothes 'but as your liverie' and reaffirms the connection between poverty and integrity:

You may take all this outside, which indeede
Is none of Grissils, her best wealth is neede,
I'll cast this gaynesse off, and be content
To weare this russet braverie of my owne,
For that's more warm than this, I shall look olde,
No sooner in course freeze then cloth of gold.

(II. ii.)

This assertion of Grissil's personal integrity gives a quite different feel to the scenes in which her patience is tested. Where Phillip's Grissil appealed to the audience for fellow feelings of maternity, an essential female characteristic, Grissil appeals as an individual who can flout the turns of fortune.[3]

The tension between static, emblematic dramaturgy and a more dynamic notion of character which transcends those definitions has important implications for the dramatic representation of women. One of the most important developments of the drama in this period was its increasing ability to create characters where a sense of an idiosyncratic personality is played off against the dramatic types imposed by notions of decorum. The decorum governing notions of 'women' was in the process continually stretched and tested in more complex dramatic structures. In part this was possible because of the slippage between symbolic and social notions of gender. In Part Two of Heywood's *If You Know Not Me*, resistance to the Armada was staged in the legendary appearance of *'Queen Elizabeth, completely armed, and Soldiers'* at Tilbury camp. True to legend, Elizabeth justifies leading her troops by the example of Zenobia and adds:

> Your Queene hath now put on a masculine spirit,
> To tell the bold and daring what they are,
> Or what they ought to be.
>
> (1964; p. 337)

The possibility of 'masculine' behaviour from a woman had always been available as a rhetorical ploy. By connecting this rhetorical possibility with the variety of ways of 'seeing' women on stage, dramatists developed the possibility of more varied and powerfully idiosyncratic female protagonists. The opposition between the Queen's known gender and her masculine spirit, represented by her armoured figure on stage, presents a simple reversal of expectations. More complex effects are created when varied images of womanhood are played off against one another. When Lady Macbeth, for example, calls on the 'spirits that tend on mortal thoughts' to 'unsex me here', a variation of the masculine/feminine opposition is in play. The opposition is later complicated by the powerful image of Lady Macbeth as a mother which is offered and then denied in the chilling speech of accusation to her husband:

> I have given suck, and know
> How tender 'tis to love the babe that milks me –
> I would, while it was smiling in my face
> Have pluck'd my nipple from his boneless gums,
> And dash'd the brains out, had I so sworn.
>
> (I. vii. 54–8)

The sense of Lady Macbeth as a dynamic individual depends upon the contrast between her essential femininity, seen in the familiar image of motherhood, and her rejection of that image as inappropriate to the particular situation.

Women characters could, moreover, quite explicitly reject the static definitions imposed on them by men. In Webster's *The White Devil*, Monticelso denounces Vittoria as a whore, expounding the word with all the familiar imagery of misogynist commonplace:

> MONT. Shall I expound whore to you? sure I shall;
> I'll give their perfect character. They are first,
> Sweet-meats which rot the eater: in man's nostril
> Poison'd perfumes. They are coz'ning alchemy,
> Shipwrecks in calmest weather. What are whores?
> Cold Russian winters, that appear so barren,
> As if that nature had forgot the spring.
> They are the true material fire of hell,
> Worse than those tributes i' th' Low Countries paid,
> Exactions upon meat, drink, garments, sleep;
> Ay even on man's perdition, his sin.
>   (III. ii. 78–88)

The dramatic power of his words, however founders on the contrast between the ugliness of the images and Vittoria's beauty, which she endorses with the opposing rhetoric of innocence abused:

> Condemn you me for that the Duke did love me?
> So may you blame some fair and crystal river
> For that some melancholic distracted man
> Hath drown'd himself in't . . .
> Sum up my faults I pray, and you shall find
> That beauty and gay clothes, a merry heart,
> And a good stomach to a feast, are all,
> All the poor crimes that you can charge me with:
> In faith my lord you might go pistol flies,
> The sport would be more noble.
>   (III. ii. 198–212)

From the narrative it is clear that Vittoria is not only an adulteress but an accessory to murder, but the local effect of the scene leaves her theatrically triumphant.

Vittoria's theatrical triumph in the trial scene is a product of a careful manipulation of dramatic form. She is allowed to step out of the Monticelso's view of her and creates, as a result, an impression of a dramatic life which extends beyond the boundary of the action. A similar effect could be obtained by combining two familiar but contrasting images of women in a single character. At the beginning of Webster's *Duchess of Malfi*, for example, the Duchess is described by her future lover, Antonio, in the language of exemplary virtuous womanhood, an image of a saint in a stained-glass window which 'stains the time past: lights the time to come' (I.ii. 132). Antonio's vision is opposed later in the opening scene by a similarly enclosing image of the lasciviousness of remarrying widows, presented in the brother's warning, and spoken across the figure of the still silent Duchess:

CARDINAL.   We are to part from you: and your own discretion
                  Must now be your director.
FERDINAND.   You are a widow:
                  You know already what man is: and therefore
                  Let not youth, high promotion, eloquence –
CARDINAL.   No, nor anything without the addition, Honour,
                  Sway your high blood.
FERDINAND.   Marry? they are most luxurious
                  Will wed twice
                      O fie:
FERDINAND.   Their livers are more spotted
                  Than Laban's sheep.
                              (I. ii. 238–45)

When the Duchess does speak she does not explicitly oppose the versions of womanhood provided by either her brothers' or Antonio's view of her. Her response literally frees her from their enclosing view with the witty and dramatically startling lines:

Diamonds are of most value
They say, that have passed through most jewellers hands.
                     (I. ii. 250–1)

She thus presents herself not as a woman worthy – the bawdy joke denies that – nor as the lascivious widow of her brothers imaginings, but as a witty woman from romantic comedy.

The possibilities for a woman character are constantly reworked by Webster throughout this play by a contrast in language and action between a number of dramatic alternatives. In the wooing scene, faced with Antonio's paralysing awareness of her position the Duchess insists that

 This is flesh and blood, sir,
'Tis not the figure cut in alabaster

Kneels at my husband's tomb.
                    (I. ii. 439–41)

This assertion of her physical vitality carries an important emotional impact at this point, but in presenting it, Webster is drawing on a traditional opposition and employing it in a startling new way.

For the notion of flesh and blood in women was vitally connected to the idea of procreation, and women's assertion of their physical vitality was inevitably circumscribed by their claims to chastity. For example, as Bertram in *All's Well That Ends Well* attempts to seduce Diana, he asserts that her chastity makes her less than human:

> If the quick fire of youth light not your mind
> You are no maiden but a monument.
> When you are dead you should be such a one
> As you are now; for you are cold and stern
> And now you should be as your mother was
> When your sweet self was got.
>   (IV. ii. 5–10)

Webster's transposition of the traditional argument of seducers to a scene of chaste wooing is part of his witty reversal of the structure of a seduction scene and creates the dramatic impression that the action is generated from the Duchess's idiosyncratic personality. It is created by giving the Duchess the attributes and the dramatic behaviour traditionally associated with a man, as Cariola makes clear in her epilogue to the scene:

> Whether the spirit of greatness or of woman
> Reign most in her, I know not. But it shows
> A fearful madness.
>   (I.ii. 496–8)

Webster, moreover, develops this strain of imagery and dramatic style through into the scenes of the Duchess's death. The opposition between maiden and monument is given a visual force by the image of the Duchess, kneeling before her own tomb, forced by her brothers into the symbolic position of submission. And at that key moment, Webster reinforces the pathos and sense of loss by invoking the essential image of motherhood:

> I pray thee, look though giv'st my little boy

Some syrup for his cold, and let the girl
Say her prayers ere she sleep.
                    (IV. ii. 215–7)

It is difficult to avoid realist sentimentality at this point, and
tempting to see in the Duchess the image of a 'real' woman, a fully
rounded character with a dramatic life outside the fiction in which
she appears. However, we can also see that this image is created
out of an interplay between available dramatic structures,
animated by a powerful poetic realisation of the discourses around
women available from contemporary polemic and dramatic
traditions.

VI

The complex dramatic structures which lie behind all the women
characters in Elizabethan drama have important implications for
feminist criticism. An insistence on dramatic structure as the sole
means of creating dramatic character closes off the direct route
from the plays to the real situation of early modern women and
locates the women characters' apparent resistance to misogyny in
a formalist dynamic of dramatic development. However, while it
is true to say that the drama as a whole developed in the direction
of more individualised characters in mimetic action, there are
important differences between the development of men and
women characters of this individualised kind. The paradigm of
the male mimetic character is Hamlet, the figure who has 'that
within than passes show', is characterised as the combination of
the soldier, courtier scholar and, through his soliloquies, develops
a direct relationship with the audience, assuring his status as the
individual, articulate about the morally complex situation in
which he finds himself. Women characters, on the other hand,
can step out of the enclosing misogyny of other characters' view of
them but are ultimately controlled by the power of the men who
control the world in which they live. Vittoria, for all her dramatic
vitality, is murdered by the avengers of those she has wronged
and the Duchess of Malfi is ultimately overcome by the political
power of one brother and the physical violence of the other.

Moreover, the sense that women characters are not definable in terms of the conventions of the *querelle des femmes* causes significant dramatic anxiety on the part of both the characters who view them and the actions in which they take part. When the emblematic figure of the iconic woman, viewed alike by both character and audience, is replaced by figures who can step out of enclosing male definitions, they are increasingly 'supervised' by the male characters in the actions in which they appear. The gap between the definition of women imposed by decorum and their behaviour in action is frequently exploited for both comic and tragic effect. In Middleton's *A Mad World My Masters*, Master Harebrain, in constant fear of being cuckolded, keeps a close watch on his wife. In spite of his close scrutiny he is continuously deceived by what he sees. He introduces his wife to Gullman, the courtesan, whom he mistakes as a 'pure virgin': the comic plot is introduced in the double bluff in which Harebrain watches the courtesan instruct his wife, as he thinks, in

> the horrible punishments for itching wantonness, the pains allotted for adultery.
>
> (I. ii. 50–1)

The courtesan, of course, teaches Mrs Harebrain the best way to deceive her husband by the further double bluff of extreme modesty. The comedy works partly through these layers of deception, with additional peaks of laughter at the description of simulated honesty and suspense as Harebrain creeps closer to try to overhear the courtesan's advice. The comic structure is evidently enlivened by the courtesan's role-playing, for Harebrain reflects admiringly:

> She puts it home, i'faith, ev'n to the quick
> From her elaborate action I reach that.
> (I. ii. 96–7)

Virtuoso performance is also the main focus for comedy in the central scene, in which the courtesan engineers a meeting between Mrs Harebrain and her would-be lover Penitent Brothel. Harebrain prevails upon his falsely modest wife to go to visit Gullman, who is pretending to be sick in bed. Before he enters, Mrs Harebrain leaves the stage with Penitent Brothel, and when Harebrain enters to listen at the bed curtains the courtesan acts out a dialogue with the apparently distraught Mrs Harebrain, as a solo act:

HAREBRAIN.   She's weeping; 't'as made her weep.
              My wife shows her good nature already.
COURTESAN.   Still, still weeping – huff, huff, huff – why, how
              now, woman? Hey, by, by, for shame, leave – sick,
              sick – she cannot answer me for sobbing.
                                              (III. ii. 195–9)

This scene presents an intersection of ways of seeing women
and the comic structures through which these discourses are
mediated in performance. The courtesan's deception acts out the
commonplace of women's inherent deceitfulness but the theatrical effect is comic rather than moralising. The moral conclusion is
held at bay both by the wit of the courtesan's act and by the
dramatic fact that Harebrain has brought this deception upon
himself.

This part of the action is closed off in a scene which plays
further on women's sexuality and male reactions to it. At the
beginning of Act Four, Penitent Brothel enters, *'a book in his
hand, reading'* (SD IV. i). The book of commonplace morality
reminds him that 'Adultery/Draws the divorce 'twixt heaven and
the soul' and brings about his repentance, couched in familiar
misogynist terms:

To dote on weakness, slime, corruption, woman!
What is she, took asunder from her clothes?
Being ready, she consists of hundred pieces
Much like your German clock, and near allied:
Both are so nice they cannot go for pride.
                                              (IV. i. 18–21)

This repentance is tested and compromised by the appearance of
a succuba in the form of Mrs Harebrain. She woos and teases and
dances round Penitent Brothel urging him to

Sieze me then with veins most cheerful
Women love no flesh that's fearful
'Tis but a fit, come drink't away
And dance and sing and kiss and play.
                                              (IV. i. 60–3)

Penitent Brothel is appalled and repelled and finally exorcises the
demon. In a later scene he tells Mrs Harebrain of his devilish
experience and together they repent. Master Harebrain, the
voyeur once again, watches their repentance and reconciles

himself with 'a wife that's modest, and a friend that's right' (IV. v. 80).

The scene between Brothel and the succuba is extremely difficult to read. Its moral weight is clear from the *sententiae* of the commonplace-book but the action is made comic in its *reductio ad absurdum* of the 'woman wooing' motif in the succuba's energetic, amoral wit. It is impossible to distinguish Brothel's serious moralising in this scene from the hypocritical pretence of earlier scenes. The succuba, moreover, would be played by the same actor in the same costume as the 'real' Mrs Harebrain and could be seen as an embodiment of her adulterous desires. However, since those desires are located in a devil, the 'real' Mrs Harebrain is not compromised by them. Interpretation depends upon performance and though Harebrain witnesses and accepts the final repentance, the context of comic deception which has enlivened the action throughout renders the conclusion comically uneasy.

In tragedy this confusion between women's essential deception and the contingent effect of theatrical action is played through with more serious consequences. In scenes where men view women's interactions with other men, the expectation of a sexual scenario is always present to be confirmed or denied. In *Hamlet*, for example, Polonius 'looses' his daughter to the prince while he and Claudius hide behind the arras expecting to see a scene of courtship or an avowal of love. What they and the audience witness in fact is a more rigorous interrogation of the truth of Ophelia's womanhood:

HAMLET.   Ha, Ha! Are you honest?
OPHELIA.   My lord?
HAMLET.   Are you fair?
OPHELIA.   What means your lordship?
HAMLET.   That if you be honest and fair, your honesty should admit no discourse to your beauty.
OPHELIA.   Could beauty, my lord, have better commerce than with honesty?
HAMLET.   Ay, truly; for the power of beauty will sooner transform honesty from what it is to a bawd than the force of honesty can translate beauty into his likeness. This was sometime a paradox, but now the time gives it proof.

(III. i. 103–15)

After this display of Hamlet's anxieties about women's actions, Claudius is shrewd enough to recognise that Hamlet's affections do not turn to love. However, the expectations of such encounters between men and women persist throughout the drama. The scene is so familiar that it can be presented in dumb show to be read or misread by the other characters on stage. In the first Cyprus scene in *Othello*, Desdemona and Cassio are seen in dumb show while their actions are 'read' by Iago as the stage is divided into observer and observed, language and action. Cassio must perform the action dictated by Iago's speech and Iago interprets the meaning that they will have for the particular action of the narrative:

> He takes her by the palm. Ay, well said, whisper. With as little a web as this will I ensnare as great a fly as Cassio. Ay, smile upon her, do; I will gyve thee in thine own courtship. You say true; 'tis so indeed. If such tricks as these strip you out of your lieutenantry, it had been better you had not kiss'd your three fingers so oft, which now again you are most apt to play the sir in. Very good; well kissed! and excellent courtesy! 'Tis so indeed. Yet again your fingers to your lips? Would they were clyster-pipes for your sake!
>
> (II. i. 165–78)

The power of Iago's images are, of course, resisted throughout the play. His efforts to engage Cassio in locker room banter after Desdemona and Othello have gone to bed are met with polite demurrals, and the whole of the great temptation scene of Act Three is a contest between Othello's and Iago's fantasies of womanhood played out on Desdemona.

The narrative power of Act Three lies in the psychological detail of Othello's growing jealousy combined with the audience's superior knowledge of the true state of affairs. On its own the narrative drive of the sequence is trivial – let housewives look to their linen – , a tale of domestic misunderstanding. A good deal of its dramatic energy comes from Iago's comic ability to wriggle out of having to expose his lies by inventing new ones. However, the scene's emotional power depends upon the characters' investment in their views of the situation. With each of Desdemona's appearances the titanic contest between men's definitions of sexuality, love and the object of that consuming attention is returned to focus. There is an almost total split between the

Desdemona of the dialogue, irritatingly insistent on her suit, showing wifely concern for Othello's health, and the silent figure of Desdemona, seen and read by the two men.

The physical figure of Desdemona on stage is again and again established as iconic, exemplary, the site of meanings generated by others. At Desdemona's first exit Othello indicates the blasphemous degree of significance which he accords her:

> Perdition catch my soul
> But I do love thee! And when I love thee not
> Chaos is come again.
> (III. iii. 91–3)

But for meaning to exist it must be endorsed by a community of understanding; Iago can easily disrupt that meaning by his refusal to answer Othello's questions. By the end of the sequence Iago's apparently unconventional understanding has gained power over Othello's simple one and Othello is resolved to 'whistle her off and let her down the wind to prey at fortune' (III. iii. 266–7). At this moment Desdemona's physical appearance on stage is enough to change his mind though once again it is to do with her iconic, exemplary power: she appears upstage (in Elizabethan theatre conditions at any rate) and Othello observes to the audience:

> Look where she comes.
> If she be false, O then heaven mocks itself!
> I'll not believe it.
> (III. iii. 281–3)

The structure of this first sequence makes the temptation scene like parallel scenes in morality drama, with Iago and Desdemona cast as evil and good angels. However, since this is not a morality play, the iconography of sainthood which attaches to Desdemona's physical appearance is overlaid with fantasy images of her status in Othello's world – the beloved hawk he would be content to lose – and with the fantasy of sexuality conjured up by Othello and Iago both:

> I had been happy if the general camp
> Pioners and all, had tasted her sweet body.
> (III. iii. 349–50)

In this contest over the truth of Desdemona's sexuality, Othello is frustrated by the increasingly apparent arbitrariness of the relation between signifier and signified. He asks:

> Make me see 't; or at the least so prove it
> That the probation bear no hinge nor loop
> To hang a doubt on.
>   (III. iii. 368–70)

Iago revels in just that ambiguity, grossly punning

> ... but how – how satisfied my lord?
> Would you, the supervisor, grossly gape on?
> Behold her topped? ...
> It were a tedious difficulty, I think
> To bring them to that prospect.
>   (III. iii. 398–402)

The dramatic power of Iago's imagery of sexual transgression depends upon language alone and though an audience knows it to be 'untrue' in narrative terms, it has all the erotic appeal of the 'dreams' of pornographic fantasy.

Throughout the rest of the action Desdemona is constructed in Othello's language and her physical presence, her beauty, her clothes, her demeanour, has less and less corrective influence. In Act Four Scene One, while contemplating the murder Othello declares:

> I'll not expostulate with her, lest her body and beauty
> Unprovide my mind again
>   (IV. i. 201–3)

There is already no room for the reality principle and in the following 'brothel scene' Desdemona's self-defence speaks from a totally different discourse of honesty and sin and the rules of evidence which has no point of contact with sexual fantasy:

> DESDEMONA.   I hope my noble lord esteems me honest.
> OTHELLO.   O, ay, as summer flies are in the shambles,
>   That quicken even with blowing ...
> DESDEMONA.   Alas what ignorant sin have I committed?
> OTHELLO.   Was this fair paper, this most goodly book,
>   Made to write 'whore' upon? What committed?
>   Committed? O thou public commoner,
>   I should make very forges of my cheeks
>   That would to cinders burn up modesty,
>   Did I but speak thy deeds.
>   (IV. ii. 66–77)

By the end, the fantasy need not even be spoken: in the final scene Desdemona's role as the recipient of images, fantasies, meanings which exist only in language is given physical embodiment. Asleep on her bed, centre stage, she is a monument to others' projected meaning. To the audience she may appear a sacrificial victim, an image of innocence wronged; in Othello's language she is both the deceptive image of 'monumental alabaster' emptied of sexuality and also the rose to be plucked. Above all she is representative, exemplary, the 'cunning'st pattern of excelling nature'.

In *Othello*, Iago's wilful misreading draws the play on to tragedy, but it is made possible, if not credible, by the structure of the scene and the narrative expectations it arouses. This play between expectation and dramatic fact, between visual gesture and verbal corroboration, can lead to a wide variety of dramatic possibilities. In Ford's *Love's Sacrifice*, for example, the doomed and thwarted affair between Fernando and Bianca is played out through a series of observed set pieces. At no point in the action do the lovers commit adultery, but Ford explores its moral and emotional possibilities by working a double bluff between the differential knowledge of the audiences on and off the stage. In Act Two the scene is varied by the familiar trope of a game of chess. Scenes in which lovers play games which provide a context for extended *double entendre* had been used in a number of earlier plays.[4] The 'true' significance of a game at chess can thus easily be taken as read by the villains Fiormonda and D'Avalos who observe the scene. As Fernando and Bianca play, knowing analogies, drawn from the dramatic tradition, are noted by the politic observers Fiormonda and D'Avalos, who have already established themselves (I. ii) as satiric if not fully reliable observers of the courtly scene.

> 'tis a Rooke to a Queene, she heaues a pawne to a Knights place;
> by'rlady if all be truly noted, to a Duke's place; and that's beside the
> play, I can tell ye.
>
> (1143–5)

D'Avalos's irony establishes the expectation of a successful seduction, but the action reverses it in Bianca's angry rejection of Fernando's plea. The scene, has, however, potential for a further twist as D'Avalos returns to watch the remainder of the action between them. The off-stage audience knows that Bianca has not succumbed but D'Avalos continues to read the action according to the convention established by his response to the chess game. He sees Fernando kneel, be raised by Bianca and kiss her hands but does not hear the dialogue. The sequence he sees is familiar to him (as to the audience) from other dramatic wooing scenes (compare the sequence of physical movements in the wooing scene in *The Duchess of Malfi*), which makes his reading as understandable as it is ironic.

Bianca's language makes the 'true' meaning of the scene quite clear. Her denunciation of Fernando's lust draws on the rhetoric of outraged chastity:

> Know, most unworthy man
> So much we hate the baseness of thy lust,
> As were none living of thy sex but thee,
> We had much rather prostitute our blood
> To some inuenom'd Serpent then admit
> Thy bestiall dalliance:
>
> (1207–12)

Nevertheless the true and false interpretations of the scene are principally counters in a complex narrative which serves to expose and exploit the rigidity of audience expectations which derive from knowledge of traditional dramatic stuctures as much as from any knowledge of the situation.

In the remainder of the play, Bianca goes through the whole gamut of possible roles for a tragic heroine. She is the seducer who approaches Fernando in bed *'her hair about her eares in her night mantle'* (SD II. iv.), but refuses to take up the apparent offer of sex. She is the lover seen *'in her night attire, leaning on a Cushion ... holding Fernando by the hand'*– and she is the sexually defiant heroine comparing her lover favourably with her physically inadequate husband. Yet throughout the action she is technically chaste and when the Duke murders her, the play moves to a disastrous conclusion.

Ford's plays occur towards the latter end of the development of Elizabethan drama and they continually draw on the available structures for particular kinds of scenes. But the virtuoso dramatic play which Ford makes of them as expectations are set up only to be reversed, demonstrates a fundamental instability which results from opening up the gap between what is shown on stage and the narrative or ideological truth of any given situation. As Othello discovers, female chastity can only be affirmed by ocular proof, frustratingly unavailable. The certainties which depend upon it constantly push the narratives in the direction of a more pressing physical searching of the bodies of their female characters. The violence against female characters which recurs on the Jacobean stage can be seen as a simulacrum of the violence perpetually wrought on women by men but it can also be seen as the formal and structural outcome of the gap which opens up between what is seen and what can be known about women. The pressing tragic question of the truth behind the role, the moral conundrum of the *theatrum mundi*, depends entirely on a stable connection between chaste appearance and true chastity.

In Chapman's *Bussy D'Ambois*, for example, the narrative dynamic depends upon the contrast between Bussy's honourable and straightforward behaviour and the political corruption of the court which he attends. He insults the court lady and kills a man in a duel, but is presented throughout as the 'glorious ruffian' whose integrity is shown by his flouting courtly form. Tamyra, his eventual mistress, is similarly presented as a woman who adheres to an absolute notion of chastity, in spite of her husband's suggestion that she condone the lustful advances of great men. When Monsieur, the politic courtier, discovers her affair with Bussy he responds according to the conventional wisdom, marvelling at 'the infinite regions betwixt a woman's tongue and her heart' (III. ii. 201). He exploits her jealous husband's anxiety to take revenge on Bussy, taunting Montsurry into finding out the truth of Tamyra's affair. Montsurry's rage is expressed in a soliloquy which expatiates on

> The unsounded Sea of women's bloods,
> That when 'tis calmest is most dangerous;
> Not any wrinkle creaming in their faces,
> When in their hearts are Scylla and Charybdis
> Which still are hid in monster-formed clouds
>   (III. ii. 286–90)

In the crisis of the action he appears '*pulling Tamyra in by the hair*', and gives full rein to his sexual fantasies, calling on her to

> Come Siren, sing, and dash against my rocks
> Thy ruff'n Galley, laden for thy lust:
> Sing and put all the nets into thy voice,

With which thou drew'st into thy strumpet's lap
The spawn of Venus; and in which ye danc'd;
That in thy lap's stead I may dig his tomb,
And quit his manhood with a woman's sleight.
                              (V. i. 60–6)

Montsurry's certainties about the 'true' nature of women arms him with the authority to torture his wife upon the rack and dissect her body for the truth about Bussy's supposed crime. The truth about seeming and reality which underpins his right to punish his wife is, for him, expressible in the rhyming commonplace:

Vice never doth her just hate so provoke
As when she rages under Virtues' cloak.
                              (V. i. 94–5)

The question of seeming is not so easily settled, however, for the truth is not to be found in Montsurry's dissection of Tamyra's body, nor in the finale of the play, where Bussy is defeated by policy and manipulation.

Montsurry's violent efforts to find the unbreachable truth in a woman's body are repeated in an almost identical scene in Ford's *Tis Pity She's a Whore* where Annabella marries her suitor Soranzo in an attempt to conceal the consequences of her incestuous affair with her brother. The opening stage direction, *Enter* Soranzo *unbraced, and Annabella dragged in* (IV. iii.), echoes Chapman's, and the ensuing scene follows a similar pattern of sexual rhetoric and physical violence. Once again the name of the unknown lover is in question and Soranzo determines to find it by dissection, using the woman's body as a surrogate for the offending man:

Not know it, strumpet? I'll rip up thy heart
And find it there . . .
                              And with my teeth
Tear the prodigious lecher joint by joint.
                              (IV. iii. 53–6)

However, where Chapman has Tamyra claim her own alternative punishment in her request to be bound to a dead woman or incarcerated in a dungeon, Ford varies the sexual display of the scene by transforming Annabella into a defiant heroine, singing as she is tormented and glorying in the beauty of her secret lover.

For if these scenes are the narrative outcome of concerns with truth and seeming, the gap between things seen and truths known, they are also dramatic moments in their own right, offering localised dramatic pleasure alongside the fulfilment of narrative and moral requirements. Whether the women are guilty or innocent of the imputed adultery, these scenes of torture offer them for display, itself a possible pleasure, and what they can reveal in that display is curtailed by the dramatic traditions inherited by and reinforced by the dramatist. Tamyra's denigration of her beauty reworks the terms of other women characters' pleas for pity and reasserts the identity and integrity of woman which transcends her merely physical attributes; Annabella's defiance picks up the type of the witty woman, though not for comic ends.

The scene with Annabella is of course, repeated in the penultimate sequence of the play. Giovanni comes to her chamber before the final banquet, not to find the truth for himself but to take it from Annabella's body in the form of her heart, which he will literally brandish before the other characters in the finale. However, in this scene Annabella's role is changed, and with it changes the character of the scene. The element of sexual display is there in the opening tableau, which presents Annabella in bed, inviting Giovanni's prurient query:

> What, changed so soon? Hath your new sprightly lord
> Found out a trick in night games more than we
> Could know in our simplicity?
>
> (V. v. 1–3)

However, Annabella's role on this occasion is to hold the emotion which will turn the violence into tragedy by creating the sense of loss:

> And know that now there's but a dining time
> 'Twixt us and our confusion: let's not waste
> These precious hours in vain and useless speech.
>   (V. v. 17–19)

The pathos mediates the violence so that, as Giovanni says, Annabella and the audience will see both death and the 'funeral tears shed on your grave'. The play on death and sexual consummation is enacted in the sexual resonances of the murder as Giovanni offers 'to save thy fame, and kill thee in a kiss'. The theatrical trope of the tortured woman is thus given full play in the exciting visual effect while the ironies and paradoxes of the poetry restore the attention to Giovanni's tragic dilemma.

Writing on women in the structures of narrative cinema Teresa de Lauretis has described how they function as 'the body to be looked at, the place of sexuality and the object of desire' (de Lauretis 1984; p. 4). In Elizabethan drama, women performed a remarkably similar set of functions. As the iconic representations of essential feminine qualities they serve to vary the emotional climate of the plays, introducing pathos and the possibility of emotional engagement for the audience. This emotional engagement often passed through the women to the concern with the heroes of the plays and their political and personal dilemmas, but it was acted out on the changing figures of the women themselves. Moreover, as the concerns of tragic drama shifted from military to sexual honour, women characters became the crucial focus of the action. The exchange of women, which seemed unproblematic in comedy as women passed more or less happily from fathers to husbands, became the problem of the tragic plays. As the parallel complexity of the visual and verbal texture of these plays engaged with notions of seeming and truth so the unknowability of women became a dramatic and emotional focal point of the drama, requiring a physical as well as a moral exploration. The naïve dramatic aim 'to represent such a Lady at such a time appoynted' became an increasingly problematic theatrical task as the meaning of 'such a lady' came under increasing ideological and dramatic stress.

Notes

1. This relationship has been analysed in complex detail in J. C. Agnew, *Worlds Apart: The Market and the Theatre in Anglo-American Thought, 1550–1750.*
2. See the discussion of the origins of these images in Alan Dessen, *Elizabethan Stage Conventions and Modern Interpreters*, p. 111.
3. See Harriet Hawkins, 'The Victim's Side: Chaucer's *Clerk's Tale* and Webster's *Duchess of Malfi*' for an alternative feminist reading of this play.
4. See, for example, *Arden of Faversham* V. i., *A Woman Killed with Kindness* scene VIII and *Women Beware Women* II. ii.
5. Leonard Tennenhouse, in *Power on Display*, presents a complex account of theatrical violence against women as neither mimetic nor theatrically determined but as a direct instrument of the ideology of the aristocratic state.

CHAPTER SEVEN

'Not for our sex but where he found us wise'

Women characters on the Elizabethan stage, 'devis'd and play'd to take spectators', owed their dramatic power and their scope for action to the structures in which they lived and moved. These structures, as we have seen, shifted and modified over the period, and a significant part in that development was played by individual dramatists. However, to consider the role of particular dramatists in relation to their women characters is fraught with the dangers of making a romantic construction of the author out of the statements of his characters or the conclusions of his plays. It is tempting to imagine that the creator of the Duchess of Malfi might have had some sympathy with women or to agree (or disagree) with Havelock Ellis's announcement that Ford

> writes of women not as a dramatist nor as a lover, but as one who has searched intimately and felt with instinctive sympathy the fibres of their hearts. (Ellis 1957; p. xvi)

One corrective to these romantic tendencies is to recognise that writers are only accessible to us through their writing, which is itself entangled with the possible ways of speaking and writing about women in the period: another would be to grapple with a writer, such as Ben Jonson, who was explicitly working with those ways of speaking and writing not only in his plays but also in the numerous poems and prose writing and conversations with which he sought to present himself as a spokesman for the culture of his time.

The work of Ben Jonson may seem barren ground for feminist reading. In his list of women characters, the familiar figures of comic misogyny recur, from the empty-headed court lady, fit only for the attentions of equally foolish men, through the unsexed middle-aged woman, affecting learning or religion, to the empty cipher of the virtuous girl who exists only as a pawn in male games of power or wit or money. The 'real lives' of Elizabethan and Jacobean women, the lives of work and family relations, are almost completely absent from his work. Like his masters Plautus and Terence, Jonson deals in his comedies primarily with the leisured male world of the street and the market-place: in that world women initiate no plots, solve no problems, and the plays offer no insight into specifically female preoccupations.

Jonson, or at any rate the persona he created in his critical writing, revelled in just that exclusion. As he forged his poetic persona in *The Forest*, X, he rejected an allegiance to Cupid, telling Venus, whom he also dismissed,

> Let the old boy, your sonne, ply his old taske,
> Turne the stale prologue to some painted maske,
> His absence in my verse is all I aske.
>
> (19–21)[1]

In the plays, Jonson's refusal to write of love results in a continuous denial of the narrative structures of romantic comedy. None of his plays ends in marriage and indeed, in *Epicoene,* the central running joke is Morose's attempt to avoid it. The ending of that play, where Morose is relieved to find that his wife is a boy and his marriage consequently null and void is a direct reversal of the romantic pattern in which the revelation of true gender serves to make marriages possible and happy endings restore social harmony. In refusing to celebrate love and, through it, social harmony, Jonson was able to insist on his sharper satiric vision.

Throughout his work the satiric persona is insisted upon. In the conversations with Drummond of Hawthornden he is the learned cynic who suffers fools ill and has privileged access to all the gossip and scandal of the metropolis. In the London context of his plays a more restrained set of personae appear who will stint neither in condemning the foolish nor in addressing their instruction to

... attentive auditors.
Such as will joyne their profit with their pleasure,
And come to feed their understanding parts:
(*Everyman out of his Humour*, Induction, 201–3)

These 'attentive auditors' were, of course, male, but women were not excluded from the ranks of the 'understanding'. The prologue to *Epicoene*, for example, offers artistic fare which will

Be fit for ladies: some for lords, knights, squires;
Some for your waiting wench, and city wires;
Some for your men and daughters of Whitefriars.
(*Epicoene*, Prologue, 22–4)

In *Discoveries*, moreover, he makes clear the judiciously discriminating character of his writing in his impatience with women

who, if they heare anything ill spoken of the ill of their Sexe, are presently mov'd, as if the contumely respected their particular: and, on the contrary, when they heare good of good woemen, conclude that it belongs to them all. (Herford and Simpson II p. 634)

Paradoxically these remarks are, in fact, misogynist for Jonson is using the comparison with women to chastise foolish men who 'take offence where no Name, Character, or Signature doth blazon them'. Nevertheless this extension of judicious discrimination to female audience, even when he is misogynist, effects the double bind which is essential to satiric success. It was an effect summed up in Nell Gwyn's epilogue to a Restoration revival of *Catiline*

I'd ne'er spoke this, had I not heard by many
He lik't one Silent Woman, above any
And against us had such strange prejudice;
For our applause, he scorn'd to write amiss;
For all this, he did us, like wonders, prize;
Not for our sex, but where he found us wise.
(Herford and Simpson vol. X; p. 243)

Like Nell Gwyn, the woman reader is aware both of being excluded by the text and also of accepting that exclusion because its reward is that she is included among the wise, the *honnetes hommes* whom Jonson constructs as his ideal readers and audience.

This inclusion of certain categories of women in the approved world of men is made explicit in some of Jonson's poems to the patronesses on whom his living depended.[2] They are of a flattery so palpable as to be inoffensive and they indicate clearly the literary methods by which women could be included in a true poet's praise. Lady Mary Wroth's family gave her status enough:

> Know you to be a Sydney, though un-named
> And, being nam'd, how little doth that name
> Need any Muses praise to give it fame?
> Which is, it selfe, the *imprese* of the great,
> And glorie of them all, but to repeate!
>   (Epigramme CIII)

Lucy, Countess of Bedford, his ideal object of love and honour in Epigramme LXXXVI, has not only 'a learned and manly soule', but also the power of all three destinies in one person (a type of the Trinity). She is furthermore the exemplar of a list of moral abstractions appropriate to the 'kinde of creature I could most desire/To honour serve and love'. Jonson's poetic strategy here is not simply the familiar Elizabethan technique of designating certain qualities masculine – Elizabeth's heart and stomach of a king; it is rather that the poetic technique constructs these women as iconographic figures who are simply given women's names, acting, as Lisa Jardine has shown, as a 'topos of female accomplishment, allegorizing humanistic competence as such' (Jardine 1985; p. 814).

For the poems, far from giving access to Jonson's 'true feelings' about women, constantly draw attention to their own techniques and their formal successes which serve to keep the anterior reality of personality and events at bay. This closed relationship between attitudes, events and the final poem is illustrated by one of Drummond's anecdotes:

> Pembroke and his Lady discoursing, the said Earl said that Woemen were men's shadowes, and she maintained ym, both appealing to Jonson, he affirmed it true, for which my Lady gave a pennance to prove it in Verse, hence his Epigrame. (*Conversations*, 142)

The resulting poem is not one of Jonson's best but it is a witty enough exercise in which the most obvious attributes of shadows are found analogies for the most obvious characteristics of a hypostatised woman:

> Follow a shaddow, it still flies you;
> Seeme to flye it, it will pursue:
> So court a mistris, shee denyes you;
> Let her alone, shee will court you.
> Say, are not women truely, then,
> Stil'd but the shaddowes of us men?
> (*The Forest*, VII, 1–6)

Given that 'women' in Jonson's poetry are simply one element of rhetorical construction, it is as easy for him to write from 'a woman's point of view' as it is for him to rehearse the clichés of literary misogyny. Two 'Lyrick Peeces' from the 'Celebration of Charis' present a pleasing image of poetic banter between sophisticated men and women. In the first, Jonson in his own persona tells how

> Charis one day in discourse
> Had of Love, and of his force,
> Lightly promis'd, she would tell
> What a man she could love well.
> (*Underwood* II, 8, 1–4)

The reply in Charis's persona, is, of course, written by Jonson too and he uses her description of a young lover to deride the taste of women for young, and by implication epicene, men:

> Eye-brows bent like Cupids bow,
> Front an ample field of snow;
> Even nose, and Cheek (withall)
> Smooth as is the Billiard Ball;
> Chin as wooly as the Peach;
> And his lip should kissing teach,
> Till he cherish'd too much beard,
> And make Love or me afeard.
> (*Underwood*, II, 9, 17–24)

This constant awareness of the satirist behind the woman speaker in the poems is evident too in 'A Song in the person of woman-kind. In defence of their Inconstancie'. The poem's opening lines take a strong stance against 'those dull and envious fooles/That talke abroad of Woman's change'. In rejecting the fatuities of conventional misogyny, the final lines of the opening stanza seem to be asserting women's rights to personal freedom:

> Our proper vertue is to range:
> Take that away, you take our lives,
> We are no women then, but wives.
> (*Underwood*, VI, 4–6)

As the poem develops, it becomes clear that these assertions of women's autonomy are part of a reversal in which morality is subordinated to wit and the woman 'poet' is displaying the moral emptiness characteristic of her sex.

The satiric persona behind all these poems makes it abundantly clear that women have no business with poetry. In the particularly scathing Epigramme on Cecily Bulstrode, *The Court Pucell*, Jonson presents women's writing as 'Tribade lust', forcing the Muse of poetry, who is, of course, female, to unnaturalnesses which only the poet, fearless and alone, can see through. For in Jonson's poems the morality which sustains his definitions of woman is perfectly stable and perfectly clear and depends on much more absolute moral categories than the mere vagaries of the debate over women. One of his most powerful poems in the *memento mori* vein is 'A farewell for a gentlewoman vertuous and noble' (*The Forest*, III). No concession is made to gender. The clear-eyed rejection of the world as 'a shop/of toyes and trifles, traps and snares' is part of Jonson's own presentation of his anti-acquisitive self; the recognition 'that I was borne/To age misfortune, sicknesse, grief' is no more courageous for being presented in the voice of a woman whose body might be thought particularly susceptible to the ills that flesh is heir to.

Nevertheless the place of women's bodies in the moral scheme is made clear by a number of the poems which, although conventional enough in structure, come at the issues in a more direct way. In Epigramme LXII, 'To Finde Lady Would-Bee', witty analogising gives way to a more direct sarcasm in the attack on a woman who has had abortions:

> The world reputes you barren: but I know
> Your 'pothecarie, and his drug sayes no.
> (3–4)

The moral basis of the poet's revulsion is clear in the sarcastic opposition of the rhymes in the final quartet:

> Oh, you live at court:
> And there's both losse of time, and losse of sport
> In a great belly. Write, then on thy wombe,
> Of the not borne, yet buried, here's the tombe.
>
> (9–12)

The sport of the court is opposed to the seemingly more eternal values of the womb and the tomb, the inescapable processes of birth and burial: the woman's attempt to control the consequences of her sexuality is seen as a choice of the transitory over the eternal, of the world against nature.

Jonson's epigrammatic attacks on sexuality are not of course restricted to women. Many of the poems act out a revulsion against the flesh and all its messy dealings.[3] What is different here is the notion that women's behaviour is open to male supervision –'I know/Your'pothecarie, and his drug sayes no'.

The notions about women which emerge from Jonson's poems are unsurprising in their historical context and they are symptomatic as much of Jonson's constant creation of an acceptable poetic persona as of particularly focused misogyny. Nevertheless they show interesting variations on the commonplaces of the *querelle des femmes*. Women are not seen as a single monolithic type to be despised or adored but are explicitly divided up into women and wives or gentlewomen 'vertuous and noble'. In part this is a reflection of the more varied literary tradition in which Jonson situated his work. For along with the debate over women, Jonson owed a particular debt to Juvenal, whose sixth Satire on women voices men's anxiety and horror at women's assumption of all kinds of freedom.

Often in Jonson's plays the misogynist tirades owe everything to Juvenal: as Drummond of Hawthornden noticed, 'his inventions are smooth and easie, but above all he excelleth in a translation'. However, the dramatic form of the plays creates interesting and complex effects with this translated misogyny. One of the most extended of these translations occurs in Act Two of *Epicoene*. Truewit, one of the witty tricksters of the play, goes to Morose's house and in defiance of the order of silence bellows his dissuasion against marriage culled directly from Juvenal. Not only is Juvenal's attack on women translated into English but the references are transposed to Jonson's contemporary London scene. Juvenal's eunuchs become 'a page, or a smooth chinn that has the despaire of a beard' (II. ii. 113–14), the lutenists and gladiators are translated as 'a vaulter, or the *Frenchman* that walkes upon ropes' (II. ii. 61–2) and the exaggerated faith in portents and priests is turned into Jonson's familiar mockery at women's devotion to radical religion.

And yet the scene is not simply a translation of Juvenal's invective, for the drama effects a curious shift in tone. The sequence is, above all, comic in its intrusion on Morose's silent world and his despairing efforts first to silence Truewit and then to know 'What I have done that may deserve this?' The lines of invective are carefully placed by direct appeals to Morose. Truewit is in no way overcome by his own rhetoric and is fully alert to the situation. In mid tirade he can suddenly swivel his attention to halt the unfortunate Mute who tries to steal away unnoticed:

Upon my faith, master servingman, if you doe stirre,
I will beat you.

(II.ii.88–9)

This dramatic placing somewhat undermines the force of Juvenal's satire. As far as Morose is concerned it is just noise and his response to it, as to the posthorn which first shatters the calm, is a matter of decibels rather than subject matter. The grotesque detail is from Juvenal, but in this context it seems playful, if not tongue-in-cheek. Juvenal, for example, tells his friend:

During Saturn's reign I believe that Chastity still
Lingered on earth, and was seen for a while.

Truewit's nostalgia about the Golden Age 'when the world/Was young, and the sky bright-new still' is by contrast turned into a comic invocation of the Saxon age:

If you had liv'd in king ETHELRED'S time, Sir, or EDWARD the Confessor's, you might, perhaps, have found in some cold countrey-hamlet then, a dull frostie wench, would have been contented with one man:

(II. 2. 36–40)

The change of reference introduces a parodic side-swipe at the arguments over the antiquity of reformed religion.[4] It shifts the balance from Juvenal's misogyny, establishing Truewit as a sophisticate, capable of more multi-layered, and current wit.

The complex interlayered effect of this scene dramatises the ambivalence of the relationship between the idea of women, the idea of morality and the debt to the ancients which informs Jonson's dramatic art. Jonson, once again polishing his persona, claimed that he used the ancients as guides not commanders, but the young men in *Epicoene* voice a rather less reverent approach. In the opening scene of the play Truewit warns Clerimont against idleness and procrastination, to which Clerimont responds:

> Foh! Thou hast read PLUTARCH'S *moralls,* now, or some such
> tedious fellow; and it shows so vilely with thee: 'Fore god, 'twill spoile
> thy wit utterly.
>
> (I. i. 2–4)

Throughout the play the use and misuse of learning and wit is dramatised in the way the foolish demonstrate their folly through their failure to discriminate between the solid learning of Seneca and such commonplace 'godly books' of popular culture as *Greene's Groatsworth of Wit* or *The Sick Man's Salve.*[5]

The issue of the right use of learning is part of a general preoccupation with art and nature, and opposition between virtue which is inbuilt and virtue which is learned. In this play (and elsewhere) women act as the central site of this discussion. Clerimont's principal objection to Lady Haughty, the president of the Collegiates, is her use of cosmetics, 'her pieced beauty', and the song which he has his page perform celebrates in elegant poetic oppositions the 'sweet neglect' which he prefers to 'th'adulteries of art'. It is a familiar poetic topos and Truewit can counter with the equally familiar opposing topos of the beauty of cultivation:

> O, a woman is, then, like a delicate garden, nor, is there one kind of
> it: she may varie, every houre, take often counsell of her glasse, and
> choose the best.
>
> (I. i. 104–7)

So far, so harmless: witty young men display their wit on a subject ever fresh. What is equally being dramatised behind this wit and style, however, is the right and the ability of men to judge women and indeed the assumption that women's actions exist for no other purpose:

> A lady should indeed, studie her face, when wee think shee sleepes;
> nor, when the dores are shut, should men bee inquiring.
> (I. i. 115–17)

Truewit's witty extension of the idea to a comparison with the decoration of the city statues of Love and Charity opens further the rhetorical and dramatic use which Jonson can make of the idea of woman. The reference is partly, as Herford and Simpson note (vol. X; p. 7), a localising of a classical reference to statues; the analogy between statues and ladies is also simply comic – it establishes Truewit as a knowledgeable man-about-town. However, it also indicates the state of conflict which exists between actual women in the drama – the conversation began about Lady Haughty – and the range of abstractions which women come to embody and personify. The statues at Aldgate were apparently of Peace and Charity:

> Implying (as I conceive) that where Peace, and love or Charity, do prosper, and are truely embraced, that Cities shall be for ever blessed.
> (Herford and Simpson vol. X; p. 7)

Truewit makes them Love and Charity – a slip of the tongue but an indication of the absolutes of womanliness by which Lady Haughty and her colleagues are to be judged. As Marina Warner has shown in detail, the process by which abstract virtues became personified as women is partly an accident of grammatical gender in the classical languages and of the iconography which arose from that (Warner 1986; p. 67). However, as she also describes:

> the misogynist strain began to cleave image and reality, and the disjunction between women and the positive ideas they traditionally represented in allegory was increasingly stressed. (Warner 1986; p. 199)

The rhetorical topos which enabled Jonson to idealise Mary Wroth as 'a Nymph, a Muse, a Grace' (Epigramme CV) is turned on its head in *Epicoene*. Abstract virtues become mere civic monuments; intellectual debates about art and nature soon degenerate into a scandalous story about a woman startled into wearing her peruke the wrong way round.

This scene contains none of the moralising clichés of patristic sermons: it neither denounces women nor praises them. However, its skilful blend of scene-setting, characterisation and humour establishes the terms in which the action around women will take place.

Dauphine's plight, which takes up the action in the next scene, involves women in another of their aspects. His uncle Morose's plan to disinherit him requires that he 'venture on a wife' but it is clear that Morose's instrumentalism requires a woman only in the most essential form

> He has imploid a fellow this halfe yeere, all over *England,* to harken him out a dumbe woman, bee shee of any forme, or any qualitie, so shee bee able to beare children:
>
> (I. ii. 22–6)

For Morose's needs, women are dowry-bringers or bearers of children, and he is prepared to forgo one element so long as he is provided with the required minimum.

This tendency is mocked even further in the scene where Morose encounters Epicoene for the first time. Having silenced all those around him, Morose dominates the scene with his own speech but the power this gives him is parodied in Cutbeard's punctuating bows and pushed to further ridiculous heights by Epicoene's refusal to answer except by a curtsy. Morose is surrounded by bobbing mutes and looks completely absurd. But the ridicule is also directed at Morose's tendency to judge his future wife entirely in terms of her suitability for *him,* as if going through a list of good parts:

> Give aside now a little, and leave me to examine her condition, and aptitude to my affection. Shee is exceeding faire, and of a speciall good favour; a sweet composition, or harmony of limmes: her temper of beauty has the true height of my blood. The knave hath exceedingly wel fitted me without: I will now trie her within.
>
> (II.v. 15–19)

Epicoene is successful as a woman because, like the fantasy she turns out to be, she can be literally all things to all men. By being less than a woman she can restore Dauphine's fortunes and by acting as the fantasy of more than a woman she can be the guarantor of La Foole's and Daw's claims to manhood. The first action provides the impetus for the main plot and the second for much of the humour of the rest of the action. When at the very end of the play Epicoene's 'true' gender is finally revealed, Truewit can insist on the distinction between lying on and lying with the silent woman, and that she has been made up of others' impressions.

Nevertheless, Jonson's apparent exposure of the manner in which Epicoene is constructed as a woman does not mitigate the play's misogyny. It is a clever manipulation of current ideas about women for comic purposes rather than a denial of their truth. The fact that Epicoene turns out not to be a woman at all does not in any way expose the fictionality of the collegiate ladies or the dreadful Mrs Otter. The *coup de théâtre* of Epicoene's revelation is a turnabout within the narrative rather than an extra-diegetic moment which reminds the audience that all of the women are played by boys. Truewit tells the ladies

here stands she that has vindicated your fames.

The fact that Epicoene's true sex calls the men's sexual boasting into question has saved the reputations of the collegiate ladies too, but it is by no means clear that they have had anything but a lucky escape. For the opposite of La Foole's and Daw's attempts to construct a fantasy of womanhood is not to grant women's autonomy but rather to place their reputations in more responsible—but still male—hands.

What is much more difficult to place both comically and conceptually is how far the wits' notions of woman, reiterated and discussed throughout the play, can be placed and modified by the play's action. At the beginning of the play they lay down the terms for the judgement of women and half way through, before the action moves towards resolution, they are once more presented as the expert judges of women in general, moving beyond the particular comic circumstances of the action. In response to Dauphine's request for advice about women Truewit presents them as desirable but easily accessible commodities to be studied in the markets of the court and then acquired by a judicious mixture of violence and guile. Nevertheless, here too the rhetoric of Truewit's advice undermines its assertions. He offers the familiar justification of rape and assumes throughout that the purpose of approaching women is sexual gratification:

> It is to them an acceptable violence, and has oft-times the place of the greatest courtese. Shee that might have beene forc'd, and you let her goe free without touching, though shee then seeme to thanke you, will ever hate you after: and glad i' the face, is assuredly sad at the heart.
>
> (IV. i. 85–9)

Nevertheless, as the speech continues, the behaviour he recommends seems more and more grotesque, so that it calls into question the value of the whole exercise. Once again Truewit is adapting a classical source, Ovid's *Ars Amatoria,* and is seen not as the expert practitioner but the laconic looker-on, saved from the folly of heterosexual relations by a learned understanding of the pitfalls they present to a man's dignity. He declines to answer Dauphine's question 'On what courtly lap hast thou late slept' in order to further the action to make the collegiate ladies fall in love with Dauphine.

If there is a central position *vis à vis* women in the play, it is one of avoidance. Both Truewit's monologue of advice to Dauphine and the remainder of the action show relations with women as both foolish in themselves and most dangerously likely to expose that folly. The character most comically embroiled in this way is the unfortunate Otter. He is the most explicitly misogynist character in the play and the most oppressed by women. His uxorious submission to the frightful, dominating Mrs Otter is a recurring comic situation which comes to a climax when he denounces her in the full flow of Dutch Courage. The misogyny of this denunciation is, once again, complicated by the multi-layered comic structure of the scene. Mrs Otter has been brought to hear her husband's daring calumny by the ever-resourceful Truewit. She can barely be restrained and her furious asides heighten the comedy of Otter's grotesque flights of descriptive disgust:

OTTER.   She has a breath worse than my grand-mothers, *profecto.*
MRS O.   O treacherous lyar. Kisse mee, sweet master TRUE-WIT, and prove him a slaundering knave.
TRUE.   I'll rather beleeve you, lady.

OTTER. And she has a perruke, that's like a pound of hempe, made up in shoo-thrids.

MRS O. O viper, mandrake!

OTTER. A most vile face! and yet shee spends me fortie pound a yeere in *mercury,* and hogs-bones. All her teeth were made i'the Blacke-Friers: both her eye-browes i' the *Strand,* and her hair in *Silver-street.* Every part o' the towne ownes a peece of her.

MRS O. I cannot hold!

(IV.ii. 82–95)

For all its rhetorical *élan*, Otter's description reveals the roots of misogyny in the suggestion that women are somehow incomplete. They can be constructed, for good or ill, in male fantasy because they are made of parts without a cohering essence. According to Otter, his wife

takes herself asunder still when she goes to bed, into some twentie boxes; and about next day noone is put together againe, like a great *German* clock.

(IV. ii. 96–8)

The image was a commonplace of misogynist wit,[6] but for Jonson, it showed, once more, the philosophical (as opposed to the social) basis on which his characters are judged. These judgements, moreover, are dealt evenhandedly among the characters according to their folly rather than their gender. La Foole, for example, is foolish not only in his foppery and his womanising but in his lack of focus and purpose, dramatised in the rambling and inconsequential character of his speech and actions. He is, as a result, fit only for the company of women, where neither his social folly nor his metaphysical incoherence will be noticed.

II

The fear that women are potential disruptions to male autonomy and coherence is particularly evident in Jonson's treatment of sexuality, both male and female. His most wittily uncompromising representation comes in the Epigramme 'On Gut', which makes no distinction between orgasm and other forms of physical evacuation:

> Gut eates all day, and lechers all the night,
> So all his meate he tasteth ouer, twise:
> And, striuing so to double his delight,
> He makes himselfe a thorough-fare of vice.
> Thus, in his belly, can he change a sin,
> Lust it comes out that gluttony went in.
>
> (Epigramme CXVIII)

This view allows none of the equivocations of lust and love, married and unmarried sex, which inform the social construction of sexuality. In Jonson's treatment, delusions about sex were only part of the hypocrisy, the concern for the trivial and transitory which served to divert human beings from a recognition of the base materiality of their lives:

> they set the signe of the Crosse over their outer doores, and sacrifice to their gut, and their groyne in their inner Closets. What a deale of cold busines doth a man mis-spend the better part of life in! in scattering *complements,* tendring *visits,* gathering and venting *newes,* following *Feasts* and *Playes,* making a little winter love in a darke corner.
> (*Discoveries,* 564–5)

In presenting sexuality on the stage, Jonson was not restricted to the sensibility or even the discourses of his own age. The language of his sensual characters, Fulvia, Volpone or Sir Epicure Mammon, draws on the traditions of sexual writing from Martial on. But the act of sex and its languages are constantly situated by narrative and poetic contexts, as the different effects of the different contexts of the song 'To Celia' reveal. When it appears as one of a collection of Songs in *The Forrest,* the poem is a version of the familiar *carpe diem* motif in which the 'sports of loue' are a means of defying time or making the most of the goods which time affords. However, far from being an open celebration of this recapture of time, the second half of the poem is a protest against the constraints which the speaker must overcome and, as the rhetorical questions imply, is far from sure of overcoming:

> Why should we deferre our ioyes?
> Fame, and rumor are but toyes.
> Cannot we delude the eyes
> Of a few poore houshold spyes?
> Or his easier eares beguile,
> So remoued by our wile?
>
> (9–14)

The feared oppositions all come from outside the implied dialogue: the lady addressed is assumed to be compliant. The form of the rhetorical question, however, leaves a textual space for a different reply, a reply which is given when the poem takes its chances in a different setting.

In *Volpone* the song is used to woo, calm and seduce Celia into accepting Volpone's sexual advances. Having cast off his disguise as the aged and bedridden invalid to whom Celia's husband has sold her, he offers himself not in the unadorned and true image of a lover but

> As when (in that so celebrated *scene*
> At recitation of our *comoedie,*
> For entertainement of the great VALOYS)
> I acted yong ANTINOUS; and attracted
> The eyes, and eares of all the ladies, present,
> T'admire each gracefull gesture, note, and footing.
> (III. vii. 159–64)

The song is now a performance within a performance, but it is one whose rhetoric signally fails to construct the appropriate response in its immediate audience. Celia completely ignores the opposition of time and secrecy which informs the song, speaking from an entirely different discourse of sexuality:

> Some serene blast me, or dire lightening strike
> This my offending face.
> (III. vii. 184–5)

For Volpone, the poet speaker of the song, the negotiations of sex involve only the considerations of the male world – Time and the 'houshold spies' who control access to women. In the context of the play, the song comes up against the other negotiation necessary for sexual consummation: that between men and women.

Celia is, to be sure, a very difficult woman to negotiate with. Not only does she insist on talking about morality, she does so in a language which belongs in a different dramatic genre. Like Bonario's cry as he rescues her from rape, 'Forbear foul ravisher, libidinous swine', her language comes from domestic tragedy,[7] and co-exists uneasily with the comic styles which up till now had been entirely in Volpone's control. As a result the issue of control and the relative theatrical power of different languages of sexuality comes into play. For both Volpone's language of seduction and Celia's of penance show the importance of male power. When Volpone fails to win Celia over with the invitation to 'act Ovid's tales' he still has access to physical power and in the last resort can command 'Yield, or I'll force thee!' (III. vii. 266).

The play offers, however, no simple contrast between male sexual violence and female morality. Volpone's role as a lover explores the full range of its narrative possibilities. In the mountebank scene, he appears as the witty trickster of new comedy, attractive both in his verbal virtuosity and by contrast with the grotesque cruelty of the familiar foolish cuckold, Corvino. The situation changes when Celia is offered as a gift in the legacy-hunting game. Her desperate unwillingness to take part in the plot exposes Corvino's obsession with winning the game but he is made doubly grotesque in using the same violent rhetoric to force Celia into adultery as he had used to punish her free response to the mountebank in Act Two. Clearly, the issue is Corvino's and Volpone's different attempts to control Celia rather than the morality of her behaviour: a question of power, not a question of chastity.

The first meeting of Doll Common and Epicure Mammon in *The Alchemist* similarly dramatises the complex tensions which lie behind sexual encounters. The scene is a masterpiece of comic double bluff as Doll and Sir Epicure go through routines of courtship which entirely fail to disguise Sir Epicure's lust and Doll's purely commercial interest in him. Doll is able to tell the truth about her lack of blood and virtue, but because those denials were so familiar, they can be read by Epicure as modesty and by Face as blunt frankness:

> MAMMON.   Were there nought else t'inlarge your vertues, to me,
>   These answers speake your breeding, and your bloud.
> DOLL.   Bloud we boast none, sir, a poore Baron's daughter.
> MAMMON.   Poore! and gat you? Prophane not . . .
> DOLL.   Sir, although we may be said to want the guilt [gilt],
>   and trappings,
>   The dress of honor; yet we striue to keepe
>   The seedes, and the materials.
> MAMMON.   I doe see
>   The old ingredient, vertue, was not lost,
>   Nòr the drug, money, us'd to make your compound.

>   There is a strange nobilitie, i' your eye,
>   This lip, that chin! Me thinks you doe resemble
>   One o' the *Austriack* princes.
> FACE.   Very like,
>   Her father was an *Irish* costar-monger
>   (IV. i. 41–57)

This play around blood and virtue is more than simple hypocrisy; it is a perversion of the considerations with which an ordered aristocratic society would ideally control and organise sexual relations.

Epicure's ludicrous view of himself as a sensual being is also presented in language and dramatic situations which allow a more sceptical view of sexuality without restricting it to a reductive morality. In his first excited fantasy about the delights afforded by the philosopher's stone, he imagines himself with

> my glasses,
> Cut in more subtill angles, to disperse,
> And multiply the figures, as I walke
> Naked between my *succubae*.
>   (II. ii. 45–8)

Epicure's fantasy presents a grotesque parody of the natural multiplication of less recondite sex: however, a moralising response is held in check by the sheer hilarity of the physical image, particularly if the actor is anything like as fat as the Falstaffian original, John Lowin.

Throughout the play, comic exposure is directed towards the fantasies which sustain and vary and aggrandise physical desire. The notion that sexual love frees individuals from the bonds of social and political duty comes in for particular mockery. Epicure imagines how with the help of his love and wealth

> when thy name is mention'd,
> Queenes may looke pale: and, we but shewing our loue,
> Nero's POPPAEA may be lost in storie!
>   (IV. i. 143–5)

Doll disingenuously suggests that this degree of liberty might attract the notice of a prince but Epicure's response is to imagine himself in an epicurean 'free state': he presents a parody of contemporary Utopias, a feast of sensuality, 'a perpetuitie of life, and lust' (IV. i. 165–6). The imaginations of political visionaries are reduced to a fantasy, fuelled by the twin desires of gut and groin.

This exposure of sexual vanity is not primarily concerned with the social realities of the double standard or the social institutions which sustained the subordination of women. As a prostitute, Doll Common is presented as a match for Sir Epicure and indeed is able to use the trick of her learned madness to escape from his embrace and to help deprive him of the stone. Her crazy talking fit as the learned Puritan lady, obsessed with Broughton's biblical chronology, is a comic parody of the aspirations of learned women. This is undoubtedly misogynist, but Jonson's misogyny does not take the form of a restricted view of women's sexuality.

Jonson fully explores the relationship between sexuality and politics; nevertheless, he is at pains to distance himself from the analogy between domestic and national politics offered by the Puritan view of patriarchy. In *Everyman in his Humour,* Thorello uses the imagery of political conspiracy to describe his fears for his wife's chastity:

> Why't cannot be, where there is such resort
> Of wanton gallants, and young revellers,
> That any woman should be honest long.
> Is't like, that factious beauty will preserve
> The soveraigne state of chastitie unscard,
> When such strong motives muster, and make head
> Against her single peace?
>
> (I. iv. 161–6)

The simple misogynist point that women's chastity needs constant surveillance is sacrificed so that Thorello's pathetic fears can be mocked. The imagery, connecting disorder in the household with disorder in the state, is a cover for his petty jealousy; the later grandiloquent references to the Golden Fleece and stolen treasure puff up his craven uxoriousness, and provide more worthy satiric targets than mere female frailty.

When Jonson did take the analogy between sexual and political corruption it was in the (for Jonson) more serious context of ancient Rome. Sexuality and politics were necessarily connected in the story of Catiline, and the connection was not merely symbolic. As Sulla's ghost urges in the opening scene, Catiline's political credentials consist mainly in his reputation for sexual vice:

Be still thy incests, murders, rapes before
Thy sense; thy forcing first a *Vestall* nunne;
Thy parricide, late, on thine owne onely sonne,
After his mother; to make emptie way
For thy last wicked nuptials; worse, then they,
That blaze that act of thy incestuous life,
Which got thee, at once, a daughter, and a wife.

(I. 30–6)

Catiline's own image of rebellion is maternal rape, a grotesque reversal of the pangs of parturition (I. 90–7), and the rewards he offers his followers are all sensual delights. For Catiline's corruption is no mere political subversion, a matter of policies and parties: Jonson presents it throughout as the corruption in which unnatural relationships within the state or the family are part of the same evil. Catiline's first action in the play shows him planning 'To make some act of mine answere thy love' (I. 122). His politics are determined by his lust. The 'fashion of freedome, and community', with which he will bind his degenerate and disgraced followers to him, is accordingly a travesty of the liberality of the true aristocrat. In place of the harmonious plenty offered in, for example, Penshurst, he asks Aurelia to join him in providing

store, and change of women,
As I have boyes; and give 'hem time, and place
And all conniuence: be thy selfe, too, courtly;
And entertayn, and feast, sit up, and reuell;

(I. 171–4)

In this context of unnatural relations, women, of course, are granted significant political influence. The second act of the play is devoted to the competition between the heterae, and opens with a dressing scene in which Fulvia indicates the symbolic allegiances in every jewel she wears. When Sempronia appears, their physical and political rivalry is dramatised by the pointed hypocrisy of their mutual charm as the conversation moves easily from the candidates for Consul to the merits of this or that tooth powder. The real role of these great whores, however, is insisted on when they turn to discussing Fulvia's lovers. She dismisses them arrogantly, insisting that she controls the terms of the transactions with them: the insulting implication is that Sempronia, for all her learning, cannot compete for influence because of her fading charms. Sempronia, however, has the last triumph since, as she leaves, Fulvia's rejected lover Curius enters the house in spite of Fulvia's commands.

By introducing these learned and influential ladies in a comic light, the text avoids any unfortunate connection with the patronesses whose similar qualities Jonson so admired. Nevertheless the misogynist effect is complicated by the theatrical power which the women gain by their rejection of conventional female roles. When Curius, impatient with Fulvia's rejection '*offers to force her*', Fulvia neither submits nor denounces him but simply '*draws a knife*' (SD. II. 283). Curius tries to find a literary explanation: 'Will LAIS turne a LUCRECE?, but Fulvia calmly refuses the analogy:

> No, but by CASTOR,
> Hold off your rauishers hands, I pierce your heart, else.
> I'll not be put to kill my selfe, as shee did,
> For you, sweet TARQUINE.
>
> (II. 283–6)

This unusual presentation of a woman working quite explicitly against both moral and literary models is not offered as a triumph of individualism but is carefully located in the politics of the situation. Curius' threats and challenges, the blustering of a rejected lover, give away Catiline's plot and Fulvia recognises the capital, in both wealth and influence, that this information provides. Sexuality and lust are not merely the symbols for political dealings: they are part of the means by which politics are conducted in the fallen world of Rome. Curius, giving way to Fulvia, concludes 'By publique ruine, private spirits must rise' (II. 362): but the whole scene has shown that dividing the affairs of state into public and private is the delusion of a man who understands neither their procedures nor their politics.

In the event Fulvia betrays the Catiline conspiracy to Cicero and the remainder of the action shows Cicero using this knowledge to save Rome and establish his own moral authority. However, the women's political role is only fortuitously on the side of justice and power. Their actions are shown to be motivated by jealousy, greed and spite. As dramatic characters, the heterae of *Catiline* are granted considerable theatrical power but their pretensions to political power are undermined by the sense that they are part of the reward for successful power-broking rather than active in its success. They are part of a symbolism of consumption and luxurious excess which dominated Jonson's satiric view of the world.

III

The satiric view that women were primarily objects of consumption is, however, double-edged. Jonson denounces women's participation in the transactions of conspicuous consumption, but he also demystifies the ways in which women themselves appeared as luxury commodities. One of Jonson's most common images for sex as consumption is Jove's appearance to Danae in a shower of gold. As Mammon prepares to encounter Doll Common, he imagines that he will

> Raine her as many shower, as IOVE did drops
> Unto his DANAE: Shew the *God* a miser,
> Compar'd with MAMMON.
> She shall feele gold, tast gold, heare gold, sleepe gold:
> Nay, we will *concumbere* gold.
>
> IV. i. 26–30)

In an extended play on Ovid's stories, Fulvia, too, rejects other versions of sexual excitement for the preferred commodity of gold:

> I am not taken
> With a cob-swan, or high-mounting bull,
> As foolish LEDA, and EUROPA were,
> But the bright gold with DANAE.
>
> (II. 179–82)

The image works very hard: it provides a simple metaphor for prostitution together with a denigration of the more usual product of ejaculation, and a reminder of the destructive power of Jove's excess on the unfortunate Danae herself.

For Jonson all sexual transactions are ultimately forms of consumption and his characters' efforts to distinguish among them are exposed as mere sophistry. Volpone, for example, denounces Corvino's greedy willingness to prostitute his wife:

> Assure thee, CELIA, he that would sell thee,
> Onely for hope of gaine, and that uncertaine,
> He would have sold his part of paradise
> For ready money, had he met a cope-man.
>
> (III. vii. 142–5)

Volpone, however, is distinguishing between styles of consumption. His contempt is for the merchant who cannot enjoy the commodities he trades in; he, on the other hand, proposes to enjoy Celia like exotic food. Celia's response, however, keeps the moral distinction in view. The buyer is as much implicated in the transaction of commodities as the seller and, as the finale of that scene shows, can if thwarted become a thief.

The focus on consumption and commercial transactions is, of course, most fully elaborated in *Bartholomew Fair*. The fate of Grace Welborne holds the action together, and she is quite explicit about her status as a 'commoditie', bought by Justice Overdo and handed, against her will, to Bartholomew Cokes. She is granted no moral authority for that recognition: she merely wishes to have some choice over her purchaser, conniving in Quarlous's theft of the licence with as little scruple as she had lamented Cokes's rightful inheritance. The moral lines are not drawn according to gender: all of the characters are involved in consumption and such distinctions as are drawn lie between consumers and producers. The comic *reductio ad absurdum* of this recognition comes in Knockem's virtuoso description of Win as if she were a horse – the commodity in which he does most of his trade:

> my delicate darke chestnut here, with the fine leane head, large fore-head, round eyes, even mouth, sharpe eares, long necke, thinne crest, close withers, plaine backe, deepe sides, short fillets, and full flankes: with a round belly, a plumpe buttocke, large thighes, knit knees, streight legges, short pasternes, smooth hoofes, and short heeles;
>
> (IV. v. 21–7)

His horse-trader's language is comically both appropriate and inappropriate. It offers ample opportunity for bawdy stage business but, most comically of all, it is a parody of the '*blazon du corps feminin*' which similarly shapes the praise of the beloved around her physical attributes, described in a similar sequence from head to foot.

The producers and the consumers use a particular form of warped logic to justify, or rather to reclassify, their actions. Just as Busy could turn eating a pig into a sanctified act so Whit, the bawd, can assure Win that 'de honesht woman's life is a scurvy dull life, indeed, la' (IV. v. 29–30) and show how she can be a lady. As well as making her a lady he will make her a 'free-woman', that is, one who is free to trade in her commodity without hindrance.

Knockem's seduction of Win to the trade is interrupted by the arrival of Alice, whose indignation reveals that the trade in commodities is regulated by market forces and conflicting interests:

> The poore common whores can ha' no traffique, for the privy rich ones; your caps and hoods of velvet, call away our customers, and lick the fat from us.
>
> (IV. v. 69–71)

The ensuing flyting between Alice and Ursula is entertaining stuff and the abuse predictably specific to women. As an event and as a dramatic scene it is no different from the similarly dramatised skirmish between Leatherhead and Joan Trash (II. ii) which opens the Fair.

Jonson's demystification of the relations of commodity production and consumption is difficult to place ideologically. At the end of Bartholomew Fair, Quarlous advises the foolish Justice Overdo to 'remember you are but *Adam*, Flesh and blood! you haue your frailty, forget your other name of *Overdoo*, and invite us all to supper' (V. vi. 96–8). This statement can be seen as an assertion of human relations which can transcend the market, restoring the harmony which is ruptured by economic competition. Within the action, however, Quarlous is in a position to be generous since he is the overall winner of the Fair's prizes: the widow and the control over Grace Welborn's money. No one escapes from the relations of the market, not the audience in the theatre, who may only judge according to the value of the seats, and not the author himself, who has provided the commodity which they are enjoying at that very moment.

The suggestion that all social relations are bound up with consumption has particular implications for feminist readings. Feminist analyses have criticised the view that women's autonomy could be assured by independent access to the market and involvement in economic and social relations outside the household.[8] It is perhaps to Jonson's credit that he includes women producers and market women in his play world but that does not, in itself, provide enough of an angle for a feminist reading. Ursula, to be sure, is a figure who does not easily succumb to patriarchal control. In her comic disquisition on her own overwork, she claims 'I shall e'en melt away to the first woman, a ribbe againe, I am afraid' (II. ii. 50–1), a mocking incorporation of both feminist and misogynist remarks about women as men's ribs. She is a match at swearing and cheating for any of the men in the Fair and is her own woman by any standards.

Nevertheless, while the local colour of her language and the detail of her commercial transaction might make her seem a figure taken from, if a little larger than, life, Ursula also has a literary ancestry in the disorderly woman of popular alehouse tales.

She comes out of a tradition which associates women with earthiness and nature and as such she offers food, sex and a public privy as well as the ale which is her main stock. Once again women's actual involvement in all these activities can be noted, but equally the accounts of them deal as much in mythologies as in facts. G. R. Quaife, for example, quotes a case from Middlezoy in which an unpopular parson's wife was accused of being 'taken in a privy' with a young man, in a case which has obvious parallels with the fate of Mrs Overdo and Win (Quaife 1979; p. 131). However, what is most clearly paralleled is less the dangers to respectable women in alehouse privies than the associations of defecation and fornication in the continuing tension between the respectable and the disorderly in which women and sexual behaviour were a central focus of comment and discussion.

In this sense Ursula exists in the play as much as an occasion for the downfall of the respectable as a 'character' in her own right. She is the physical embodiment of misogynist fears about women's all-consuming sexuality. Quarlous asks Knockem

Is shee your quagmire, Dan. Knockem? Is this your Bogge? hee that

would venture for't, I assure him, might sinke into her, and be
drown'd a weeke, ere any friend he had, could find where he were.

(II. v. 90–7)

This anxiety is only one of the pieces of ammunition in the sex
war conducted by Quarlous. He teases Ursula to make her display
the full range of her comic performance and in doing so indicates
his superior male status as the judge of female sexuality and its
controller. She can defend herself only by contrast with other
women who might be in competition with her for male sexual
attention:

> Aye, aye, Gamesters, mocke a plaine plumpe soft wench o' the
> Suburbs, doe, because she's juicy and wholesome: you must have
> your thinne pinch'd ware, pent up is the compasse of a dogge collar
> (or 'twill not do) that lookes like a long lac'd *Conger*, set upright, and a
> greene feather, like fennel, i'the jowl on't.

(II. v. 83–8)

Once again the imagery shows her offering food and sex and sex
as food while the men can anger her further by a reminder of their
rights to control her:

> Doe you thinke there may be a fine new Cuckingstoole i'the Faire, to
> be purchas'd? one large inough, I meane. I know there is a pond of
> capacity, for her.

(II. v. 117–19)

Ursula, of course, can trade insults with the best, but her attack
on the men is not in terms of their appearance or sexual
desirability but in terms of their empty claims to wealth and
status and their putative ancestry:

> you were engendred on a she-begger, in a barne, when the bald
> Thrasher, your Sire, was scarse warme.

The quarrel can end when Knockem, another man, intervenes,
and the conflict moves from angry insults exchanged by men and
women with different honour leagues to insults dealt by men who
inhabit the same world of honour which can grow into a physical
challenge.

The main emphasis of the scene is, of course, primarily comic
and one cannot but admire the rhythmic and shapely way it
moves towards chaos. It may seem a little solemn to analyse it in
terms of value systems and the conflict between men and women.

Nevertheless it is clear that Jonson has constructed both his characters and their comic encounters in terms which re-enact and work through conflicts, familiar from 'real lives' of early modern women. The relationship between the comic world of *Bartholomew Fair* and the social world of the church courts requires, however, further scrutiny. The Fair world is not simply a reflection of the real world but a reworking of the values which exist in both. Ursula's gross comic garrulity, which would certainly invite action in the real world, is given licence in the Fair world, for it represents a comically controlled version of a mythologised form of woman. Ursula's behaviour offers no threat to the order of the real world and no more does the insubordinate behaviour of any of the women in the play. They are there to be laughed at and, like Quarlous, the audience can turn aside when the amusement value fades or they 'finde by her *similes* shee wanes a pace' (II. v. 140–1). Within the text, the women of the Fair exist to expose the hypocrisy and futility of the godly, Zeal of the Land Busy and Justice Overdo, who pettily attempt to control or resist the world of the Fair.

In supporting the popular against the godly, Ben Jonson gives a full rein to his comic art. He was also taking the conservative side in contemporary social conflict. David Underdown has pointed to the importance of 'elite sponsorship' of may-games and popular festivities, the process whereby 'local defenders of traditional customs could usually rely on central authority to protect them' (Underdown 1985; p. 67). He shows further how the popular festivities, so deplored by the godly, were part of an ideology of the harmonious and hierarchical society and served as entertainment for the gentry in a way that did not threaten their status, or their hold on the political stability of their communities (64–7). The popular culture of Bartholomew Fair is not, of course, the benign festivity of seasonal customs; it has been sullied by its contact with the market. The Fair-people's behaviour is closer to the 'high contempt' which the godly feared would be the result of popular licence. Nevertheless, even this 'high contempt' is still comic for those who feel superior to it and can be easily outwitted by the clever gallants who have made no investment in its values or its world. By presenting versions of popular culture in the theatre, Jonson offered it to be judged in terms laid down by the narrative and dramatic structures. He thus neutralised its threat and, in spite of his Induction's acknowledgement of different standards and tastes, ensured that the judgement of the urbane young wits, uninvolved in the social structures of popular culture, would prevail.

For the central political conflict which was fought out over popular festivity was not between the popular and the élite but between opposing governing groups. In taking sides against the Puritans, Jonson was attacking a group who were much more of a threat to political stability than the disorderly and criminal.

In the Induction, the scrivener explicitly warns against the '*state-decipherer,* or politique Picklocke of the Scene' who 'search out who was meant by the Ginger-bread-woman, who by the Hobby-horse-man'. Despite his disclaimers, however, Jonson seems unusually pointed in his satire of the godly in *Bartholomew Fair*. E. A. Horsman has discussed the parallels between Justice Overdo and Thomas Hayes, Lord Mayor of London (Horsman 1960; p. xviii), and Zeal of the Land Busy may be based on Richard Whately, the Banbury mercer who was involved in the conflict over the Banbury maypole which he denounced as the work of Dagon (see Collinson 1982; p. 145). Be that as it may, Jonson's comic treatment of Zeal of the Land Busy offers no mitigating sympathy or understanding of his aspirations. From his first introduction, 'fast by the teeth i' the cold turkey-pie' (I. vi. 35), to his final discomfiture at the hands of the puppets he is presented as gross and contemptible both in his physicality and in his hypocritical self-delusion. The only possible regeneration for such a character is to abandon his religious aspirations complete-ly, as Busy does at the end with his humiliated recognition that 'I am confuted, the Cause hath failed me' (V. v. 113).

Jonson is similarly ungenerous in his construction of women characters who claim autonomy and status through their religion. The autonomy of an Ursula, based in a recognition and acceptance of physicality and licence, is venial comic material but the Puritan women arouse more scorn than comedy. The Puritans provided Jonson (and other playwrights) with obvious sources of comedy in their singular and outlandish behaviour. Names like Sindefy and Win the Fight, together with the inflated rhetoric of their preaching, were easy targets and Jonson parodies their piety with great effect in the language and style of Busy and Dame Purecraft. In the context of seventeenth-century England, however, the Puritans were not simply an easily identifiable object of mockery; they constituted a coherent opposition within the politics of the church and state, not least in the involvement of women.[9]

Jonson's attitudes to these women might have been the same as those church leaders who denounced them as 'womanish brabble', particularly as his view on dissent in religion was that 'In the Church some errors may be dissimuled with less inconvenience then can be discovered' (*Discoveries*, 596). However, once again the attack on what Jonson saw as religious hypocrisy is delivered in terms of sexual self-deception. He reported to Drummond the scurrilous story of how

> [a] Gentlewoman fell in such a Phantasie or Phrensie wt one Mr Dod a Puritan preacher yt she requested her husband that for the procreation of ane Angel or saint he might lye wt her, which having obtained, it was bot ane ordinarie birth. (*Conversations*, p. 151)

This witty tale moreover had further misogynist ramifications, for Dod was 'a preacher renowned as much for his "practical divinity" embodied in his treatise on godly household government as any extremist "puritan" position on church government or theological controversy' (Collinson 1965; p. 128).

Jonson's characterisation of Dame Purecraft in *Bartholomew Fair* is as an adjunct to Zeal of the Land Busy, and her eventual marriage to Quarlous is one of the frail links which hold the plot together. Nevertheless the descriptive monologue by Quarlous which precedes her entrance into the play brings together two different strands of misogyny in a powerful way. Quarlous's contempt for Winwife's widow-hunting combines horror at the sexuality of an old woman with an almost equal horror of being in a subordinate position to her:

> I'll be sworne, some of them, (that thou art, or hast beene Suitor to), are so old, as no chast or married pleasure can ever become 'hem . . . thou must visit 'hem, as thou would'st doe a *Tombe*, with a Torch, or three hand-fuls of linke, flaming hot, and so thou mai'st hap to make 'hem feele thee, and after, come to inherit according to thy inches.
>
> (I. iii. 70–7)

It does not take a complex psychological reading to understand this obscene attack on women as a projection of male sexual anxiety. Moreover, it is matched by contempt for the religiosity which will circumscribe the unfortunate husband's peace and pleasure:

> Dost thou ever thinke to bring thine eares or stomack, to the patience of a drie *grace*, as long as thy Tablecloth? and droan'd out by thy sonne, here, (that might be thy father;) till all the meat o'thy board has forgot, it was that day i'the kitchin? Or to brooke the noise made, in a question of *Predestination*, by the good labourers and painefull eaters, assembled together, put to 'hem by the Matron your Spouse; who moderate with a cup of wine, ever and anone, and a Sentence out of *Knoxe* between?
>
> (I. iii. 87–96)

Dame Purecraft has little comic action; she simply displays herself in the terms that Quarlous describes, with the additional folly of falling in love with a madman. When Quarlous, disguised as the madman, rejects her offer of marriage she confesses her corruption in a crude and static exposure which is designed to deny all of the claims to religion which Quarlous has feared.

In this play the widow is corrupt, Ursula is the embodiment of fleshly appetite, providing endless nourishment, Punk Alice provides sexual services, Mistress Overdo and Win can be persuaded to do the same, and Grace is a commodity which can be bought and sold to the wittiest man. Quarlous's anxieties, and perhaps those of his audience, can be easily assuaged and the potential for conflict glossed over in the assertion that all are joined by the unity of the flesh and blood of Old Adam.

However comically attractive, the other assertive women in Jonson are similarly undermined with the imputation of folly, emptiness, hypocrisy if not downright vice in their claims to attention. In the familiar double bind which encircles silenced and oppressed groups, their very assertions of power render them suspect. Mistress Polish in *The Magnetic Lady*, for example, is the type of the garrulous woman displayed to great comic effect. However, her comic garrulity is explicitly placed as a form of insubordination. When Palate urges her to 'heare your betters speake' she announces:

> Sir, I will speake, with my good Ladies leave,
> And speake, and speake againe;
>
> (I. iv. 23–4)

This she proceeds to do at great length, with the empty
circumlocution and fatuous platitudes which Jonson used to mark
the self-important fool. She is not explicitly designated a Puritan,
but her folly takes on the form particularly mocked in Puritan
styles of speech and argument. She is quite impervious to the
learned sarcasm of the men who try to stem the flow. When
Compass sarcastically compounds her miscalling Arminians
'Armenians' by asking about the Medes and the Persians she is
quite undaunted and assimilates them to the description of
Puritan sects:

POLISH   The *Armenians,* he would say, were worse than Papists!
              And then the *Persians,* were our Puritanes,
              Had the fine piercing wits!
COMPASS.   And who, the *Medes?*
POLISH   The middle men, the Luke-warme Protestants!
RUT   Out, out!
POLISH   Sir, she would find them by their branching:
              Their branching sleeves, brancht cassocks, and brancht
                 doctrine,
              Beside their Texts.
                                                     (I. v. 17–25)

Her indomitable resistance to the logic of men's argument, her
cavalier name-dropping and her insistence on the anti-logical and
anti-reasoned rightness of her stance mark her as Puritan:

Sir, I am mad, in truth, and to the purpose.
                    (I. v. 29)

They also grant her a certain comic energy and vitality and the
comedy of this scene need not be entirely at her expense.
However, it is a comic energy which is denied any outlet in
action, and her energy remains directed to and confined within
the female world.

Mistress Polish's main role in the plot is in the device of the
changed children. She had, as nurse to them both, substituted
her own daughter for Placentia Steel in the hope of gaining a
portion for her. When Placentia turns out to be pregnant, the
hero Compass marries Mistress Polish's daughter Pleasance and
reveals the device. Characteristically, Compass's device is presented as wit since it thwarts the greed of Sir Moth and assigns
the dowry to the rightful heir – or rather the rightful heir's

husband. The old women's device is presented as a cruel treachery, tainted with the physicality of childbirth and other arcane female rites.

Mother Chair proposes that the birth shall be hushed up:

> Will you goe peach, and cry yourselfe a foole
> At Granmam's Crosse? be laughted at, and dispised?
> Betray a purpose which the deputie
> Of a double Ward, or scarse his Alderman,
> With twelve of the wisest Questmen could find out,
> Imployed by the Authority of the Citie!
> Come, come, be friends: and keepe these women-matters,
> Smock secrets to ourselves, in our owne verge.
>
> (IV. vii. 34–41)

The autonomy of women, their control over fertility and childbirth, is thus reduced to 'smock secrets', a means of deceiving the men and trammelling the rightful passage of money and inheritance from one generation to the next. Nor is this area of women's control shown as providing solidarity among them. When the matter of Placentia's pregnancy first emerges it becomes the occasion for a fight in which Polish accuses the wet nurse Keep of failure to keep a close watch on the young woman. Once again the invective drives towards comedy:

> Out thou catife witch!
> Baud, Beggar, Gipsey: Any thing indeed,
> But honest woman.
>
> (IV. iv. 1–3)

In her fury Polish uses all the abuse of comic misogyny:

> Thou art a Traitor to me,
> An Eve, the Apul, and the Serpent too:
>
> (IV. iv. 5–7)

Polish's intemperate lack of logic is very funny, but it also reveals how the women in the play accept the terms which locate them in the conventional sexual hierarchy. When Mother Chair's ruse seems to solve the problem, Keep and Polish are reconciled and Keep gradually mollified:

> Nothing Griev'd me so much, as when you call'd me Baud:
> Witch did not trouble me, nor Gipsie; no,
> Nor Beggar. But a Baud, was such a name!
>
> (IV. vii. 52–5)

Words which imply sexual deviance carry greater weight than other forms of insult. This title is the only one Keep deserves but the joke also shows how the women accept sexual conventions even when they violate them. Such self-delusion makes them the object of mockery rather than sympathy, for the comic world of the play accords no value to the women's work of child rearing. Sir Moth, on the other hand, who has been in charge of the portion but not the girl, claims that the profit he has made on the money between receiving it and paying it out to Placentia's husband is to 'pay/Me for my watch, and breaking of my sleeps', not while he tends the child but while he worries about the money. The familiar analogy between breeding and taking interest is twisted to present financial dealings as a parody of child care. The young women in question are in the play as commodities, fully constructed and assessable in terms of their value in the market.

What, then, can a feminist reading of Ben Jonson conclude? Simply to gird at his misogyny would be a self-defeating undertaking, for it would result in a denial of his comic power and a simplification of the powerful contradictions dramatised in his plays. For Jonson, or rather the 'Jonsons' of his constructed personality, do not offer approval or disapproval of women. What emerge as representations and constructions of women are a feature of the comic poetic forms in which he wrote. The idealised lady of Penshurst, 'noble, fruitful, chaste withal', is the central focus of his panegyric, but deviations from that ideal are given large degrees of comic vitality, particularly in the city comedies where dramatic form and energetic language and action appear to grant an autonomy to the women characters, liberating them from the constraints of the moral formulae of writing on women and even from the misogyny of Jonson's classical sources.

Nevertheless a critique of Jonson cannot remain at the formalist level, for both his plays and his poems are clearly situated within the contradictions of Elizabethan/Jacobean ideology. In particular, his plays work through conflicting attitudes to the growth of a consumer culture which exercised politicians, economists and moralists alike. Jonson's deep distrust of consumer relations and their apparent disruption of more familiar hierarchies is apparent throughout his work and, like many of his contemporaries, he used the bonds between men and women as the model for the corruption of nature by consumption. This, together with his cynicism about men's capacity for self-delusion, particularly in aggrandising their greed and lust, informs an apparently clear-eyed demystification of the 'real' relations between men and women, the true nature of the marriage market, and pathetic emptiness of male sexual fantasy and the locus of power within sexual relations.

This comic exposure makes Jonson an attractive writer for feminists, whose principal concerns since the nineteenth-century women's movement have been to demystify these very features first of the social construction of women and, more recently, of male appropriation of female sexuality. It should be clear, however, that Jonson's intelligent demystification is not in the service of women's autonomy and sexual freedom. His sarcastic outrage at women's pretensions to learning or religious enthusiasm, his passionate contempt for their attempts to regulate their sexuality or to find a direct access to creativity are in the service of an equally mystified notion of a stable hierarchy of aristocracy and learning and hospitality which he felt to be under threat. The seductive positioning of some women among the judicious, the wise appreciators of his satire, cannot be allowed to mitigate the more fundamental misogyny which lay at the heart of his satiric vision.

Notes

1. All quotations are from *Ben Jonson,* ed C. H. Herford and Percy and Evelyn Simpson, 10 vols (Clarendon Press, 1925–53).
2. On the role of one of Jonson's patronesses see David Lindley, 'Embarrassing Ben: The Masques for Frances Howard'.
3. See especially Jonson's Epigramme 'On Gut', discussed below p. 172.
4. For a full discussion of the origins and political implication of this idea see Christopher Hill's essay, 'The Norman Yoke' (Hill, 1986).
5. The role of these books in popular culture is addressed by Margaret Spufford (1983).
6. See Herford and Simpson, vol. X, p. 33 for a full account of this commonplace.
7. See the discussion of domestic drama in Chapter 6 above, pp.123–57.

8. See Miranda Chaytor's and Jane Lewis's critique of Alice Clark in *The Working Lives of Women in the Seventeenth Century,* introduction pp. xxxi-ii.
9. See Chapter 2 above, pp. 27–56.

CHAPTER EIGHT

'A maidenhead, *Amintor*, at my yeares!'

A maidenhead, *Amintor*, at my yeares!
(II. i. 193–4)

Evadne's show-stopping line from *The Maid's Tragedy*, addressed to her bewildered husband on their wedding night, presents a paradigm case of the difficulties involved in offering a feminist reading of the plays of Fletcher.[1] The line's arch sarcasm throws down a challenge to all the assumptions of Elizabethan writing, from poems to coy mistresses and handbooks on conduct to tragedies, often by Beaumont and Fletcher themselves, in which the loss of maidenhead is enough to shake the very foundations of the family and the state. The line brings to a halt all Amintor's coyly expressed assumptions about the behaviour of brides, throwing into question both the narrative and the social conventions which assume that marriage will achieve the happy and automatic conjunction of social form and sexual pleasure.

In response to Evadne's line, Amintor articulates quite clearly the implications for the sexual politics of future ages:

> *Hymen* keepe
> This story (that will make succeeding youth
> Neglect thy ceremonies) from all eares.
> Let it not rise up for thy shame and mine
> To after ages, we will scorne thy lawes,
> If thou no better bless them; touch the heart
> Of her that thou hast sent me, or the world
> Shall know, ther'es not an altar that will smoake
> In praise of thee; we will adopt us sonnes,

Then virtue shall inherit and not blood;
If we do lust, we'le take the next we meet,
Serving our selves as other creatures doe,
And never take note of the female more,
Nor of her issue:

(II. i. 214–27)

In this speech Amintor quite clearly acknowledges the political connection between the sexual control of women and the maintenance of social order. Amintor is evidently appalled at the prospect of such anarchy but the connection itself can be (and has been[2]) seen as evidence of a subversive and radical sexual politics in these plays. However, the argument over the precise ideological import of such scenes demonstrates the dangers of readings which are 'readings' and no more. In the case of this scene, all its radical potential, the acceptance of female sexuality and its ,connections to the social order, are shaped and modulated by its complex theatricality. It is a theatricality which brings ideas *into play* in the sense both of 'into operation' and 'into playfulness'. The serious ideas about sexuality and the state, the family and social stability which are central to Jacobean absolutism are also, in this scene, material for a series of twists and reversals which play along the delicate balance between comedy and horror.

The preamble to the scene, in which Evadne is undressed by her attendants, plays through opposing literary versions of the subject of wedding-nights. Dula, one of the ladies in waiting, offers 'a dozen wanton words' to make Evadne 'livlier in her husband's bed' while Aspatia, whose beloved Evadne has married, presents a gloomy reminder of the dangers of thwarted passion. The sequence ends with each attendant singing a song, Aspatia's of unrequited love – 'Lay a garland on my hearse, /Of the dismal yew' – and Dula's a celebration of sexual adventuring.

I could never have the power
To love above an houre,
But my heart would prompt mine eie
On some other man to flie

(II. i. 83–6)

This opposition, crystallised in the songs, holds the movement of the rest of the scene in suspense, showing that its action will be concerned with a love-affair, but not revealing if it will be tragic or comic, true or false.

The ensuing scene reverses not only all the expectations established by the songs but also the very range in which these expectations can function: it shifts to a different and totally unexpected narrative line. The story initiated by Evadne's line is not one of true love betrayed as in Aspatia's song, nor, as in Dula's song, of sexual pleasure enthusiastically enjoyed; it is a story in which sexual relations are simply the context in which other stories of honour and power are enacted. Evadne's defiant assertion of her sexual experience turns out to refer not to her autonomy as a sexually experienced woman, but to the prior claims on her favours held by the King. In spite of Amintor's passion, his threats of rape and murder, he finds in the very name of King 'a word that wipes away all thoughts revengeful', and the scene ends in a quiet coda of resignation.

The story of honour and power, however, does not wipe out the story of sex and unrequited love. Evadne's two reversal lines, one about maidenhead and the other naming the king, are equal poles around which the scene is structured, creating the link between sex and politics which informs the remainder of the play. The situation offers the scope for extended ironies: in the morning-after scene, both Melantius, Evadne's brother, and the King mistake the situation, assuming the marriage has been consummated. Both Melantius' teasing congratulation and the King's suppressed anger at the couple's supposed disobedience are equally painful to the newlyweds and theatrically tense for the audience. The situation is, moreover, reworked throughout the action: Melantius is eventually astonished into understanding his sister's situation and reacts to it as Amintor did. He interrogates Evadne as Amintor did and she, repentant, overcomes the scruples of their honour in order to kill the King herself.

Because of this initial situation, other issues are continually placed in sexual terms, and the theatrical pleasure which many of the scenes offer is sexualised too. In the scene with Amintor, Evadne is undressed and ready for bed and the action constructs her (whether played by a boy or a woman) in the classic position of the tease. She refuses the sex which the occasion seems to demand, at the same time making quite clear that her refusal is no matter of 'A maidens strictness':

> Looke upon these cheekes,
> And thou shalt finde the hot and rising blood
> Unapt for such a vow; no, in this heart
> There dwels as much desire, and as much will
> To push that wish'd act in practise, as ever yet
> Was knowne to woman, and they have been showne both.
>
> (II. i. 286–91)

The images of heart and will and blood are commonplaces of Jacobean writing about sexuality: the placing of the lines and the context of the action make possible a seductive delivery with considerable voyeuristic appeal. However, it is not sex but knowledge which is first withheld and then released. The narrative information that the King is Evadne's secret lover is banal enough but is made more exciting by the audience's knowledge that this kind of scene should culminate in sex but will always avoid it in view of what is possible on stage. The audience are thus entertained both by the image of the scantily dressed character on stage and by the narrative problem of how the consummation will be avoided.

A similar effect of sexualised suspense occurs in the scene where Evadne kills the king. The sexual tone is established from the beginning as Evadne approaches the King asleep in bed: on waking to find himself tied up, he enquires

> What prettie new device is this Evadne?
> What, doe you tie me to you? by my love
> This is a queint one: come my deare and kisse me.
> *Ile* be thy *Mars*, to bed my Queen of love,
> Let us be caught together, that the gods may see,
> And envie our embraces.
>
> (V. i. 47–52)

The reference to Mars and Venus, caught in a net by Venus' husband, Vulcan, both ironises the King's speeches and shows the playfully sexual world which he inhabits.[3] Evadne's new role, however, comes from a different theatrical context. She begins the scene with a self-searching speech reminiscent of Hamlet's over Claudius at prayer. The teasing dialogue which ensues when the King wakes up (and he takes comically long to do so) is the result of the interplay between his comic sense of the scene and her insistence on its tragedy. But the teasing also plays with the audience's expectation of seeing a king killed on stage, with all the resonances of that act which have been built up throughout the action.

Beaumont and Fletcher's play with narrative knowledge, with audience expectation and with dramatic conventions, is further developed in their treatment of the cross-dressed heroine. Aspatia, Amintor's former lover, rejected for the King's convenience, is presented through most of the action as an emblem of wronged virginity. Her mournful presence on stage places her in the long line of such victims, from 'the nymph Oenone/When Paris brought home Helen' to Dido and Ariadne. However, she also has the dramatic potential to save the situation, presenting a tragi-comic counter action to the tragic plot with Evadne and the King. In Act Five, she appears 'in man's apparell', presenting herself as her own brother, come to demand a reckoning from Amintor. To her frustration (and the audience's delight), Amintor will not quarrel with her, and the hoped-for consummation of death has, literally, to be kicked out of him. Amintor does eventually fight and fatally wound her just as Evadne enters with a bloody knife to claim Amintor as her reward for killing the King.

As Amintor's summary to Evadne makes clear, this is the moment in which all the possibility of a romantic happy ending is denied:

> Behold
> Here lies a youth whose wounds bleed in my breast,
> Sent by his violent Fate to fetch his death
> From my slow hand, and to augment my woe,
> You now are present, stain'd with a King's bloud,
> Violently shed: this keepes night here
> And throwes an unknowne Wildernesse about me.
> (V. iii. 144–50)

The unknown wilderness of Amintor's imagination is the wilderness where love, marriage and sexual obedience are not inextricably linked into a neat narrative pattern of challenge and restoration. Evadne kills herself and Amintor returns too late to stop her; Aspatia, who has been dying throughout the scene with Evadne, wishes to live when she realises that Amintor still loves her but is too badly wounded to survive; Amintor kills himself in despair.

The play, of course, does not end on this note of chaos. Behind the lovers' action there has been a skeletal plot of Calianax, Melantius and Lysippus, and it is brought to the foreground in the final scene, ensuring the rightful succession of Lysippus, the King's son, who states a comfortable moral as the final lines of the play:

> May this a faire example be to me,
> To rule with temper, for on lustfull Kings
> Unlookt for suddaine deaths from God are sent,
> But curst is he that is their instrument.
>
> (V. iii. 292–5)

Lysippus' closing moral sounds dully conclusive after the witty refusal of consummation elsewhere in the play. It closes off the play's world in the commonplacely political, which suits the conventions of drama set in the court but makes no contribution to the play with sex and knowledge, convention and form which has animated the principal action. It demonstrates the problematic relationship between reductive versions of ideology – sexual or political – and the dance of wit with which Beaumont and Fletcher transform its implications.

II

For the treatment of sex and power was not simply a matter of ideology. The dramatic forms which Fletcher and his collaborators had at their disposal permitted very different theatrical treatments of the same material. In *The Custom of the Country*, for example, the motif of the lustful ruler again provides the initial impulse of the plot, but since the corrupt prince is now pitted against a witty heroine rather than a tragic hero, the action provides a different variety of discussions around the characters' dilemmas and their attitudes to sex. Arnoldo, the heroine's lover and potential victim of the lustful ruler, takes a characteristically fatalistic view of the situation. But the potential for a tragic action is comically cut off by his brother Rutilio's guying mockery. He responds to the news of the custom of *ius primae noctis*, which will thwart Arnoldo of his bride's virginity, with an enthusiastic comic envy of the Duke's position:

How might a man achieve that place? a rare Custom! An admirable
rare custom:

(I.i.)

The energy of Rutilio's enthusiastic endorsement of male
promiscuity derives from a wit which acknowledges no allegiance to
conventional morality or conventional power. He is equally witty at
the expense of the Duke's exploitative lust, denouncing him as

A Cannibal, that feeds on the heads of Maids
Then flings their bones and bodies to the Devil
(I.i)

and the same spontaneous vitality informs his contempt for the
heroine's father's craven plan to solve the problem of the Duke's
lust by marriage:

Would any man of discretion venture such a gristle,
To the rude claws of such a Cat-a-mountain?
You had better tear her between two Oaks; a Town Bull
Is a meer Stoick to this fellow, a grave Philosopher,
And a Spanish Jennet, a most vertuous Gentleman.
(I.i)

The language of satire, whose frame of reference is most
frequently misogynist, is here used to mock male lust. However, this
treatment of lust is concerned less with moral opprobrium than with
vulgarity. The Duke's behaviour is less a decline from what is
expected of princes than a ludicrous narrowing of what is expected
from a man.

This witty reworking of the conventional language of sex and
sexual relations, however, serves dramatic as much as ideological
demands. As so often in Fletcher's work, a possible closure of the
action in keeping with one version of a solution is teasingly
proffered at the beginning of the play when the heroine's father
suggests that she might marry the Duke. By rejecting that offer,
Zenocia, the heroine, saves the action of the play as well as
endorsing the ideal of her own sexual autonomy. The dramatic
function of these ideals is evident in the scene between Zenocia
and the Duke himself. Having rejected one version of a plot in
which a Duke marries a commoner, the text exploits the
ideological language of that scenario. Zenocia rejects the Duke's
sexual advances, not by stressing her chastity but by disingenuously and comically insisting on her unworthiness:[4]

I must not think to marry you,
I dare not, Sir, the step betwixt your honour
And my poor humble state . . .

(I.i)

She then pushes the point further by elaborating on the disadvantages of marriage, made familiar by the long tradition of misogynist diatribes against her sex.

The intense competition between men and women, the exploitation of lust by power, the tussle between desire and social control – all these issues are evident in the action. However, they are rendered wittily, so that they amuse rather than threaten. The characters invite the audience to share a knowing play with ideas; ideological struggles become grist to a theatrical mill. As in *The Maid's Tragedy* the subversive potential of this mockery of convention is held in check in the conclusion, though even there the rewards and punishments seem part of the game. Rutilio has his attitude to sex thoroughly chastened by an exhausting stint in a male brothel, and after adventures with pirates and a nymphomaniac and her vengeful son, the characters combine in conventional ways. The pleasure of the play lies less in the happy and conventional conclusion than in the wit with which Fletcher holds such potentially offensive material within the bounds of decorum while mocking decorum at every turn.

In part, Fletcher's success at achieving this witty play with dangerous questions of sex and power lay in his ability to disentangle dramatic from social convention. For, as we saw in Chapter six, marriage and sexual relations were as much dramaturgic elements which could be combined in different ways as they were social institutions. The ways in which they held both the narrative structures of the drama and the institutions of society together were analogous; but they were not the same. Early in his career, Fletcher indicated his interest in the dramatic and theatrical potential of sexuality and sexual relations. In *The Faithful Shepherdess* he presents, in a highly decorated poetic form, a round dance in which chastity is set off against lust, successful against unsuccessful love. Where earlier treatments of sexual relations had concerned the conflict over love thwarted or restored, the acquisition of sexual partners or the trials of wifely obedience, *The Faithful Shepherdess* focused very squarely on chastity. There is no social context for the action: the sexual identities of the characters are given rather than dramatically constructed. Amoret and Perigot, the chaste lovers, are simply opposed to unchaste lovers such as Cloe, whose comic enthusiasm for lust – 'It is impossible to ravish me, I am so willing' – is an equally static characterisation.

The play demonstrates the difference between an ideological and a theatrical treatment, for although chastity is discussed in familiar moral terms, it only has a narrative and theatrical interest when it is beseiged. The sense that chastity is infinitely precarious is established from the beginning of the play. The Priest of Pan lists while exorcising the 'wanton, quick desires/That do kindle by their fires' and as soon as the couples who make up the cast find themselves in the wood where the action takes place, they are subject to just those torments and temptations which the Priest has warned against. Given the static characterisation, however, none of the chaste can become lustful or the lustful chaste and so the whole of the action turns on a magical plot in which no one is what they seem.

In this context, where action is controlled by situation and clearly established character types, ideas about lust and chastity can be given free play. The play's characteristic style is endless poetic scrutiny of the meaning of sexual behaviour in which the poetic effects have a certain autonomy from the moral direction of the play. Chaste love is described in the most sensual terms and the opposing horrors of lust are dramatised with all the power of the language of satiric misogyny; but the two can be combined in the same dramatic moment. When Perigot, for example, reassures Amoret that the assignation he proposes will be chaste, he vividly reminds her and the audience of the alternative to chastity:

> some dame
> Whose often prostitution hath begot,
> More foule diseases, then ever yet the hot
> Sun bred through his burnings, whilst the Dog
> Pursues the raging Lyon, throwing fog
> And deadly vapour from his angry breath,
> Filling the lower world with plague and death.
> I. ii. 131–7)

The familiar division between coy women and lustful men is completely abandoned, not only in the action but in the language.

For example Amaryllis, rejected by Perigot, announces

> I must enjoy thee boy,
> Though the great dangers twixt my hopes and that
> Be infinite:
>
> (I. ii. 191–3)

and Cloe, finding no outlet for her eager lust, enquires

> Is it not strange, among so many a score
> Of lusty bloods, I should picke out these thinges
> Whose vaines like a dull river farre from springs,
> Is still the same, slowe, heavy, and unfit
> For streame or motion?
>
> (I. iii. 146–50)

Fletcher's innovation here is not in presenting women who are not chaste; it is rather in simply transposing the discourses of male lust on to them, making the connections between gender, language and action arbitrary and thus infinitely malleable to the dramatic action.

The same free play with character and sexual identity is evident in the plot device of the 'false Amoret', the lustful Amaryllis who transforms herself into Amoret's double, causing confusion about identity and dismay at the unpredictability of lovers' behaviour. The two parts would have been played by the same boy actress and the confusion between the two characters allows for dramatic variation in the scenes with Perigot as well as suggesting the coexistence of chaste and lustful feelings in love. When 'false Amoret' makes the first pass at Perigot, he coyly replies

> Forbeare deare soule to trye,
> Whether my hart be pure: Ile rather dye,
> Then nourish one thought to dishonour thee.
>
> (III. i. 293–5)

Perigot's response comes from the plots of other comedies, which underscores the humour of his situation, but it is also usually a woman's line, which makes it funnier still. His coldness then prompts the question 'thinkst thou such a thinge as Chastitie,/Is among women' (296–7). A misogynist generalisation is wittily turned into a seduction when spoken by a woman. This reversal of theatrical convention, together with the disguise, neutralises the scene's potential for engaging the audience emotionally. The possibility of resolution is kept open even when Perigot's horror at false Amoret's lust turns to violence.

The more dangerously ironic sequence occurs when the true Amoret comes on stage and Perigot stabs her. However, the rhyme and the pattern of the verse show that these events are merely another turn in the dance:

AMORET.   My *Perigot*
PERIGOT.   Here
AMORET.   Happye.
PERIGOT.   Haplesse first:
            It lights on thee, the next blow is the worst. [*Wounds her*]
AMORET.   Stay *Perigot*, my love, thou art unjust.
PERIGOT.   Death is the best reward that's due to lust.
                                                (III. i. 343–6)

The spectacle of the chaste victim falsely accused offers up its theatrical pleasures in cameo form, and the sequence is actually repeated later in the play, after Amoret has been rescued and healed by the god of a magic spring. Other couples are similarly tried and tested and the problems of ocular proof of chastity, so difficult to achieve in the social world, are solved with the aid of a magic taper. In the end, of course, the lustful are humiliated, the chaste lovers restored and the irredeemable held up as an example. However, the morals of closure are the predictable end which allows the pleasures of spectacle and songs and lush poetic protestations free play. The value of chastity is somehow taken for granted, held in abeyance, while the kinds of scenes which the seige of chastity can generate are explored to the full.

III

It is difficult to know how to read *The Faithful Shepherdess*'s treatment of sexuality. At one level the text acts out fantasies of women who are infinitely available and infinitely controllable. The play has no social context in which women are exchanged in culturally sanctioned ways, so their definition purely in sexual terms has no boundaries. Male sex can be withheld from the lustful or imposed on the chaste while any ensuing danger will be annulled by the arrival of the God of the River, or the Priest of Pan, or the morning which heralds the end of the dream. The very ease of this reading, however, renders it suspect, for it says nothing of the poetic and theatrical pleasures of the text which are offered to the audience so as to complicate thematic or moralising reading. The most severe censure of lust in a reading, for example, could not exceed the poetic denunciations of Perigot, nor the most libertine advocacy the enthusiasm of Cloe or the brutality of the Sullen Shepherd. In its thorough coverage of all the possible ways of talking about sexuality and sexual relations, the text is constantly one jump ahead of any account which is restricted to 'interpretation'. If, however, we go beyond 'interpretation' to the 'conditions for making'[5] the text, we might ask about the circumstances of production in which these poetic and theatrical pleasures were made available.

Our understanding of those circumstances of production is made a little easier by the fact that the play failed at its first performance: the real reasons can never be fully known, but the terms in which it was defended by Fletcher and his contemporaries reveal the conflicting attitudes within the profession. Fletcher was clear that his audience was in the wrong. He wrote a prefatory epistle to the printed text of the play, distinguishing the kind of European-influenced aristocratic pastoral which he was writing from the popular dramatic tradition of 'country hired Shepheards, in gray cloakes, with curtaild dogs in strings ... whitsun ales, creame, wassel and morris dances' (Bowers vol. III; p. 497). Jonson and Chapman, too, in their commendatory verses, defended the play against the taste of the vulgar, Jonson pouring characteristic scorn on the whole audience and Chapman contrasting Fletcher's play with 'a thing/That every Cobler to his patch might sing' (Bowers vol. III; p. 493). Their dismissal of the ignorant audience was, however, more than a venting of pique; it was contributing to the definition and construction of a new audience for their plays.

The new audience was constructed only partly in terms of social class: equally important was its sophisticated awareness of the role and use of theatre. In *The Knight of the Burning Pestle*, for example, Beaumont comically portrayed the kind of audience he felt his plays were up against. The citizen and his wife who interrupt and take over the play are a delightful couple but they are the antithesis of a sophisticated audience. The Citizen Grocer insists in spite of the prologue that the new drama intends to abuse the city:

> if you were not resolv'd to play the Jacks, what need you study for new subjects, purposely to abuse your betters? Why could not you be contented, as well as others, with the legend of *Whittington*, or the life and death of sir *Thomas Gresham*?
>
> (Induction, 16–20)

By her own admission, the citizen's wife 'was nere at one of these playes as they say, before' (Induction, 50–1), and the last time she was promised such an outing it was to see the old-fashioned *Jane Shore*.[6] As a result her judgement is constantly faulty, not only in preferring the outdated heroic style of a Grocer errant to the city comedy of *The London Merchant* but more particularly in her moral assessment of the characters and their behaviour. One of the actions in the play involves Jasper, the apprentice, planning to elope with his master's daughter. Both the citizen and his wife ignore the narrative convention at work, and denounce the immorality of the characters:

> Fye upon am little infidels, what a matters here now? well, I'le be hang'd for a halfe-penny, if there be not some abomination knavery in this Play, well let 'em looke toot, *Rafe* must come, and if there be any tricks a brewing . . .
>
> (I. i. 61–4)

Sophistication, for Beaumont and Fletcher, was not merely a matter of independence of judgement – 'In his owne censure an explicite faith', as Beaumont puts it in his commendatory epistle – but also a willingness to recognise the difference between the play with theatrical form and the moral and commercial calculations of social existence. An old-fashioned perception of the drama was equated with an old-fashioned, instrumental sexual morality. *The Knight of the Burning Pestle*, like many of the other contemporary parodic plays[7] presented an image of its ideal audience. It flattered the aspirations and taste of those who could appreciate the conventions and style of the drama by distinguishing them from 'the common prate of common people': it created a sense of a coterie, knowledgeable in both artistic and moral matters, indulging in a fashionable, because exclusive, exercise.

The definition of this audience was, in the early years of the century, rather unstable. *The Knight of the Burning Pestle*, like *The Faithful Shepherdess*, was unsuccessful at its first appearance and the terms of the reception of the new drama had to be reiterated again and again in prefaces and epistles and prologues. By the 1630s, however, Fletcherian drama was the dominant mode of the fashionable theatre. *The Faithful Shepherdess* was successfully revived at court in 1633 and the terms of the new style's success were explicitly laid out in the commendatory verses to the Folio of Beaumont and Fletcher's plays compiled by Humphrey Mosely after the closing of the theatres.

The intellectual function of the drama continued to be insisted on but the familiar aesthetic formula of profit and pleasure was now presented with a different emphasis. James Shirley, who succeeded Fletcher as principal dramatist to the King's Men, described the

> [a]uthentick witt that made Blackfriars an Academy, where the three howers spectacle while Beaumont and Fletcher were presented, were usually of more advantage to the hopefull young Heire, then a costly, dangerous, forraigne Travell . . . it cannot be denied but that the young spirits of the Time, whose Birth and Quality made them impatient of the sowrer wayes of education, have from the attentive. hearing these pieces, got ground in point of wit and carriage of the most severely employed Students, while these Recreations were digested into Rules, and the very Pleasure did edifie. (Glover 1905; vol. I; p.xi)

Shirley's suggestion that the plays could replace traditional modes of education was partly tongue-in-cheek, a joke which is compounded by its extension to 'passable discoursing dining wits' who 'stand yet in good credit upon the bare stock of two or three single scenes'. Nevertheless his description suggests a more explicit recognition of the financial implications of profit together with the recognition that the education of a man about town had less to do with learning than with fashion and style: points of wit and carriage, recreations, pleasures.

Shirley's preface showed how the theatre had become commercially available leisure, addressing its audience as consumers and offering a commodity which would enhance their lives. As we saw in Chapter four, many comments on the conspicuous consumption of theatre were vaguely disapproving, distancing the desired audience from the fop, the groupie and the unlettered parvenu. In Fletcher's work, however, the notion that a play was a commodity was treated quite matter-of-factly: as the epilogue to *Valentinian* unapologetically concludes, 'We have your money and you have our wares.'

The impact of this new relationship between the production and consumption of drama on the plays themselves is difficult to assess and is complicated by other aspects of the dramatic and theatrical tradition. The relationship with the audience constructed by the plays is, moreover, not the same as the actual social relationships in the audience for any given production. Nevertheless, the commendatory verses seem to suggest that by the time of the closing of the theatres the plays were appreciated in terms of the theatrical pleasures of newness, wit and value for money:

> When thou wouldst Comick be, each smiling birth
> In that kinde, came into the world all mirth,
> All point, all edge, all sharpnesse; we did sit
> Sometimes five Acts out in pure sprightful wit,
> Which flowed in such true salt, that we did doubt
> In which scene we laught most two shillings out.
> Shakespeare to thee was dull, whose best jest lies
> I'th' Ladies questions, and the Fooles replies;
> Old fashioned wit, which walkt from town to town
> In turn'd Hose which our fathers called the Clown.
> (Glover and Waller; p. xxxix)

This shift in artistic taste seems to have involved, among other changes, a particular focus on the sexual dimension of the actions portrayed.

In *Philaster*, for example, the 'serious concerns'[8] are to do with dynastic competition resolved by sexual exchange. Philaster's kingdom has been taken over by Arethusa's father in a war. The King now seeks to consolidate his heir's right to the throne by marrying her to Pharamond the Prince of Spain, who would thus usurp Philaster's right. The narrative problem is of course solved by Arethusa marrying Philaster, neatly endorsing both inheritance by right and inheritance by force of arms. The tone of the play, however, and the means by which it works out the action, are very different. Far from taking the exchange of women for dynastic purposes for granted, the action is accompanied by continuous commentary which suggest a series of very different views of the roles and functions of women at court. It is Arethusa who first presents Philaster with the conundrum of her desire for both Kingdoms:

> *Philaster*, know
> I must enjoy these Kingdomes
> (I. ii. 53–4)

Her earlier conversation with a waiting lady had firmly set the context of love and creates a romantic if not a sexual resonance around her. Philaster, for the moment, is unmoved and finds it unworthy of his future fame that he should give

> His right unto a Scepter, and a Crowne,
> To save a Ladies longing.
> (I. ii. 60–1)

In the main action 'a Ladies longing' is seen as a trivial counterweight to the politics of men but it is nevertheless just those questions of longing which drive the action.

Set against Arethusa's role as a means of consolidating political deals is the figure of Megara, who is described by Dion in terms which play on sexual and political meanings:

> Faith, I thinke she is one who the state keepes for the Agents of our
> confederate Princes: She'll cog, and lye with a whole Army, before
> the league shall breake: her name is common through the Kingdome,
> and the Trophies of her dishonour, advanc'd beyond *Hercules* pillars.
> She loves to try the severall constitutions of mens bodyes; and
> indeede, has destroyed the worth of her owne body, by making
> experiment upon it, for the good of the Commonwealth.
> (I. ii. 47–54)

In the commentary which accompanies the first encounter between Philaster, Pharamond and the King, the relative political suitability of each of the princes, discussed by the men, is contrasted with the ladies' comments on their relative attractiveness. Dion had noted at the beginning that Arethusa does not seem to love Pharamond – a common enough way of indicating unsuitability – but this is made quite explicitly sexual in Megara's appreciation of Pharamond:

but eye yon stranger, is he not a fine compleate Gentleman? O these
strangers, I doe affect them strangely: they do the rarest home things,
and please the fullest: as I live, I could love all the Nation over and
over, for his sake.

(I. ii. 284–8)

Megara and Pharamond are, of course, the villains and a good
deal of the action concerns Megara's spiteful accusation of
unchastity directed at Arethusa. Nevertheless they have a lusty
vitality, like Chloe in *The Faithful Shepherdess*, which is
appreciated by the commentators on stage, who guide the
responses of the theatre audience.

The action of sexual revenge begins when Megara is caught in
Pharamond's lodging, an action which is presented in a confusing
mixture of tones. Dion at first informs the King in comic bawdy
language that he has been unable to find Megara. The scene then
shifts to one of suspense as the courtiers knock on Pharamond's
door and he tries to forbid their entry. Finally, in a comic
moment, Megara appears on the upper level presenting herself
with a mixture of pathos and anger to threaten revenge and
foreshadow the next movement of the plot. What is most
surprising in this scene, however, is the courtiers' final comment.
It offers no moral judgement or fear at the outcome but presents a
frank enjoyment of the comic possibilities. The King has asked
that the disgraced Pharamond be conducted 'to my lodging and to
bed'. After his exit Cleremont jokes:

Get him another wench, and you bring him to bed indeed

and Dion comments:

'Tis strange a man cannot ride a stage
Or two, to breathe himselfe, without a warrant:
If this geere hold, that lodgings be search'd thus,
Pray God we may lie with our owne wives in safety,
That they be not by some tricke of state mistaken.

(II. iv. 129–33)

Megara's appearance on the upper level was greeted, in her
words, by 'your hootings and your clamours' and a similarly
unrestrained comic reaction is possible to a number of other
sequences in the play. For in spite of Pharamond's villainy he is

also presented as a comic stud. After his first appearance and his speech of courtship to Arethusa, Cleremont notes

> This speech calls him *Spaniard*, beeing nothing but a large inventory of his owne commendations.
>
> (I. i. 152–3)

Pharamond's vanity is completely sexualised and his conflict with Philaster over the kingdom is presented as an unseemly display of male bravado before Arethusa, whose sexual rather than political response is at issue. Pharamond ends the scene by making a gross pass at her which confirms his unsuitability as a hero. However, when he complains, in an aside, 'The constitution of my body will never hold out until the wedding', he also confirms his comic role.

Alongside this comic treatment of morally outrageous behaviour, the play offers other moments of blatant sexual display. A good deal of the action hinges on the young page, Bellario, whom Philaster uses as his go-between to the princess. The character would have been played by a boy actor since in the denouement he disproves all the accusations against Arethusa by proving he is a girl. As a result although his/her sex is not revealed until the end of the play there is an androgyne quality to his performance, reinforced by the way he is introduced in a poetic set piece as an emblem of pathos

> sitting by a fountaines side,
> Of which he borrowed some to quench his thirst,
> And payd the Nymph againe as much in teares.
>
> (I. ii. 114–16)

His passion for Philaster is expressed by his skirting round the discourses of homosexuality, and there is a similar tinge to the scene in which he and Arethusa talk of love. Arethusa is indeed accused by Megara of being unchaste with Bellario. This generates the central section of the action, but more important than the plot is the argument about sex and sexuality which this accusation provokes. When Philaster is told that Arethusa and Bellario have been caught together he responds at first with the sophisticated argument that she could find no pleasure in an inexperienced boy. When Philaster accuses Bellario he proceeds by a voyeuristic interrogation about Arethusa's behaviour to him and his opinion of her:

Tell me gentle boy,
Is not she parrallesse? Is not her breath,
Sweete as *Arabian* winds when fruits are ripe?
Are not her breasts two liquid Ivory balls?
Is she not all, a lasting mine of joy?
                                          III. i. 200–4)

The other side of these fantasies is of course the misogynist fantasy of women's perfidy indulged by the King against Megara and by Philaster against Arethusa. Megara's and Arethusa's behaviour is quite different but that is, anyway, irrelevant to these outbursts, which conjure up myths of women's total availability, bypassing all constraining social forms.

This wished lack of constraint culminates in the violence of the famous hunting scene. The title page of the 1609 quarto depicts Arethusa with her breasts exposed, the *country fellow* (here transmuted into a *'countrie Gentleman'* beside her and Philaster slinking off into the trees. The change of scene from court to country offers the possibility of a further range of sexualised fantasy. It opens with Philaster speaking a paraphrase from Juvenal's sixth Satire, contrasting the evils of women with the pastoral joys of earlier ages which include 'some mountaine girle, Beaten with winds, chaste as the hardned rocks' (IV. iii. 7–8). What he actually finds in the woods are first Bellario, pursuing him with unwanted devotion, and then Bellario with Arethusa in his arms. At this moment tragicomedy teeters between farce and disaster. Philaster is given an entrance speech in which he resolves to explain the situation calmly to Arethusa but this is followed by a potentially comic double take which launches a speech of melodramatic excess, followed by speeches in which the lovers express mutual deference over who is to die. The culmination is also knocked off balance by the arrival of the country fellow, who interprets the ritual both with his vulgar desire to see the sights and his simple morality of

Hold, dastard, strike a woman.
                    (IV. v. 85)

With such a variety of effects the scene can offer no single coherent point of view, for pleasure in classical tropes and passionate rhetoric vies with comic undercutting, a sense of aristocratic moral virtuosity with the country fellow's simple

views, the simple excitement of a stage fight with the more drawn
out sado-masochistic wounding of Arethusa.

The scene is similar in structure to the one in *The Faithful
Shepherdess* in which Amaryllis is rescued by the Satyr, though
the pleasures there were offered in a more abstract form. In
Philaster, the narrative framework is tighter and the action can go
through further complications and false endings until the final
revelation, startling even the audience, that Bellario is a girl. The
whole plot had been predicated on contrasting fantasies, drawing
on a range of literary styles enacted through a sophisticated
dramaturgy of obvious sexual display. Teasing innuendo is
accompanied by a comic undercutting of the very fantasies which
sustain the main action. The serious concerns of the play have to
fight for attention against literary games and theatrical effects
which can be turned in either a comic or a tragic direction.[9]

IV

This witty treatment of sex as commodity and pastime offers
welcome relief from the more common Jacobean display of
women as victims, and necessarily complicates any monolithic
account of 'ideology' concerning women and sexual relations in
the period. The problem for a feminist reading, nevertheless, is
how to connect the varied treatment of women as heroines with
the construction of women as an audience for these displays.
Women were addressed directly in both the commendatory verses
to the Folio and in prologues and epilogues to the plays
themselves. Together these texts address an audience of women
who were felt to bring a particular sensibility to the theatre
audience. Richard Lovelace, the Cavalier poet, wittily attributed
the invention of tragicomedy to Fletcher's concern for the ladies'
feelings:

> But ah, when thou thy sorrow didst inspire
> With Passions, blacke as is her darke attire,
> Virgins as *Sufferers* have wept to see
> So white a Soule, so red a Crueltie;
> That thou hast griev'd, and with unthought redresse,
> Dri'd their wet eyes who now thy mercy blesse;

> Yet loth to lose thy watry jewell, when
> Joy wip'd it off, Laughter straight sprung't agen.
>
> (Glover 1905; p. xxiv)

The dramatists too, presented themselves as the ladies' champions:

> Ladies to you, in whose defence and right,
> Fletcher's brave muse prepar'd herself to fight
> A battaile without blood, 'twas well fought too,
> The victory's yours, though got with much ado.
>
> (*The Woman's Prize* prologue 1–4)

The battle which was so easily won once again involved art as well as morality. It repudiated the old-fashioned misogyny of the quarrel over women as both clichéd and tedious but recognised that men and women quarrelling had significant theatrical potential. In *The Woman Hater*, Gondarino's misogyny is mocked as affectation but it does produce comic sequences in which the witty woman is more than a match for the railing man. Oriana teasingly pretends to love Gondarino and then Gondarino to love Oriana, with the comic contrast between true and false feeling opposing different ways of talking about sex made even funnier by the knowing way in which they are used by each character. Oriana gloats sarcastically over the way Gondarino was taken in by her pretence:

> by my troth good Lord, and as I am yet a maid, me thought 'twas
> excellent sport to heare your Honour sweare out an Alphabet, chafe
> nobly like A Generall, kicke like a resty jade and make ill faces:
> Did your good Honor thinke I was in love?
> Where did I first begin to take that heat?
> From those two radiant eyes, that piercing sight?
> Oh they were lovely, if the balls stood right;
> And there's a legge made out of dainty stuffe,
> Where the Gods be thanked, there is calfe ynough.
>
> (III. i. 213–23)

Gondarino, for his part, can just as easily put aside the satiric prose of his usual attitude to women –

> Hee that shall marry thee, had better spend the poore remainder of his
> dayes in a Dung-barge
>
> (III. i. 231–2)

– for the poetic courtship of

> Shall I find favour Ladie?
> Shall at length my true unfained penitence
> Get pardon for my harsh unseasoned follies?
> (III. i. 235–7)

Gondarino's final punishment is to be tied to a chain and have all the ladies court him.[10] It was a scene which dramatised the theatrical triumph of witty women over misogynist men, an artistic preference for Beatrice over Griselda.

This artistic shift, however, does not necessarily affirm a feminist triumph on Fletcher's part. The witty play with dramatic style, the ability of each character to act the roles of love and hatred equally well, plays once again on anxiety about how far the truth of sexuality can be known. The plot still turns on a woman's chastity and Gondarino can worry even the urbane Duke, Oriana's beloved, with the familiar problem of ocular proof:

> Doe's your Grace thinke, wee carry seconds with us, to search us, and see faire play: your Grace hath beene ill tutord in the businesse; but if you hope to trie her truly, and satisfie your selfe what frailtie is, give her the Test . . . put her too'it without hope or pittie, then yee shall see that goulden forme flie off, that all eyes wonder at for pure and fixt, and under it, base blushing copper . . .
> (V. ii. 47–54)

The test consists of abducting Oriana and locking her in a brothel; a courtier is then sent to tell her that she has been condemned by the Duke but could escape by lying with the courtier. She resolutely refuses, is threatened with rape and rescued by the Duke who has been watching the whole scene. The sequence encapsulates the basic plot of so many plays on women's chastity, demonstrating the constant and repetitious necessity for women to display their virtue to men. The witty, ingenious, virtuous, theatrically imaginative women must throughout this drama submit to the test of chastity. For the theatrical pleasures of Gondarino baited by women or Oriana threatened with rape are offered to those who can distinguish wit from tedium but who also control those definitions.

A similar reworking of theatrical misogyny is offered in *The Women's Prize*, which presents an updated sequel and contrasting response to *The Taming of the Shrew*. Petruchio has now remarried Maria, who is determined not to follow in Katherina's footsteps. She distinguishes herself from the trained hawk of Shakespeare's play, claiming triumphantly that she is

> The free Haggard
> (Which is that woman that has wing, and knowes it,
> Spirit, and plume) will make a hundred checks,
> To shew her freedom, saile in ev'ry ayre,
> And look out ev'ry pleasure; not regarding
> Lure, nor quarry, till her pitch command
> What she desires.
>
> (I. ii. 149–55)

The speech is a powerful assertion of independence. However, the play presents sexual relations less as a reversal of male supremacy than as a kind of bargaining, a negotiation of terms in the free market. The dramatic initiative is handed over to the women who withhold their sexual favours until better terms are agreed.

The precarious link between sexual relations and the ideology of marriage is exposed in the debate between Maria, Petruchio and her father. Maria refuses to obey her father on the grounds that she, and her allegiances, have now been transferred to her husband. Petruchio is then offered the apparently reasonable arguments of the new contractual mode of married relations in which the husband and wife are bound by mutual obligations:

> As I take it, sir, I owe no more
> Then you owe back again . . .
> You do confesse a duty or respect to me from you again
> That's very neere, or full the same with mine?
>
> (I. iii. 198–234)

However, when Petruchio accepts the new terms, Maria throws it back with

> Then by that duty, or respect, or what
> You please to have it, goe to bed and leave me,
> And trouble me no longer with your fooling.
>
> (I. iii. 235–8)

This sophisticated discussion of contesting ideologies, however, is grist to a comic mill. It takes place in a parody of a parley scene as Maria and her friends, fortified on the upper acting level, threaten Petruchio and his forces with full chamber-pots. Their relative positions dramatise the threat of male violence which underlines the argument and the measures the women take to defend themselves. If the women have, literally, the upper hand in these scenes, the men console themselves with the familiar solace of witty misogyny. Rowland and Tranio amuse the audience with a discussion of the 'great Schoole question' 'Whether that woman ever had a faith/After she had eaten' (II. iii. 7–8) and Jacques produces a mock heroic set piece describing the advancing army of city wives who come to Maria's support (II. iv. 42–84).

As the frustration mounts, so the rhetoric of misogyny becomes more violent. Petruchio's soliloquy (III. iii. 146–71), addressed directly to the 'Gentlemen' of the audience, vividly describes his past unquiet marriage, with explicit emphasis on the problem of sex, presented as rape, a matter for violent insistence and a source of humiliation for the unfortunate man:

> had I ever
> A pull at this same poor sport men run mad for,
> But like a cur I was faine to shew my teeth first,
> And almost worry her.
>   (III. iii. 162–5)

The issue here is less the struggle for power between men and women than a negative view of monogamy. Marriage is no longer presented as a sacred institution: rather it is seen as a limit on free sexual activity in the market returning it to an arena where restrictions render it a matter either for constant miserable negotiation or violent rapine. Neither of these is an attractive prospect for an urbane audience. As Mike Bristol explains,

> Although every individual husband has a compelling interest in his wife's sexual fidelity . . . men collectively desire the subordination and sexual availability of all women. . . . The much more arduous and difficult choice is that between marriage on any terms at all, and the freedoms and privileges of the unattached male. (Bristol 1986; p.164)

Petruchio's soliloquy addresses the audience as a collection of unattached males for, whatever its actual composition, that is the point of view from which the jokes and the narrative make sense. The play no longer imposes obedience by violence in the interests of 'an awful rule and right supremacy'[11] but after the comic gags are over Maria must recognise that she loves Petruchio and come to an agreeable understanding with him.

The process by which these plays comically modify the excesses of both patriarchy and predatory sexuality reinforces the values and the self-image of the urbane young men who were their original audience. The highly polished gloss in which this audience viewed itself reflected similarly urbane images of the witty woman and the wife who sought more civilised relations with men. For the wittiest and most attractive women of these plays are those who accept the terms of sexual relations offered by the new consumerist ideology. For when sex becomes a matter of commodity relations women occupy the ambiguous position of sharers in this consumption and the commodity themselves. Berkenhead's verses to the First Folio praise

> Thy Sence (like well-drest ladies) cloath'd as skinn'd
> Not all unlac'd, nor City starch't and Pinn'd.
>
> (xiii)

It was a common enough critical trope, but the extension of the metaphor and the precision of its reference locate it as especially applicable to the taste of urbane gentlemen. This particularity of appeal is rendered even more precisely in the Epilogue to *Valentinian*, where the audience are urged to accept the play

> has yee would choose a Misse,
> Only to please the eye a while and kisse,
> Till a good wife to got:
> (18–20)

The plays, like mistresses, were to be seen as the pastimes of a young, free, urbane male audience for whom pleasure and value for money lay behind their social as much as their commercial transactions.[12]

The dangerous prospect for men in this world is that the free market is equally available to women. When Maria uses her sexuality as a bargaining counter, she accepts that her husband might find the commodity elsewhere. However, as a free agent on the open market she too can find other purchasers:

PETRUCHIO.   Well there are more Maides then Maudlin, that's my comfort.

MARIA.   Yes, and more men then Michael.

PETRUCHIO.   I must not to bed with this stomach, and no meat Lady.

MARIA.   Feed where you will, so it be sound and wholesome,
                Else live at livery, for I'le none with ye.
                                              (I. iii. 221–5)

The really desirable, up-market version of sex is to be found
among women who hold themselves chaste for wit or for virtue,
but it is available elsewhere. Maria's image of sex as horseflesh
available either as the accoutrements of a gentlemen or for more
mundane purposes 'at livery' is then extended by her associate
Byancha, who advises Petruchio:

> You had best back one of the dairy maids, they'l carry.
> But take heed to your girthes, you'l get a bruise else.
>   (I. iii. 226–7)

For the plays make a very clear distinction between the witty
chaste women whose individualism and wit match those of the
new men and women who, since they merely service their needs,
are the butts of their wit, meeting the pleasures of sex and
laughter at the same time.

This distinction between the sexual behaviour of different
classes is a further complication in the dramatisation of misogyny.
In *The Scornful Lady*, the eponymous heroine has plotted
successfully to humiliate her lover Elder Loveless, and he vents
his rage in a misogynist soliloquy which reveals a number of the
pressures which lie behind this witty and urbane presentation of
sex:

> This senselesse woman vexes me to th' heart,
> She will not from my memory . . .
>   Sure shee has
> Some Meeching raskall in her house, some hinde,
> That she hath seene beare (like another *Milo*)
> Quarters of Malte upon his backe, and sing with't,
> Thrash all day, and ith evening in his stockings,
> Strike up a hornepipe, and there stink two houres,
> And nere a whit the worse man; these are they,
> These steelechind rascalls that undoe us all.
> Would I had bin a carter, or a Coachman,
> I had done the deed ere this time.
>   (V. i. 1–2, 11–20)

Ferdinand has a similar fantasy about his sister in *The Duchess of
Malfi* but where Ferdinand's vision is presented as that of a
pathological villain, The Elder Loveless's dramatic status is in no

way affected by this misogyny. His fault in the play is rather that
he loves too well and his dramatic development consists of
learning to trick and humiliate his mistress as she had tricked and
humiliated him earlier in the action. For the Scornful Lady is a
witty woman who, unlike Maria, is not controlled by being
married to the object of her wit and the play has to calculate the
value of her wit in making her a suitable partner for the hero
against the danger that her wit might get the better of him.

Throughout the action this procedure is worked through by a
play with literary convention and a rejection of the familiar fit
between old-fashioned ideology about sex and old-fashioned
dramatic expressions of it. The plot opens conventionally enough
with the lady sending her lover away because he has revealed their
love, but the language and style of the discussion reveals a social
world in which matters of chastity and love, socially accepted
behaviour and individual integrity coexist uneasily with a
constant potential for breakdown and disaster. The language,
however, also displays an energetic lack of piety about the
situations described. The Scornful Lady's language is not that of
the morally righteous but that of the stylishly wilful: and the
marriage described less one of sacrament than of the fulfilment of
certain social rites:

> Believe me; if my Wedding smock were one,
> Were the gloves bought and given, the Licence come,
> Were the Rosemary branches dipt, and all
> The Hipocrists and cakes eate and drunke off,
> Were these two arms incompast with the hands
> Of Bachelers to lead me to the Church;
> Were my feete in the dore, were *I John*, said,
> If *John* should boast a favour done by me,
> I would not wed that yeare.
>
> (I. i. 144–52)

A similar pragmatic air pervades the action where Elder
Loveless returns to charge his lady with cruelty. She pretends to
swoon and die at this treatment but, when he repents his
harshness, revives to laugh at him. The conventions of misogynist
denunciation, the references to face painting or a taste for coaches
which had become the stale commonplaces of complaint, are
revived in this exchange partly by the rhetorical *élan* with which
they can be delivered but also by the sense that they arise out of

the particularities of the relationships. The language of patronage
and service, of the old-fashioned poetic notions of sexual
alliegance, are turned into sarcastic rejection of a set of ideals
which cannot any longer be lived up to:

> You have us'd me, as I would use a jade,
> Ride him off's legges, then turn him into the Commons;
> If you have many more such prettie Servants,
> Pray build an Hospitall, and when they are old,
> Keepe um for shame.
>
> (IV. i. 190–4)

This extension and combination of metaphors of older ideals of
love and service is witty in itself, and even though the audience
knows that Elder Loveless is only trying his mistress. However,
the rhetoric indicates a cynicism about love and service which
says more for the characters' wit than their integrity. Loveless, in
ridding himself of the old allegiances, is liberated into placing
love where it belongs – as a luxury commodity to be enjoyed like
art and music:

> O 'tis brave
> To be one's owne man. I can see you now
> As I would see a Picture, sit all day
> By you and never kisse your hand: heare you sing,
> And never fall backward; but with as set a temper
> As I would heare a Fidler, rise and thanke you . . .
> I can eate mutton now, and feast my selfe
> With my two shillings, and can see a Play
> For eighteene pence againe.
>
> (IV.i. 207–18)

In this scene the Elder Loveless is humiliated for his railing by
the lady's trick of pretended horror which brings about his
repentance. But the action of the play endorses his view that the
Scornful Lady must be tamed, though by a wittier trick than
denouncing her virtue.

In the hilarious denouement, the Elder Loveless pretends to
be about to marry a country wench, in fact his friend Welford in
disguise. The Lady in a fit of pique insists on his earlier vows to
her and marries him before she can find out the truth. The scene
with Welford in disguise has all the comedy of farcical cross-
dressing, but it is also the occasion for working through yet more
of the questions of regarding women and correct sexual relations.

The Lady is at first completely unfazed by the strange apparition. When Welford goes into his routine as the paradigm submissive wife seeking only to please her lover and proud that she uses 'no paint, not any drugs of art' to enhance her beauty, her behaviour is seen as prodigious rather than exemplary and the lady enquires disingenuously

> Why, what thing have you brought to shew us there?
> Doe you take money for it?
>
> (V. ii. 101–2)

The Elder Loveless insists that his new love transcends the cash nexus as 'a Godlike thing not to be bought for mony' and praises her virtues in contrast with those of the Lady who has rejected him:

> She cannot sound in jest, nor set her lover tasks, to shew her peevishnes, and his affection: nor crosse what he saies, though it bee Canonicoll. Shee's a good plaine wench, that will doe as I will have her, and bring mee lusty boyes to throw the Sledge, and lift at Pigs of lead: and for a wife, shee's farre beyond you: what can you doe in a houshold, to provide for your issue, but lye a bed and get um? your businesse is to dresse you, and at idel houres to eate; when she can doe a thousand profitable things: She can doe pretty well in the Pastry, and knows how pullen should be cram'd: she cuts Cambricke at a third: weaves bone-lace, and quilts balls: And what are you good for?
>
> (V. ii. 176–86)

The force of Loveless' speech is complex; his charge that the lady is but an idle ornament carries some weight. However, the parody of marriage handbooks shows that the alternative to a sophisticated lady is not a virtuous country companion, who would prove no match for a witty man about town. In the end the desirable attributes are those of a woman whose wit can match the man's, but only enough to appreciate the merits of his superior trickery.

The action, the language and the imagery of this play show a writer who had a most acute understanding of the conflicting arguments over women and sexual relations and who could assume his audience did so too. The older ideals of chastity and service would clearly no longer do as theatrical conventions, either. The wit which makes the plays more entertaining can also bring more tangible rewards. Elder Loveless's hopeless and humiliating passion for the lady is contrasted with the careless attitude of his friend, Welford who gets the best of the action too. His part in Elder Loveless's plot results in him going to bed, still disguised as a country wench, with the Scornful lady's sister. His wit thus brings him an heiress and they are bound together by a shared joke, not by bonds of service or patriarchy.

The style and ethos of *The Scornful Lady* were repeated with more or less good humour in numerous other comedies until the closing of the theatres. They offered their urban audiences an image of a world where sex was significantly more important than honour and where relations with women had to be renegotiated, unfettered by older conventions of chastity and service and the smooth passage of women from fathers to husbands. The humanised patriarchy of Shakespearean comedy is transferred to a world of competitive individualism which was liberating for those women with the wit and the resources to survive within it. However, the release from the familiar narrative and moral patterns of the *querelle des femmes*, the contest between misogyny and adulation, was only a release into patterns of wit and urbanity in which women could as often be the victims as the heroines of the action. Moreover, it is impossible to tell how far these shifts in the representation of women were a result merely of the play with theatrical conventions, and how far they indicated that women as well as men were in a position to renegotiate the terms of their sexual relations. In an elegant play with the titles of some of Fletcher's comedies, G. Hill's commendatory verses claim that Fletcher

> taught (so subtly were their fancies seized)
> To Rule a wife, and yet the Women pleas'd.

Hill confirms that the terms by which sex acted as the narrative and social dynamic of these plays had shifted to include a more pleasing image of women, but that the rule of the father, the tyranny of the lustful king, was replaced by the rule of witty men even over the women who consented to become their partners in wit.

Notes

1. In order to avoid the minefield of the authorship of the Beaumont

and Fletcher canon, I am using 'Fletcher' to refer to plays by Fletcher and his collaborators. Where possible I have used the editions prepared under the general editorship of Fredson Bowers, *The Dramatic Works in the Beaumont and Fletcher Canon*.

2. See, for example, Herbert Blau, 'The Absolved Riddle: Sovereign Pleasure and the Baroque Subject in the Tragicomedies of John Fletcher'. Suzanne Gosset in 'Marrying the Rapist' discusses some Fletcher plays in the context of dramatic treatments of rape in the period.

3. Compare Volpone's inappropriate invitation to Celia to 'act Ovid's tales', discussed in Chapter 7 above.

4. Compare the scene between Epicure Mammon and Doll Common in *The Alchemist*, discussed above p. 174–5.

5. See the more general discussion of this problem at the beginning of Chapter 3 and, in particular, its reference to Macherey, *A Theory of Literary Production*.

6. Jokes about the occasional, inexperienced visitor to the theatre abound. In *Playgoing in Shakespeare's London*. Andrew Gurr quotes Peacham's anecdote about a citizen's wife who mistook a pickpocket's advances as sexual. Its mockingly superior tone is very similar to that of Fletcherian comedy.

7. See R. A. Foakes's account of the importance of this dramatic development in 'Tragedy of the Children's Theatres after 1600'.

8. See Peter Davidson, 'The Serious Concerns of Philaster'.

9. For a fuller account of these plays, in particular the different comic and tragic treatment of the 'lustful tyrant' motif, see my section in Lois Potter *et al.*, *The Revels History of Drama in English. volume IV, 1613–1660*, pp. 188–94.

10. Compare the end of the anonymous *Swetnam the Woman Hater Arraigned by Women*, in which the misogynist is tried and found guilty by a court of women who punish him with violent pinching. The play is discussed at length in Linda Woodbridge, *Women and the English Renaissance*, pp. 300–22.

11. See *The Taming of the Shrew* v. ii. 109. See also Kathleen McLuskie, 'Feminist Deconstruction: Shakespeare's *Taming of the Shrew'*.

12. This connection has been fully documented by Jean-Christophe Agnew, whose *Worlds Apart: The Market and the Theatre in Anglo American Thought, 1550–1750* appeared as this book was nearing completion. It corroborates with fascinating complexity my basic thesis about the theatre and commercial culture.

CONCLUSION

Feminism, History
and Theatre

Since this work was begun, feminist criticism of Shakespeare, and sometimes of his contemporaries, has grown and flourished. Feminist Readings of Renaissance Drama can now be embarked on in teaching and research, supported by a range of theoretical and analytical work from a variety of different sources and different critical positions.[1] These developments have, of course, generated debate: as Carol Neely has shown most recently,[2] the critical activities of new historicists, cultural materialists and feminist critics, though overlapping in their common impulse to understand Renaissance culture and the role of literary texts within it, are divided by both aims and method. Professor Neely feels that the focus on ideology and the power relations within Renaissance culture, which characterises the work of what she calls the 'cult-historicists', has led to a regrettable blurring of the clear feminist commitment of earlier work. It imposes, she claims, a sense of the inescapable character of ideology, the determinism of linguistic structures and cultural discourses which make any sense of the power and resistance of early modern women disappear. She calls instead for a committed feminist criticism which involves, as its theoretical basis, an insistence on

> some area of femaleness that is part biological, part psychical, part experiential, part cultural and that is not utterly inscribed by and in thrall to patriarchal ideology and that makes possible female discourse, a women's literary history, a feminist critique which can do more than lament its own inevitable co-optation or suppression.
> (Neely 1988; p. 7)

This 'area of femaleness' is apparently to be located in historical accounts of women's lives, such as church court depositions which

> document gender conflicts, social contradictions, women's oppression and women's unruliness (ibid. p.18)

The historical documentation of the existence of these women will then endorse a feminist reading of literary and theatrical texts, permitting the modern feminist to celebrate the subversive potential of their unruly heroines.

Plays by Renaissance dramatists certainly provide voices in which women characters speak of their struggles over marriage, the commodification of sexuality and the restrictions which their gender imposed on their lives. There is, moreover, no shortage of evidence that women in early modern communities showed energy and vitality and independence of spirit. The static model of hierarchical sexual relations and appropriate female behaviour was daily recognised as a consoling fiction, offered by moralists and social legislators in the face of pressure from the demographic and related subsistence crisis which made manifest nonsense of the stable images of patriarchal hierarchy.[3] Widows and *femmes seules* ran their own households and businesses without men[4] learned women and women artists showed that their skills could transcend the common notion of appropriate womanly accomplishments[5] and literate women resisted quite explicitly their denigration as the inheritors and perpetuators of Eve's primal sin.[6] They quarrelled with, and sometimes murdered, their husbands over the vexed and contentious question of their share of domestic work and their rights to the products of their labour. Most importantly, the language and images of reformed religion provided them with a point of leverage with which to contest their subordination through the competing claims of their duty to God, revealed by faith, and their duty to husbands and fathers demanded by the exhortations of the church and the state.

Nevertheless, the problem still remains of how we read the evidence of women's engagement with the culture of their time. The terms, 'gender conflict', 'women's oppression', 'social contradiction' and 'women's unruliness' all present metaphors of social interaction which elide different and, I think, opposed, models of historical analysis. 'Gender conflicts' and 'women's oppression' imply a model of explicit conflict between men and women, conscious of themselves as gendered agents in competition for resources or power. 'Women's unruliness' and 'social contradiction' suggest a rather more random process in which change in social relations between men and women occurs as a result of their reactions to larger forces of material change.

Men and women were, of course, constructed as gendered subjects by the discourses of the law and the church and manifold social and material formations from sartorial regulation to the conditions of work in the early modern economy. However, the extent to which gender was a site of explicit conflict is much less clear. The church court depositions, for example, often deal with women anxious to secure and ratify their relations with men, to establish themselves within the family and to protect themselves, often against other women, from the material and social implications of an independent existence. The social harmony and community values in whose name such women were controlled were often precisely those which were being upheld by women when they seemed at their most insubordinate. The remarrying widow, the scolding woman who accused her neighbours of fornication, even the witch who cursed her neighbours for lack of charity, acted as often as a result of the material pressures on their lives as out of explicit rebellion against constraining social ideology. The conflicts which men and women experienced had, of course, a gendered dimension. Women had relatively less control over their material lives than men and, when they were accused of deviance, their judges would have been men. A feminist historian would well note the disproportion of unruly women to unruly men and the different treatment each were afforded. She might seek explanations in the ways in which women were subordinated by their differential access to status and resources and by the community response which suggested that social order and harmony were felt to depend on women's behaviour.[7] For history which concerns itself with the analysis of women's struggle within social contradictions must be called feminist. It is, however, different from a history of feminism which seeks to identify the point at which unruliness and disobedience on the part of individual women become a political movement presenting a more concerted challenge to patriarchal power.

This insistence on the specificity and difference of women's experience is a vitally important element for feminist readings of early modern culture. It is clear that women in the period had a different relationship with their culture than men. They were less likely to be the producers of literary and theatrical culture and were only problematically its consumers.[8] Moreover, their difference was insisted upon within the culture itself. Writers used 'women' as the locus for discussions of a number of problems from the organisation of the godly family, to the control of sexuality to the emotional power of narrative and theatrical representation. However, the relationship between women's experience and the construction of women in cultural representations is the most problematic area for feminist criticism. The feminist critic must place women at the centre of her enquiry, but feminist theory has taught her that 'women' is also an ideological category, the site of constant struggle.

As a result, the representation of women in Elizabethan culture cannot be regarded as purely mimetic since it was constantly being negotiated around conflicting paradigms of womanhood. The complex and flexible terms and language which early modern women had to think and talk about themselves were able, for the time being, to hold the contradictions of their experience in place. Queen Elizabeth, in the most contradictory position of all, could, as she appeared in armour at Tilbury, resolve the contradiction of having the 'weak and feeble body of a woman' along with the 'heart and liver of a king' by a metaphoric slide from gender to status. In a society where the language of social stratification was firmly fixed, the language of gender could be accommodated around it. For women can be defined in terms of their bodies or their social roles – an identity part biological, part psychical, part experiential, part cultural – but the social meanings of those definitions are always being negotiated within the terms available in particular cultures.

The analysis of textual material is, consequently, vitally important, for it reveals the terms and forms of that negotiation. However, it is precisely because texts are engaged in negotiation that the business of analysis is so complex. If we examine the relations of power or the sexual politics of Renaissance drama, we cannot assess their ideological force simply in terms of analogous practices in social relations or handbooks of propaganda, far less as a reflection of our own political dreams and nightmares. Dramatic texts are primarily theatrical productions, inscribing and producing social material from pre-existing ideas or political positions, as well as images and speeches, jokes and songs, working through and against genre and conventions of narrative and dramatisation. The ways in which marriage and heterosexual relations held both the narrative structures of the drama and the institutions of society together may have been analogous but they were not the same.

The direct pressures on Renaissance dramatists were artistic and commercial as well as ideological. The opposition between Griselda and Beatrice, Lady Macbeth and Anne Frankford, the Duchess of Malfi and Moll Cutpurse can be seen as a function of contrasting narrative roles, the need for variety and surprise, and the appeal of an unusual twist to an old story. For contrasts between the paradigms of 'woman' and the vital individuality of particular women characters was also part of the dramatic development from the abstractions of morality drama to the contingent particularity of mimetic narrative.[9] In addition, Renaissance dramatists in all their writing faced the practical problem of how to construct satisfactory women characters for their boy actors to inhabit. It may have been this pressure, as much as ideological concerns which focused attention on the construction of women out of and in contrast to received ideas about women's behaviour and characteristics. The variety of styles and theatrical effects in this body of drama provides, moreover, an insight into the complex process by which social concepts are formed, indicating the importance of distinguishing between which views of women are frightening and which are funny, which are subversive and which are reassuring, and the contradictory ways in which they can be all of these simultaneously.

Dramatised misogyny, and its mirror image, the adulation of women, was (and is) undoubtedly part of the ideological process which sustained patriarchal power. However, it was also a source of jokes and horror and the contradictory ways in which dramatic texts modulate its influence to sustain and humanise its impact reveal the process by which different forces within contemporary ideology can co-exist at one and the same time. To read dramatic texts in search of 'the possibility of resistance or even subversion' would be to ignore the seductive pleasures of narrative closure, tragic engagement and comic containment. To see them, on the other hand, as powerful displays in the interests of the ruling order, is to ignore both the alternative informing tradition of religious and political opposition[10] and the extent to which the drama often fails to impose the pleasures of closure, allowing for quite alternative readings of its key events.

Moreover, assertions about subversion or containment beg the question of the relative effectivity of cultural forms as against material forces.[11] They leave undiscussed the political and social relations between writers and the ruling order, and between audiences in the theatre and those represented on stage. If idealist realm. Resistance and subversion become mere gestures. which they share with other texts, then conflict, whether directed towards social change or social stasis, takes place in an entirely idealist realm. Resistance and subversion become more gestures of discourse rather than explicitly political procedures directed to social transformation.

As a political movement, feminism is directed to social transformation. When feminist critics and theatrical practitioners encourage audiences in the theatre and the classroom to see the clarity with which Renaissance plays deal with women and their social relations, they are engaged in a cultural struggle. However, the effectiveness of that struggle depends on recognising the double historical existence of the Renaissance play. Alerting attention to a Renaissance play's treatment of sexual politics today subverts its status as a timeless cultural monument, reminding the audience of the role of culture in the modern exercise of power. That political aim cannot be served by asserting the timelessness of feminism, turning the struggles of early modern women into costume drama versions of our own.

Notes

1. Ann Thompson, 'The Warrant of Womanhood': Shakespeare and

Feminist Criticism in Graham Holderness, ed *The Shakespeare Myth* provides a full account of feminist criticism of Shakespeare to 1987.

2. Carol Neely, 'Constructing the Subject: Feminist Practice and the New Renaissance Discourses' gives a full account of the debate with an extensive bibliography.

3. See above, Chapter 2.

4. See Alice Clark, *Working Life of Women in the Seventeenth Century*.

5. See Lisa Jardine, 'The Myth of the Learned lady in the Renaissance', and Griselda Pollock and Rosika Parker, *Old Mistresses, Women, Art and Ideology*.

6. See Elaine Hobby, *Virtue of Necessity English Women's Writing, 1649–88* and Germaine Greer, Jeslyn Medoff, Melinda Sansone and Susan Hastings, *Kissing the Rod: An Anthology of Seventeenth Century Women's Verse*.

7. For a particularly telling example of complex and contradictory treatment of female unruliness, see David Underdown's account of Agnes and Margaret Davis of Nettleton, accused of scolding in 1612, 1613 and 1614. 'The incident exemplifies ... a preference for persuasion rather than legal process; informal mediation by the clergy; official connivance ... at failure to punish a law-breaker; finally a resort to direct action to counter the authorities' neglect of community feelings.' *Revel, Riot and Rebellion*, p.17.

8. See above, Chapter 4 and Chapter 8.

9. For a fuller discussion of this developement in drama see Kathleen McLuskie 'When the Bad Bleed: Elizabethan and Jacobean Tragedy' forthcoming in M. Hattaway and A. Braunmuller (eds) *The New Cambridge Companion to Elizabethan and Jacobean Drama*.

10. Discussed by Margot Hienemann, 'Political Theatre' forthcoming in M. Hattaway and A. Braunmuller (eds) *New Cambridge Companion to Elizabethan and Jacobean Drama*.

11. Debated, for example, in Raymond Williams, *Politics and Letters*, pp. 350–5, and in Perry Anderson, *Arguments within English Marxism*.

SELECT BIBLIOGRAPHY

Agnew, J. C., *Worlds Apart: The Market and the Theatre in Anglo-American Thought, 1550–1750* (Cambridge University Press, Cambridge, 1986)

Amussen, S., 'Gender, Family and the Social Order, 1560–1725', in Fletcher and Stevenson, pp. 196–217

Anderson, P., *Arguments within English Marxism* (Verso, London, 1980)

Anger, J., *Jane Anger: Her Protection for Women* (London, 1589), reprinted in Ferguson, pp. 58–73

Anon., *Swetnam the Woman Hater Arraigned by Women*, ed. C. Crandall in *Swetnam the Woman Hater: The Controversy and the Play* (Purdue University Studies, Lafayette, Indiana, 1969)

Anon., *Everywoman in her Humour*, ed. A. M. Tyson (Garland, New York and London, 1980)

Anon., *Haec Vir: or the Womanish Man* (London, 1620)

Anon., *Hic Mulier: or the Man Woman* (London, 1620)

Anon., *The Maid's Metamorphosis*. ed, R. W. Bond in *The Complete Works of John Lyly* (Oxford University Press, Oxford, 1902)

Aston, E., 'Outside the Doll's House: A Study in Images of Women in the English and French Theatre 1848–1914', Ph. D. thesis, University of Warwick, 1987

Barker, F., *The Tremulous Private Body: Essays on Subjection* (Methuen, London and New York, 1984)

Barker, F., Hulme, P., Iverson, M. and Loxley, D., (eds), *Literature, Politics and Theory, Papers from the Essex Conference 1976–84*) (Methuen, London, 1986)

Barker, H., with Middleton, T., *Women Beware Women* (John Calder, London, 1986)

Barker, S., 'Images of the Sixteenth and Seventeenth Centuries as a History of the Present', in Barker, Hulme, Iverson and Loxley, pp. 173–89

Barish, J., *The Antitheatrical Prejudice* (California University Press, Berkeley, 1981)

Beauman, S., *The Royal Shakespeare Company: A History of Ten Decades* (Oxford University Press, London, 1982)

231

Beaumont, F., and Fletcher, J., *The Dramatic Works in the Beaumont and Fletcher Canon*, 6 vols, general editor F. Bowers (Cambridge University Press, Cambridge, 1966–82)

Beaumont, F., *The Works of Francis Beaumont and John Fletcher*, ed. A. R. Waller (Cambridge University Press, Cambridge, 1910)

Belsey, C., *The Subject of Tragedy* (Methuen, London, 1985)

Bentley, G. E., *The Jacobean and Caroline Stage* (Clarendon Press, Oxford, 1941–68)

Bergeron, D. M., 'Women as Patrons of English Renaissance Drama', in G. F. Lytle and S. Orgel (eds) *Patronage in the Renaissance* (Princeton University Press, Princeton, 1981), pp. 69–78

Berry, H., 'The Globe Bewitched and El Hombre Fiel', *Mediaeval and Renaissance Drama in England*, 1, 1984, 211–30

Blau, H., 'The Absolved Riddle: Sovereign Pleasure and the Baroque Subject in the Tragicomedies of John Fletcher', *New Literary History*, 17, 3, 1986, 539–54

Brecht, B., with Auden, W. H., (adaptors), *The Duchess of Malfi*, in R. Mannheim and J. Willet (eds), *Brecht Collected Plays*, vol. 7 (New York, Vintage Books, 1974)

Bristol, M., *Carnival and Theatre: Plebeian Culture and the Structure of Authority in Renaissance England* (Methuen, London, 1985)

Brown, J. R., *Shakespeare and his Theatre* (Penguin, Harmondsworth, 1982)

Butler, M., *Theatre and Crisis 1632–1642* (Methuen, London, 1983)

Cavanaugh, J., 'Lady Southwell's Defence of Poetry', *English Literary Renaissance*, 14, 1984, 284–5

Chapman, G., *Bussy D'Ambois*, ed N. Brooke (Methuen, London, 1967)

Chaytor, M., 'Household and Kinship: Ryton in the Late Sixteenth and Early Seventeenth Centuries', *History Workshop Journal*, 10, 1980, 25–60

Churchill, C., 'Vinegar Tom', in *Plays 1* (Methuen, London, 1985)

Clark, A., *Working Life of Women in the Seventeenth Century*, Introduction by M. Chaytor and J. Lewis (Routledge & Kegan Paul, London, 1982)

Clark, A. M., *Thomas Heywood Playwright and Miscellanist* (Russel and Russel, New York, 1967)

Clark, P., 'The Alehouse and the Alternative Society', in Pennington and Thomas, pp. 47–72

Clark, Sandra, *The Elizabethan Pamphleteers. Popular Moralistic Pamphlets 1580–1640* (Athlone Press, London, 1983)

Clark, Stuart, 'Inversion, Misrule and the Meaning of Witchcraft', *Past and Present*, 87, 1970, 98–127

Clemen, W., *English Tragedy before Shakespeare: The Development of Dramatic Speech* (Methuen, London, 1961)

Collinson, P., 'The Role of Women in the English Reformation Illustrated by the Life and Friendships of Anne Locke', in G. J. Cuming *Studies in Church History*, 1965, pp. 258–72

Collinson, P., *The Elizabethan Puritan Movement* (London, Methuen, 1967)

Collinson, P., *The Religion of Protestants. The Church in English Society 1559–1625* (Oxford University Press, Oxford, 1982)

Cook, A. J., *The Privileged Playgoers of Shakespeare's London, 1576–1642* (Princeton University Press, Princeton 1981)

Culler, J., *On Deconstruction: Theory and Criticism after Structuralism* (Ithaca, N. Y., Cornell University Press, 1982)

Daly, M., *Gyn/Ecology. The MetaEthics of Radical Feminism* (The Women's Press, London, 1978)

Davies, K., ' "The Sacred Condition of Equality". How original were Puritan doctrines of marriage?', *Social History* 2, 5, 1977, 563–78

Davies, W. R., *Shakespeare's Boy Actors* (Dent, London, 1939)

Davis, N. Z., *Society and Culture in Early Modern France* (London, Duckworth, 1975)

Dekker, T., *The Dramatic Works*, general editor F. Bowers, (Cambridge University Press, Cambridge, 1953–60)

Dekker, T., *The Non Dramatic Works* ed. A. B. Grosart (reprinted Russel and Russel, New York, 1963)

Dekker, T., with Ford, J., and Rowley, W., *The Witch of Edmonton*, ed. S. Trussler (Methuen, London, 1987)

de Lauretis, T., *Alice Doesn't: Feminism, Semiotics, Cinema* (Indiana University Press, Bloomington, 1984)

Dessen, A., *Elizabethan Stage Conventions and Modern Interpreters* (Cambridge University Press, Cambridge, 1984)

Dollimore, J., and Sinfield, A., *Political Shakespeare: New Essays in Cultural Materialism* (London, Manchester University Press, 1985)

Dunbar, W., *The Poems of William Dunbar*, ed. W. M. Mackenzie (The Porpoise Press, Edinburgh, 1932)

Elliot, V. B., 'Single Women in the London Marriage Market: Age, Status and Mobility, 1568–1619' in R. B. Outhwaite (ed.), *Marriage and Society. Studies in the Social History of Marriage* (Europa, London, 1981), pp. 81–100

Ellis, H., *John Ford, Five Plays* (Hill and Wang, New York, 1957)

Ferguson, M., (ed.), *First Feminists. British Women Writers 1578–1799* (Indiana University Press, Bloomington, 1985)

Fitzgeffrey, H., *Satires and Satyricall Epigrams* (London, 1617)

Fletcher, A., and Stevenson, J., *Order and Disorder in Early Modern England* (Cambridge University Press, Cambridge, 1985)

Foakes, R. A., 'Tragedy of the Children's Theatres after 1600. A Challenge to the Adult Stage', in D. Galloway (ed.), *Elizabethan Theatre* (Macmillan, London, 1970), pp. 37–59

Foakes, R. A., *Illustrations of the English Stage 1580–1642* (Scolar Press, London, 1985)

Foakes, R. A., with Rickert, R. T., *Henslowe's Diary* (Cambridge University Press, Cambridge, 1961)

Foucault, M., *Discipline and Punish: The Birth of the Prison*, translated by A. Sheridan (Allen Lane, London, 1977)

Gataker. T., *A Good Wife God's Gift: and A Wife Indeed: Two Marriage Sermons* (London, 1624)

Gibbons, B., (ed.), *Elizabethan and Jacobean Comedies* (Ernest Benn, London, 1984)

Goldberg, J., *James I and the Politics of Literature* (Johns Hopkins University Press, Baltimore, 1983)

Goodcole, H., *The Wonderfull Discoverie of Elizabeth Sawyer, a Witch* (London, 1621)

Gosset, S., ' "Best Men are Molded out of Faults": Marrying the Rapist in Jacobean Drama', *ELR*, 14, 3, 1984, 305–27

Gosson, S., *The School of Abuse* (London, 1579)

Gouge, W., *Domesticall Duties* (London, 1622)

Greenblatt, S., *Shakesperian Negotiations: The Circulation of Social Energy in Renaissance England* (Clarendon Press, Oxford, 1988)

Greer, G., *et al., Kissing the Rod: An Anthology of Seventeenth Century Women's Verse* (Virago, London, 1988)

Gurr, A., *Playgoing in Shakespeare's London* (Cambridge University Press, Cambridge, 1987)

Haltaway, M., and Braunmuller A., *The New Cambridge Companion to Elizabethan and Jacobean Drama*, (Cambridge University Press, Cambridge 1989)

Hankey, J. (ed.), *Richard III* (Junction Books, London, 1981)

Harbage, A., *Shakespeare's Audience* (Columbia University Press, New York, 1941)

Hawkes, T., *That Shakespeherian Rag* (Methuen, London, 1984)

Hawkins, H., 'The Victim's Side: Chaucer's *Clerk's Tale* and Webster's *Duchess of Malfi', Signs*, 1, 2, 1975, 339–62

Hazlitt, W. C., *Remains of the Early Popular Poetry of England* (John Russell Smith, London, 1866)

Henderson, K. U., and Macmanus, B. F., *Half Humankind: Contexts and Texts of the Controversy about Women in England, 1540–1640* (University of Illinois Press, Urbana and Chicago, 1985)

Heywood, T., *An Apology for Actors* (London, 1610)

Heywood, T., *Guneikeon: or Nine Bookes of Various History Concerninge Women* (A. Islip, London, 1620)

Heywood, T., *The Dramatic Works* (Russel and Russel, New York, 1964)

Heywood, T., *A Woman Killed with Kindness*, ed, R. W. van Fossen (Methuen, London, 1961)

Heywood, T., *The Fair Maid of the West*, a programme/text with commentary by S. Trussler, (Methuen, London, 1986)

Higgins, P., 'The Reactions of Women, with Special Reference to Women Petitioners', in B. Manning, (ed.), *Politics, Religion and the English Civil War* (Edward Arnold, London, 1973), pp. 179–224

Hill, C., 'The Norman Yoke', in *Puritanism and Revolution: Studies in*

Interpretation of the English Revolution of the Seventeenth Century (Penguin, Harmondsworth, 1986)

Hill, C., *The World Turned Upside Down: Radical Ideas during the English Revolution* (Temple Smith, London, 1972)

Hobby, E., *Virtue of Necessity: English Women's Writing 1649–88* (Virago, London, 1988)

Hoby, Lady M., *The Diary of Lady Margaret Hoby*, (ed) D. M. Meads (Routledge & Kegan Paul, London, 1930)

Holderness, G., *The Shakespeare Myth* (Manchester University Press, Manchester 1988)

Homilies, *Certain Homilies Appointed to be read in Churches in the time of Queen Elizabeth* (SPCK, London, 1908)

Houlbrooke, R. A., *Church Courts and the People During the English Reformation 1520–1570* (Oxford University Press, Oxford, 1979)

Howard, J., 'The New Historicism in Renaissance Studies', ELR, 16, Winter, 1986, 13–43

Ingram, M., *Ecclesiastical Justice in Wiltshire, 1600–1640 with Special Reference to Cases Concerning Sex and Marriage* (unpublished D. Phil. thesis, University of Oxford, 1977)

Ingram, M., 'Ridings, Rough Music and Mocking Rhymes in Early Modern England', in B. Reay (ed.), pp. 166–97

Ingram M., 'The Reform of Popular Culture? Sex and Marriage in Early Modern England', in B. Reay (ed.), pp. 129–65

Jardine, L., *Still Harping on Daughters: Women and Drama in the Age of Shakespeare* (Harvester, Brighton, 1983)

Jardine, L., ' "O decus Italiae virgo" or, The Myth of the Learned Lady in the Renaissance', *The Historical Journal*, 28, 1985, 788–819

Jeffreys, S., (ed.), *The Sexuality Debates* (Routledge & Kegan Paul, London, 1987)

Jensen, E. J., 'The Boy Actors: Plays and Playing', *Research Opportunities in Renaissance Drama*, 18, 1975, 5–11

Johnson, J. T., 'The Covenant Idea and the Puritan View of Marriage', *Journal of the History of Ideas*, 32, 1971, 107–18

Jonson, B., Herford, C. H., and Simpson, P. and E., (eds), *Ben Jonson* (Clarendon Press, Oxford, 1925–53)

Jonson, B., *Bartholomew Fair* (ed.) E. A. Horsman (Methuen, London, 1960)

Juvenal, *The Sixteen Satires*, translated P. Green (Penguin, Harmondsworth, 1967)

Kyd, T., *The Spanish Tragedy*, ed. P. Edwards (Methuen, London, 1959)

Lamar, V., 'English Dress in the Age of Shakespeare' in L. B. Wright and V. Lamar, *Life and Letters in Tudor and Stuart England* (Cornell University Press, Ithaca, 1958)

Lanyer, A., *Salve Deus Rex Iudeorum* (London, 1611)

Larner, C., *Enemies of God: The Witch-hunt in Scotland* (Chatto & Windus, London, 1981)

Larner, C., *Witchcraft and Religion: The Politics of Popular Belief* (Blackwells, Oxford, 1984)

Laslett, P., *Family Life and Illicit Love in Earlier Generations* (Cambridge University Press, Cambridge, 1977)

Leigh, D., *The Mother's Blessing* (London, 1621)

Lenz, C., Green, G., and Neely, C., (eds), *The Woman's Part: Feminist Criticism of Shakespeare* (University of Illinois Press, Urbana, 1980)

Levin, R., *New Readings vs Old Plays: Recent trends in the reinterpretation of English Renaissance drama*. (University of Chicago Press, London, 1979)

Lindley, D., 'Embarrassing Ben: The Masques for Frances Howard', ELR, 16, 1986, 343–59

Longhurst, D., ' "Not for All Time, but for an Age": an Approach to Shakespeare Studies', in P. Widdowson (ed.), *Re-reading English* (Methuen, London, 1982), pp. 150–63

Macdonald, M., *Mystical Bedlam: Madness, Anxiety and Healing in Seventeenth Century England* (Cambridge University Press, Cambridge, 1981)

MacFarlane, A., *Witchcraft in Tudor and Stuart England: A Regional and Comparative Study* (Routledge & Kegan Paul, London, 1970)

MacFarlane, A., *The Family Life of Ralph Josselin, A Seventeenth Century Clergyman: An Essay in Historical Anthropology* (Cambridge University Press, London, 1970)

MacFarlane, A., *The Diary of Ralph Josselin, 1616–1683* (Oxford University Press, London, 1976)

MacFarlane, A., *Reconstructing Historical Communities* (Cambridge University Press, London, 1977)

Macherey, P., *A Theory of Literary Production*, translated Geoffrey Wall (Routledge & Kegan Paul, London, 1978)

McLuskie, K., 'Feminist Deconstruction: Shakespeare's *Taming of the Shrew*', *Red Letters*, 12, 1982, pp. 15–22

Manningham, J., *The Diary of John Manningham of the Middle Temple*, 1602–1603, ed. R. P. Sorlien (University Press of New England, Hanover, 1976)

Marston, J., *Antonio and Mellida*, ed. G. K. Hunter (Edward Arnold, London, 1965)

Mendelson, S., 'Stuart Women's Diaries and Occasional Memoirs' in M. Prior, *Women in English Society, 1500–1800* (Methuen, London, 1985)

Middleton, T., *Women Beware Women*, ed. R. Gill (Benn, London, 1984)

A Mad World my Masters, ed. G. Salgado, *Four Jacobean City Comedies* (Penguin, Harmondsworth, 1975), pp. 111–88

Middleton, T., and Dekker, T., *The Roaring Girl*, ed. A. Gomme (Ernest Benn, London, 1976)

Miller, J., *Subsequent Performances* (Faber & Faber, London, 1986)

Munda, C., (pseud.) *The Worming of a Mad Dogge; or a Soppe for Cerberus the Iaylor of Hell* (London, 1617), reprinted in Henderson and Macmanus, pp. 245–63

Nashe, T., 'Pierce Penniless his Supplication to the Devil', in *The Unfortunate Traveller and other Works*, ed. J. B. Steane (Penguin, Harmondsworth, 1972)

Neely, C. T., 'Constructing the Subject: Feminist Practice and the New Renaissance Discourses, *ELR* 18, 1988, pp. 5–18

O'Donovan, K., *Sexual Divisions in Law* (Weidenfeld & Nicholson, London, 1985)

Pearse, N. C., *John Fletcher's Chastity Plays. Mirrors of Modesty* (Bucknell University Press, Lewisburg, Pa., 1973)

Peele, G., *The Old Wife's Tale*, ed. C. W. Whitworth, in B. Gibbons (ed.), pp. 4–62

Pennington, D., and Thomas, K., *Puritans and Revolutionaries: Essays in Seventeenth Century History Presented to Christopher Hill* (Clarendon Press, Oxford, 1978)

Peter, J., *Complaint and Satire in Early English Literature* (Clarendon Press, Oxford, 1956)

Phillip, J., *The Play of Patient Grissil* (The Malone Society, London, 1909)

Pollock, G., with Parker, R., *Old Mistresses, Women's Art and Ideology* (Routledge & Kegan Paul, London, 1981)

Potter, L., with G. E. Bentley, P. Edwards and K. E. McLuskie, *The Revels History of Drama in English, Volume IV, 1613–1660* (Methuen, London, 1981)

Quaife, G. R., *Wanton Wenches and Wayward Wives: Peasants and Illicit Sex in Early Seventeenth Century England* (Croom Helm, London 1979)

Reay, B., (ed.), *Popular Culture in Seventeenth Century England* (Croom Helm, London, 1985)

Rollins, H., (ed.), *A Pepysian Garland: Blackletter Broadside Ballads of the Years 1595–1639* (Cambridge University Press, Cambridge, 1922)

Seville, D., 'Political Criticism and Caricature in Selected Jacobean Plays', (M. Phil. thesis, University of Sheffield, 1986)

Shakespeare, W., *The Complete Works* ed. Peter Alexander (Collins, London and Glasgow, 1951)

Sharpe, J., *Defamation and Sexual Slander in Early Modern England: The Church Courts at York*, Borthwick Papers 58 (St Antony's Press, York, 1981)

Shepherd, S., *Marlowe and the Politics of Elizabethan Theatre* (Harvester, Brighton, 1986)

Shepherd, S., *Amazons and Warrior Women: Varieties of Feminism in Seventeenth Century Drama* (Harvester, Brighton, 1981)

Smith, B., 'Sexuality in Britain 1800–1900: Some Suggested Revisions', in M. Vicinus (ed.), *A Widening Sphere: Changing Roles of Victorian*

Women (Methuen, London, 1980) pp. 180–98

Sowernam, E., (pseud.) *Ester Hath Hang'd Haman ... With the Arraignment of Lewd, Idle, Froward and Unconstant Men, and Husbands* (London, 1617). Excerpted in Ferguson, pp. 74–9. Reprinted in Henderson and Macmanus, pp. 217–44

Spufford, M., *Contrasting Communities: English Villages in the Sixteenth and Seventeenth Centuries* (Cambridge University Press, Cambridge, 1974)

Spufford, M., *Small Books and Pleasant Histories: Popular Fiction and its Readership in Seventeenth Century England* (Methuen, London, 1981)

Spufford, M., 'Puritanism and Social Control?', in Fletcher and Stevenson (eds), pp. 41–57.

Stuart, S. M., 'The Annales School and Feminist History: Opening Dialogue with the American Stepchild', *Signs*, 7, 1981, 135–41

Stubbes, P., *A Christel Glass for Christian Women: Contayning an excellent Discourse of the Life and Death of Katherine Stubbes* (London, 1591)

Stubbes, P., *The Anatomy of Abuses* (J. R. Jones, London, 1583)

Swetnam, J., 'The Arraignment of Lewd, Idle, Froward, and Unconstant Women' (G. Purslow for T. Archer, London, 1615). Reprinted in Henderson and Macmanus, pp. 189–216

Tennenhouse, L., *Power on Display: The Politics of Shakespeare's Genres* (Methuen, London, 1986)

Thomas, K., 'Women and the Civil War Sects', in T. Aston (ed.), *Crisis in Europe, 1560-1660: Essays from Past and Present* (Routledge & Kegan Paul, London, 1965) pp. 317–40

Thomas, K., *Religion and the Decline of Magic: Studies in Popular Beliefs in Sixteenth and Seventeenth Century England* (Penguin Books, Harmondsworth, 1971)

Thomas, K., 'The Place of Laughter in Tudor and Stuart England', *TLS*, 21 January, 1977, p. 78

Thompson, A., 'The Warrant of Womenhood': Shakespeare and Feminist Criticism in G. Holderness ed. *The Shakespeare Myth* (Manchester University Press, Manchester 1988)

Thompson, E. P., ' "Rough Music", Le Charivari Anglais', *Annales ESC* xxvii 1972, 285–312

Thornton, A., *The Autobiography of Mrs Alice Thornton*, ed. C. Jackson (Surtees Society, Durham, 1825)

Tourneur, C., *The Revengers Tragedy* ed. R. A. Foakes (Methuen, London, 1966)

Underdown, D., 'The Taming of the Scold: The Enforcement of Patriarchal Authority in Early Modern England', in Fletcher and Stevenson, pp. 116–36

Underdown, D., *Revel, Riot, and Rebellion: Popular Politics and Culture in England 1603-1660* (Clarendon Press, Oxford, 1985)

Utley, F. L., *The Crooked Rib: An Analytical Index to the Argument about Women in English and Scots Literature to the End of the Year 1568* (Octagon Books, New York, 1970)

Walter, J., 'Grain Riots and Popular Attitudes to the law: Maldon and the Crisis of 1629', in J. Brewer and J. Styles (eds), *An Ungovernable People: The English and their Law in the Seventeenth and Eighteenth Centuries* (Hutchinson, London, 1980) pp. 47–84

Warner, M., *Monuments and Maidens: The Allegory of the Female Form* (Weidenfeld & Nicolson, London, 1985)

Wayne, Don E., 'Drama and Society in the Age of Jonson: An Alternative View', *Renaissance Drama*, XIII 1982, 103–29

Weeks, J., *Sexuality and its Discontents* (Routledge & Kegan Paul, London, 1985)

Webster, J., *The Displaying of Supposed Witchcraft* (London, 1677)

Webster, J., *The White Devil*, ed. J. R. Brown (Methuen, London, 1960)

Webster, J., *The Duchess of Malfi*, ed. J. R. Brown (Methuen, London, 1964)

Wickham, G., *Early English Stages*, vol. III part 1 (Routledge & Kegan Paul, London, 1963)

Willett, J., (ed. and translator) *Brecht on Theatre: the Development of an Aesthetic* (Methuen, London, 1964)

Williams, R., *Problems in Materialism and Culture* (Verso, London, 1980)

Williams, R., *The Country and the City* (Chatto & Windus, London, 1973)

Williams, R., *Politics and Letters: Interviews with New Left Review* (New Left Books, London, 1979)

Wilmot, R., *Tancred and Giusmunda*, in R. Dodsley *A Select Collection of Old English Plays* (B. Blom, New York, 1964)

Wilson, E., 'The Context of "Between Pleasure and Danger": The Barnard Conference on Sexuality', *Feminist Review*, 13, 1983, 35–41

Wilson, E., *Adorned in Dreams* (Pandora Press, London, 1985)

Woodbridge, L., *Women in the English Renaissance* (University of Illinois Press, Urbana and Chicago, 1984)

Woodbridge, L., 'New Light on *The Wife Lapped in Morel's Skin* and *The Proud Wife's Paternoster' ELR*, 13 1983, 3–35

Woolf, V., 'Notes on an Elizabethan Play' in *Collected Essays* (The Hogarth Press, London, 1971)

Woolf, V., *A Room of One's Own* (Penguin, Harmondsworth, 1945)

Wrightson, K., *English Society, 1580–1680* (Hutchinson, London, 1982)

Index

241